Masculinity in Children's
Animal Stories,
1888–1928

Masculinity in Children's Animal Stories, 1888–1928

A Critical Study of Anthropomorphic Tales by Wilde, Kipling, Potter, Grahame and Milne

WYNN WILLIAM YARBROUGH

McFarland & Company, Inc., Publishers
Jefferson, North Carolina, and London

LIBRARY OF CONGRESS CATALOGUING-IN-PUBLICATION DATA

Yarbrough, Wynn William.
    Masculinity in children's animal stories, 1888–1928 : a critical study of anthropomorphic tales by Wilde, Kipling, Potter, Grahame and Milne / Wynn William Yarbrough.
        p.   cm.
    Includes bibliographical references and index.

    ISBN 978-0-7864-5943-8
    softcover : 50# alkaline paper ∞

    1. Children's stories, English — History and criticism.
2. Masculinity in literature. 3. Animals in literature.
4. Anthropomorphism in literature. 5. Adventure stories, English — History and criticism. I. Title.
PR830.C513Y37   2011
823'.8099282—dc23   2011017219

BRITISH LIBRARY CATALOGUING DATA ARE AVAILABLE

© 2011 Wynn William Yarbrough. All rights reserved

No part of this book may be reproduced or transmitted in any form or by any means, electronic or mechanical, including photocopying or recording, or by any information storage and retrieval system, without permission in writing from the publisher.

Front cover image: "The Piper at the Gates of Dawn," frontispiece to *The Wind in the Willows*, Paul Bransom, 1913

Manufactured in the United States of America

McFarland & Company, Inc., Publishers
  Box 611, Jefferson, North Carolina 28640
  www.mcfarlandpub.com

Contents

Preface	1
Introduction — Play's the Thing	3
ONE • Adventures, Escapes and Violence	23
TWO • Aestheticism, Christianity and Spirituality: Masculinity in Flux	58
THREE • Reputation, Hierarchy, Masculine Logic, Law and Codes	90
FOUR • Collaboration, Compromise, Group Performances	125
Conclusion — The Hidden, the Subversive, the Traditional	163
Chapter Notes	179
Works Cited	183
Index	187

Preface

This study of masculinity is an interdisciplinary study incorporating elements of psychology, sociology, new historicism, gender studies, and textual based criticism. While many critics and scholars have examined the works of Oscar Wilde, Rudyard Kipling, Beatrix Potter, Kenneth Grahame, and A. A. Milne, there hasn't been a book that brings them together in an interconnected study. I examine masculinity in this work, attempting to tease out the variety of factors and expressions that surround ideas of what being British and male meant to these writers of anthropomorphic tales.

I must set out a few disclaimers and limitations to this study. I have left out the adult works of Oscar Wilde, Rudyard Kipling, and A.A. Milne (as this is a study of children's literature). I have also not included Kipling's *The Just So Stories for Little Children* (1902) and *Puck of Pook's Hill* (1906): the first because of its nature as a collection of origin or creation stories; the second because as a historical fantasy, it doesn't use animals. The focus of anthropomorphism in this study reveals how the pressures on masculinity could be more freely expressed and exhibited under the cover of animal or, in Mowgli's case, feral skin.

I owe thanks to a great many people. The first people to thank are my parents and family for "talking me down from the roof" several times and for supporting me in the long haul of writing a book. I would like to also give thanks to Nandita Batra and Vartan Messier for their interest and support of my first forays into this study with a chapter on Kipling in *Of Mice and Men: Animals in Human Culture* (Cambridge Scholars Press, 2009). Also I owe recognition to a great many friends for reading several parts of this manuscript in a variety of forms: Jennifer Geer, Keith Dorwick, Liberty Kohn, Michael Howarth, Jeff Hill and Alex Martin. And I couldn't have made this book without the insightful reading, questioning, and criticism of these people.

Preface

Finally, I need to thank the Children's Literature Association. Besides the camaraderie and opportunities they've provided me in publishing, conferences, and membership, they've established this field of children's literature as both a legitimate and necessary field of scholarship. In particular, I want to thank Jackie Horne and Donna White for their focused and informed editing of my essay "Animal Boys, Aspiring Aesthetes, and Differing Masculinities," in *The Wind in the Willows: A Children's Classic at 100* (Scarecrow Press, 2010). Their work was an invaluable experience in revising and editing which I hope I brought to this work.

INTRODUCTION

Play's the Thing

This book explores how masculinity is performed and represented in selected children's works of Oscar Wilde, Rudyard Kipling, Kenneth Grahame, Beatrix Potter, and A. A. Milne. Masculinity is a range of expressions, not a fixed identity, and is responsive to social, historical and cultural forces that permeate the consciousness of the writers I've chosen and the time periods of their works (1888 through 1928). I have constructed several categories, which are not exhaustive on the subject of masculinity, but which I hope will show a range of performances and reveal the collusion of various forces at work in this rich period of British literary history.

Many literary critics have investigated masculinity in British society and adult texts, calling attention to a "hegemonic masculinity" (Connell) and responses or revolts to this hegemony (see Nelson, Roper, Sedgwick, and Tosh). While queer theorists like Sedgwick have scrutinized adult texts like *The Picture of Dorian Gray* and historians like John Tosh, Susan Kingsley Kent and Leo Braudy have examined nineteenth- and twentieth-century representations of masculinity in its relationships to society, family dynamics, and war, how masculinity is represented in children's texts is a work still in progress. While studies in children's literature have focused on the specific animal tales of Wilde, Kipling, Grahame, Potter and Milne, there is no connected study of these writers whose responses to the anxieties that surround masculinity were related and often written in response to each other. Gender theory, queer theory, historiography, Marxism, sociology, literary analysis, close readings, even Bahktinian analysis can provide an interdisciplinary analysis of masculinity as it is performed and represented in these texts.

But this scholarship largely uses readings of the texts themselves: the connections and disruptions in how authors scripted the performances of their various characters. Then I proceeded to read these characterizations against biography, history, sociology and literary criticism. Such a method will be heavy on textual analysis, but, I hope, rewarding because of the connections and shifting portraits these writers give of masculinity and the forces behind these portraits.

Depictions of masculinity in the works I examined are deeply connected to the historical forces at work in this transformative period in Britain's history (the fin de siècle to the interwar period of "Bright Young People"), often with intertextual references and connections to specific events, people, and other literary works. While I will elucidate hegemonic performances of masculinity, marginalized, subordinate, and complicit representations of masculinity are also visible in how masculinity can be understood (Connell). Disruptive and subversive behaviors; troubling violence, homosocial/homoerotic bondings; reconfigured, egalitarian marriage; and celebrations and denunciations of aestheticism (among many other representations and characterizations of masculinity) are connected to public policy, social history, literary production and influence, and biographical evidence in Oscar Wilde's *The Happy Prince and Other Stories* (1888) and *A House of Pomegranates* (1891); Rudyard Kipling's *The Jungle Book* (1894); Beatrix Potter's tales (1902–1930); Kenneth Grahame's *The Wind in the Willows* (1908); and A. A. Milne's *Winnie the Pooh* (1926).

Examining gender with human characters presents different modes of characterizations and more direct opportunities to reveal anxieties and prejudices of both the writer and their respective historical era. Using nonhuman characters who act, speak and think like humans can allow for a remarkable amount of freedom and transgressive characterization. Works for children have used animals from Aesop's fables (*The Ant and the Grasshopper*) through fairy tales (*Cinderella*), from folktales (*Little Red Riding Hood*) through fantasy (*The Golden Compass*). In fact, anthropomorphism has been a mainstay of children's literature, exciting the child's mind with magic and uncertainty that animals bring to a human-centered consciousness while simultaneously portraying human foibles and characteristics. But though many of the stories that use animal characters have tried to impart morals or instruct the young reader/listener in correct or socially sanctioned behavior, the human in the animal can't help revealing gender slippage, gender inscription, gender coding, and anxieties over gender.

My reading of gender in these works is directly influenced by the work of Judith Lorber and Judith Butler. In Butler's performative theory, gender is "a corporal style, an 'act,' as it were, which is both intentional and performative, where 'performative' suggests a dramatic and contingent construction of meaning" (177) and is a rich filter to employ when examining children's texts, specifically works where authors use nonhuman characters to not only forward plot, but to construct versions of innocence, facilitate relationships, and establish power dynamics among characters. Lorber contends that gender is a social institution, like religion or class, and reveals gender's relationship to power and the fluidity of gender (*Paradoxes of Gender*). She asserts that "gender has changed in the past and will change in the future" (6). My study of gender representations will demonstrate its highly performative nature, its relationships to societal expectations and social institutions (marriage, bachelorhood, business, etc.) as well as identify how gender representations illuminate differences in how masculinity is represented as exploitation, ordering/ranking, and marginalization.

The categories of gender I have used for examining these works began with my reading of the texts. But I was influenced by John Stephens, in "Gender, Genre and Children's Literature," who uses schemata from David Rumelhart's "Schemata: The Building Blocks of Cognition":

> Understanding of a text, as a product of both the text's own discourse and a reader's prior knowledge, is mediated by the schemata societies use to organize concepts around the world. Schemata represent the concepts which underlie objects, situation, events, sequences of events, actions, sequences of actions, character types, patterns of behaviour, participant interactions and narrative closure [Stephens, 17, quoted in Rumelhart, 34].

From this understanding of schemata, Stephens (18–19) constructs his own categories of gender representation in children's works thusly:

Schema for Masculinity	*Schema for Femininity*
Strong	Beautiful (therefore, good)
Violent	Non-violent
Unemotional, hard, tough	Emotional, soft, yielding
Aggressive, authoritarian	Submissive, compliant
Transgressive	Obedient, pleasing
(= "nature" when + sexual)	(= "culture" when + sexual)
Competitive	Self-effacing, sharing
Rapacious	Caring
Protective	Vulnerable
"Hunter"; powerful	"Victim"; powerless

Introduction

Schema for Masculinity	*Schema for Femininity*
Player	Prize
Independent	Dependent
Active	Passive (active = evil)
Analytical	Synthesizing
Thinks quantitatively	Thinks qualitatively
Rational (= culture, civilization)	Intuitive (= nature, the primitive) [intuition = "lateral thinking" when + male]

I found these schemata helpful when examining these anthropomorphic works and intriguing when positioned next to a study of masculinity as it must encounter the historical circumstances of late Victorian through early Georgian literature, the influences of literary production, the church, the Imperial mission, evolving aesthetics, social history, etc. Many of these schemata are obviously influenced by traditional notions of gender. As such, they prove useful to the student of gender and children's literature. But the categorization of characters' performances against these schemata as well as understanding notions of Victorian and Edwardian gender codes reveal some slippage and range, in terms of gender performance. For my study, masculinity is positioned as a performance traditionally associated with being male. When I use the term gender, I am employing the sexual neutral sense of the word and am specifically concerned with experiences characters undergo in these stories that reveal the process of engendering, i.e. making masculine.

Historical Forces

The late Victorian, Edwardian and Georgian eras (1888–1926) provide a glimpse of a society warring with itself and ripe for the self-questioning that occurs in any society that seeks to expand and colonize. Changes to the heteronormative code, changes in the class system, changes in colonial relationships brought about freedoms, interdependence, and renewed focus on issues of children's health, education, and advancement at home. The "waning" empire was forced to tackle the excesses of industrialization, the burgeoning inequity between owner and worker, and the increasingly educated and legally marginalized female. Perhaps the two most important historical events to be tied to masculinity or, indeed, to how the public viewed sexuality were based on legal proceedings. The first

Play's the Thing

case was the Cleveland Street scandals (1889) where boy prostitutes were linked to aristocracy, specifically Prince Albert Victor. The second case was the government's case against Oscar Wilde. Oscar Wilde's libel trial in 1895 against the Marquess of Queensbury turned into his arrest and subsequent conviction on May 25 under Section 11 of the Criminal Law Amendment Act of 1885:

> Any male person who, in public or private, commits, or is a party to the commission of, or procures or attempts to procure the commission by any male person of, any act of gross indecency with another male person, shall be guilty of a misdemeanor, and being convicted thereof shall be liable at the discretion of the court to be imprisoned for any term not exceeding two years ... [swarb.co.uk/acts/1885Criminal_Law_Amendment Act].

Both cases were *causes célèbres*, and demonstrated that the public had become fearful of degeneration and any public figures or works who/which would espouse a masculinity that contested Victorian norms. Certainly, the public found models of masculinity more "robust" and "muscular" in Christian virtue in boy's magazines and periodicals and, more importantly, with works in the adventure story tradition: *King Solomon's Mines, Allan Quatermain,* and *Treasure Island.* The romantic conceptions of masculinity these books produced, aimed at the children readers, extolled the native virtues of the Englishman abroad. The idea of masculinity as tested in colonial expansion and colony retention was tied to social ideas the public had concerning masculinity and promoted the martial qualities that would eventually lead to war. As Susan Kingsley Kent describes it:

> "New Imperialism" gained momentum from the social Darwinist theories that saw in competition with the other European powers ... the means by which to create a robust society of virile men and proper, moral women.... In the eyes of many who embraced Darwin's notions of the survival of the fittest and applied them to the species of human beings as well, war constituted a positive good.... Through war, the "effeminate" could be weeded out, the manly preserved [*Gender and Power in Britain: 1640–1990*, 236–237].

And when rebellions flared up, manliness was called to its test. The Boer War (1899) was the first test and the effects of this test were far reaching. The Dutch/Afrikaaner farmers were able to resist British troops at first and though finally subdued, revealed weaknesses in the concept of Britain's imperial might: "British officials [Army Medical Corps] discovered that fully one-third of those who sought to enlist did not meet military

Introduction

standards of physical health.... The 'New Town Type' could not stand up to the rigors of physical training and war" (Kent, 237). The "splendid isolation" policy of Britain was tested (though not officially ended until the 1902 Japanese–Anglo Alliance) and the "degeneration," which social commentators like Max Nordhaus chronicled, became manifest in problems with military strategy and preparedness, increasing the anxiety over masculinity heightened by Wilde's trial.

One of the heroes of the Boer War was R. Baden-Powell, who first made his name during the Siege of Mafeking. During the siege, the resistance to the Boers included young, underage boys serving functions that would later influence Powell's conception of the Boy Scouts. Baden-Powell's *Scouting for Boys* (1908) included a section that reads as if it came from Mowgli's experiences in *The Jungle Book*:

> Real men in every sense of the word, and thoroughly upon scout craft ... understand living out in jungles, and they can find their way anywhere, are able to read meaning from the smallest signs and foot-tracks.... They are accustomed to take their lives in their hands, and to fling them down without hesitation if they can help their country by doing so [Kent, 238].

Kipling's work, where masculinity is constructed in the wild, far away from "New Town Types" and the degeneration of England, was admired by Powell and led to his use of the "wolf" and "cub" as rank in the Boy Scouts. In many ways, the adventure story hero was to be trained on native grounds with what had been learned abroad.

Different pressures on masculinity existed at home. From the 1880s through the first decades of the twentieth century, labor unrest became more commonplace in Britain. The famous Matchmakers Strike (1888) and Great London Dock Strike (1889), as well as strikes by the railway workers (1907) and shipbuilders and coalminers (1908), ushered in a new era of unskilled labor organizing in unions to protect wages and promote better working conditions. This unionization as well as the third Reform Act (1884) and the Representation of the People Act (1918) had extended voting rights to all men and women over 30. These forces generated fear among the middle-class and we see this fear evidenced in the literary works of writers from Charles Dickens to Frances Hodgson Burnett.

In many ways, these revolts and society's attempt to deal with them speaks about class. Fears and suspicions of the working-class are products of the rapidly changing nation, according to James Eli Adams:

> The language and experience of social class become especially insistent themes in the [Victorian] novel in conjunction with new forms of social mobility in nineteenth-century Britain, but such mobility in turn frequently generates crises of understanding because it strains existing categories ["'The Boundaries of Social Intercourse': Class in the Victorian Novel," 48].

We will see, throughout this work, how masculinity responds to class differentiation paralleling Britain's response to industrialism, colonialism and the end of empire: with such responses as rigidity (Grahame and Potter) and idyllic escape (Milne).

The caste system of the 1700s had not produced open class warfare and neither did the Victorian era, most likely because members of society could move upwards monetarily at least. Grahame and Potter prove as much: Grahame, from abandoned son with no "expectations" to speak of to Secretary of the Bank of England. And Potter, though she came from a wealthy family, demonstrates that women, through rigorous and careful attention to career and marriage, could prosper in both personal wealth and artistic reputation.

Richard Altick has called the Victorian era's class system an "open society," where individuals could rise (19). But there are many divisions, even in the class system: "partly social, partly religious, partly occupational, partly demographic" (Altick, 18). As we will examine masculinity in this work, we see that class is not a homogenous concept with definitive lines and categories. The "blunt and independent ... manner" (Altick 19) of the north in England was different than the "agricultural south, where vestiges of the feudal pattern of degree and deference lingered" (Altick 19). And as we examine class, we may see the "vestiges of the feudal pattern of degree and deference" (Altick, 19) in the agricultural south where Grahame and Milne situate their tales. How the writers I've examined script masculinity will demonstrate fears of working-class characters and suppression of their interests (Kipling, Grahame) as well as a paternalistic devotion to the lower classes reminiscent of aristocratic duty (Wilde, Potter).

Masculinity can also be read against the burgeoning women's movement. In 1903, the Women's Social and Political Union (WSPU) formed, and allied with the Independent Labour Party, with the slogan "Deeds, Not Words" to usher in a new push for the vote. This group held rallies, burned buildings, practiced sit-ins, endured prison hunger strikes, and collectivized women into a political group mobilized against disenfranchisement. The WSPU would resort to arson and property damage and, in an odd turn of events, become a patriotic group during World War One (still lobbying for women to have the right to work in the trade unions), putting enfranchisement on hold during the war.

But the United Kingdom had changed. Fears of the working class and of the "New Woman" are even evident in the children's works of Grahame, Potter, and Milne. Anthropomorphism breathes more than human life into nonhuman characters; fears, anxieties and desires are also animated, be it a former Bank of England Secretary (Grahame), conservative feminist and conservationist (Potter), or former soldier and dramatist (Milne).

Another complication of masculinity and its representation in these literary works can be traced to the history of marriage in the early part of the twentieth century. Marriage, as an institution, was no longer the only option for women, in terms of a collaborative union or economic survival. The idea of marriage as a partnership and not as a prison became realized in the Royal Commission on Divorce (1923), which instituted equalization of grounds for divorce. Feminists even used the language of commerce in their attacks on marriage:

> The adoption of a commercial idiom to speak about the institution most exalted by Victorians helped to demonstrate that the private sphere of women — the realm where generosity, compassion, kindness and decency were to prevail — had been tainted by the intrusion of the public, male sphere, symbolized for Britons by greed, competition, exploitation, and lust [Kent, 249–250].

It is no wonder that Potter, a conservative female author who opposed women getting the vote, would also be extremely astute in the business of publishing and in acquisition of property. Her characterizations of female characters demonstrate femininity in flux: business owners, farmyard killers, single mothers. In terms of masculinity, her male characters who are married demonstrate more equal and frequently subdued roles in opposite-sex unions. For the male writers in this study, their worlds and depictions are largely marriage free. The unnerved British male could find escape in the Arcadian settings of Grahame and Milne: areas "free of the clash of sex" (qtd. in Kuznets, *Kenneth Grahame*, 13).

Another important historical element in this study is World War One.

Play's the Thing

The fervent reactions to Wilde's trial, fears over "degeneration," the boisterous and seemingly overpowering working class, the rise of the "New Woman," and the declining image of Britain's imperial might abroad led to a crisis over masculinity that had, as one result, the easy entrance into World War One. A. A. Milne was such an Englishman who was thrust into World War One and emerged as a damaged survivor of war's masculinization process, reflected in his *Winnie the Pooh*. As Carol Stanger has observed,

> He [Milne] could not write about the filth, the smells, the lice, the rats, the lack of any privacy, the constant fear. He could not describe the corpses, including the suicides, and the men executed for cowardice or desertion — all the things that life in the Army meant on the Somme in 1916. He could not write now about the meaningless lunacy of the whole horrible business [177].

Milne's experiences at the Somme led him to write a play with a confrontation between a soldier and his war-profiteering uncle in *The Boy Comes Home* (1918) as well as in pamphlets like *Peace with Honour: An Enquiry into War Convention* (1934). But, for this study, we experience how Milne renegotiated masculinity in *Winnie the Pooh*, as a result of his experiences in World War One.

There have been historical moments when sexuality and history have collided to visibly challenge an era's gender norms. Most observers of history would agree that white, middle and upper class males formed the dominant power structure in the late Victorian era through the Georgian era in Great Britain. However, when we speak of gender, we can get lost in the idea of "progress," as if there were a point to reach, while "process" might be a more accurate concept for the framing of any sort of gender study that stretches over a period of time. The implications of this "reprocessing" can be profound. As Michael Roper contends in "Between Manliness and Masculinity: The 'War Generation' and the Psychology of Fear in Britain, 1914–1950," "In gender history the focus has, of course, been on men as agents of patriarchal power rather than as victims. This overlay of a gender approach onto earlier formulations has left an awkward and still unresolved legacy" (361). In many of the stories and episodes in the works I've included in this study, the process of identity formation makes every character a victim in some way. The categories I've used have elements of masculine privilege (such as Adventures and Hierarchy), but they also demonstrate this idea of renegotiated gender norms (such as Collaboration and Aestheticism). As I see it, gender is, and most likely will remain, a painful series of inscriptions where no final conception of masculinity is presented and where more liberated expressions of identity exist when sexuality and society are unyoked from the system of establishing order and control. Examining these works by Wilde, Kipling, Grahame, Potter and Milne may allow us to see how children's authors have been vital to understanding culture's influence on sexuality and identity.

The legacy of Wilde and aestheticism is evident in every writer I've chosen for this study. While "muscular Christianity" certainly held sway with the public and in the public schools' "official" voices, aestheticism as it was transmitted from John Ruskin's lectures and Walter Pater's talks and books, filters into Wilde's writings prominently, and is evident in *The Happy Prince and Other Stories* and *A House of Pomegranates*.[1] Grahame's Toad is said to have been modeled on Wilde by some critics (see Green, Lerer, and Gauger) and Potter's Jeremy Fisher is modeled on Toad (bachelor fisher in dandy attire). There are even intertextual references to Wilde's work in Grahame and Milne, and the legacy of aestheticism can be no more evident that in the return of Pan in *The Wind in the Willows*. But aestheticism had its detractors and its enemies. Indeed, as the nineteenth century ended, aestheticism becomes more sinister and the age produces a "masculinity under fire" (229) according to Susan Kingsley Kent, perhaps begun by the debates over Wilde's trial and leading up to inevitable war on the continent. Leo Braudy has suggested, in *From Chivalry to Terrorism: War and the Changing Nature of Masculinity*, that

> war on the horizon [provoked] the need to purge the national body of those who were perceived as less than men or as men of the wrong kind, picked up speed and urgency in the 1890s and as the century turned. Pervading the atmosphere was a great hostility to whatever was different ... [354].

Aestheticism reveals itself as an ideological force in each author's work I examine, whether it is in specific reactions to Wilde, masculinity in crisis, or even in artistic or aesthetic choices concerning characterization, dialogue, and action. "What was different" was manhood, with "manliness" held hostage to world war.

Manliness, as conceived of by the traditional public and developed for war, found a "godfather" in Lord Baden-Powell. Baden-Powell wrote his *Aids to Scouting* (1903) in an effort to combat the sickly state of manliness in turn-of-the-century England. The Scouting movement became hugely popular in Britain and America as young men from different social classes camped, trooped, trained, and became inculcated with ideas of manliness tied to nature, discipline, service, obedience, and godliness. Scouting isn't the first nor the only "youth movement" of the late nineteenth and early twentieth century attempting to re-orient manliness into a relationship with nature and away from cosmopolitan decadence. As Jon Savage in *Teenage: The Creation of Youth Culture* asserts,

> After Wilde and Nordau's *Degeneration* [1902], the decadent aesthete was both obsolete and vilified. The only option was to explore male sensitivity in a different way. Organized within various groupings, this impulse elevated spontaneity of instinct and emotional expression and the nature mysticism to be found in the outdoor life [104].

In Germany, this new manliness would be found in the Wandervogel (trans. wandering bird), a mixture of romantic and utilitarian impulses to steer youth, in particular young men, towards more simple and "natural" manhood. We see the influence of these youth movements (Scouting, the Wandervogel, Caravanning, etc.) in Grahame and Milne's work, as boys, located in rural settings, attempt to construct a relationship with nature while rejecting urban, cosmopolitan influences that could taint a middle-class child (like Toad).

But the youth movement, on the continent and in England, began before Baden-Powell. More importantly, for this study, scouting reaffirmed an "essentialist" argument in gender: men need to be organized in hierarchies; need to obey older, more paternal leaders; and need to be physically active and engaged in relationships with nature and the natural world rather than the industrial cities with their noxious influences. Encouraged and sanctioned by its leaders, war became a great test of manhood and patriotism and ended in the bloody intersection of new technology and an unquestioning allegiance to patriarchy.

Animals and Authors

As a whole, studies of animals in children's literature have recently had more attention as we launch into the twenty-first century. For example,

Introduction

Tess Coslett's recent *Talking Animals in British Children's Fiction, 1786–1914* (2006) provides an excellent introduction to the context of works like *The Jungle Book, The Wind in the Willows* and Beatrix Potter's tales. Her work also traces the use of the talking animal convention from the Romantic Era through the Edwardian Era. But my study seeks to focus on the representations of multiple aspects of masculinity as expressed by the uses of a variety of author's nonhuman characters. And, while reliant on historical, cultural, and literary frameworks, the main basis for this study is the texts of the works themselves and what they reveal about the respective age's (late Victorian and early Edwardian) notions of gender. For this reason, it is helpful to quickly review the scholarship on the various authors I examined.

Most of the critical studies on Oscar Wilde, though certainly addressing sexuality from almost every conceivable angle, rarely address his children's works. This is changing. Recent calls for papers from the Children's Literature Association and critical re-evaluations of Wilde's work have brought *The Happy Prince and Other Stories* (1888) and *The House of Pomegranates* (1891) more conclusively into the scholarly fold. Elizabeth Goodenough has traced (and critiqued) the typical characteristics of fairy tales in Wilde's children's work, while Naomi Wood has examined pederasty and the influence of Pater on Wilde's creations. But, as I said earlier, most critics investigate gender and gender issues in his adult works. And numerous critics (Sedgwick, Glick, Riquelme, Charlesworth, and others) have investigated gender, decadence, dandyism and the gothic elements in Wilde's work specifically through *The Picture of Dorian Gray* (1890).

Rudyard Kipling has generated a great amount of critical work from a post-colonialist angle, but very little in reference to his work for children, specifically when read next to gender. There are several articles I will address when examining masculinity as it is represented in the tales (see Stevenson, Roper, Nelson). But most critics have focused on *Kim* or read Kipling in relation to his positions on colonialism. Particularly useful in positioning masculinity and the forces at work when Kipling wrote is Claudia Nelson's "Sex and the Single Boy: Ideals of Manliness and Sexuality in Victorian Literature for Boys." Her examination of Victorian culture as it regulated gender development and Laura Stevenson's "Mowgli and His Stories: Versions of Pastoral" provide a useful pairing of critical articles in fluidity of both gender and in the way Kipling's artistic process worked.

Stevenson chronicles how Kipling actually wrote the stories of *The Jungle Book* and put the novel together, revising gendered depictions, specifically of Raksha, the wolf mother. Stevenson's article makes an excellent case for why biographical criticism can offer up truly remarkable readings of a text as approached from textual criticism. Hopefully, this will be evident when I discuss the construction of *The Jungle Book* and its depictions of masculinity. The reader will also notice that I include Mowgli as an anthropomorphic character in my examination of *The Jungle Book*. His characterization is such that Kipling's uses him as a character who exhibits human characteristics despite his "otherness" and "outsider" status in the human village.

Beatrix Potter's works have been explored, particularly for their depictions of women, by various critics (Kutzer, Mackey, Hollinsdale). Exploring Potter's work through a feminist lens has been productive in extracting both personal and societal context from the anthropomorphism she employed in her classic texts. But an evaluation of masculinity has not been done. More importantly, my study of masculinity and the categories I've constructed demonstrate that Potter's work is every bit as concerned with masculinity and multiple representations of masculinity, replete with the anxieties that mark writers like Grahame and Kipling. The sheer variety of Potter's characters reveals anxieties over identity and roles that men and women in the Edwardian age sought to define and, consistently, redefine.

Kenneth Grahame's depictions of masculinity are both varied and, by virtue of how he ends *The Wind in the Willows*, could be considered an attempt at unification of masculine identity. Michael Mendleson has provided an excellent source for this construction and various critics have commented on the "closing down" of the novel by way of Grahame's construction of the ending and the characterization of Badger as a source of patriarchy in the novel (Kuznets, Gilead, Peter Hunt). My study will attempt to demonstrate that aestheticism and "aesthetic masculinity" are evident in Grahame's work and provide an alternative to "muscular Christianity" and middle-class expectations of masculinity as represented in the novel. Perhaps Grahame's greatest achievement is the range of masculine expression his characters perform. Peter Green's excellent biography, *Kenneth Grahame, 1859–1932: A Study of His Life, Work and Times*, has provided both biographical sources as well as the history of the production of the text, which, like Laura Stevenson's article on Kipling, demonstrates Grahame and Kipling's awareness of audience in their composition. This awareness reflects concerns about manliness fueled by the anxieties over trade unionism, war and marriage, particularly in Grahame.

Criticism of A. A. Milne makes a case for the need for more research. Perhaps Frederick Crews' *The Pooh Perplex* and *The Postmodern Pooh* has silenced critics? But scholars and writers have tackled the book and unpacked the characters as representatives of adult figures and stereotypes (see Lurie, Wullschlager, and Carpenter). Carol Stanger's article, "*Winnie the Pooh* Through a Feminist Lens," provides a rationale for my assertion that masculinity as it is represented has been tempered by war. Though elements of the adventure story tradition are evident, jokes, logic play through language, and farcical representations of authority subvert the heroic or heteronormative representations of masculinity seen in Kipling and even Grahame. But Milne's connection to the beginning of this study are evident: his adoption of *The Wind in the Willows* for the stage (*Toad of Toad Hall*) includes notes on a casting decision that is reminiscent of Wildean characters in his work: "As regards their relative size, Toad should be short and fat, Badger tall and elderly, Rat and Mole young and slender. Indeed Mole might be played by some boyish young actress" (*Toad of Toad Hall*, 15).

Masculinity and Range of Being

This book is divided into chapters containing a wide range of masculine performances exhibited in the works I've chosen to examine. This "range" allows for inherited traditions of masculinity as well as paradoxes, alternative representations, and challenges to heteronormative depictions of British masculinity. These categories reveal genre developments in children's literature as well as a remaking of the anthropomorphic tradition. One might argue that these Victorian and Edwardian writers are only extending the tradition of using animals made famous by Aesop and used by writers like Sarah Trimmer, Anna Sewell, and Charles Kingsley to carry overt morals for the child reader. But the use of animals to represent humans necessarily carries context. The categories I use will hopefully make the social, political, and biographical contexts more visible and more understandable during the course of my analysis. For this study, I focused on active masculinity as evidenced in adventure, escape, rebellion and violence; in aesthetic and spiritual characterizations; in the use of reputation, hierarchy, language, logic, and law; and, finally, in collaborations, compromise, and group performances. My greatest hope would be for the reader to encounter these categories and speculate on their own categories or to revise mine, especially with an eye towards diverse masculinities.

Chapter One, "Adventures, Escapes and Violence," examines characters as they act out escapist and adventure-oriented impulses. Often these impulses contain violence and illuminate how violence is used in terms of character identification and in terms of power relationships. The adventure story tradition was a strong factor in the publishing market of the late 1800s. Defoe, Stevenson, Haggard and other writers constructed English heroes in exotic settings where manliness was proven by resilience, courage, individualism, and physical prowess.

Various characteristics of this "adventurer" exist in characters as diverse as Mowgli, Toad, Peter Rabbit, and Pooh. Frequently, class bias emerges, particularly in the forces aligned against the character but, more importantly for this study, in the actions taken by principal heroes where "othered" groups receive violence. Violence instills the plots with energy, action and drama, but also reveals a code of masculinity that favors force and punishment as a means towards establishing control, however illusory that control may be. I do not restrict violence, in this analysis, to male characters. Both Kipling and Potter, social conservatives in many ways, use violence to reinforce domestic sites as settings where control is illustrated by female's agency as enacted through actions popularly reserved for males in children's literature from their respective eras.

Escape dominates much of these animal's actions, even if that escape may be thwarted. This first chapter positions escape as a performance authors attempt to encourage, thwart, or manage; this management encourages a scholar to position these escapist behaviors in relation to historical context. For example, Kenneth Grahame and A. A. Milne employ Arcadian settings where bachelorhood and all-male company provide evidence of a society that yearned for sentimental landscapes fit for plot construction that rewards the escapist impulses, indeed cements them as part of popular culture and necessary for a picture of masculinity that differs

Introduction

from writers such as Rudyard Kipling and Beatrix Potter who often punish the same.

Chapter Two, "Aestheticism, Christianity and Spirituality: Masculinity in Flux," examines aestheticism and spirituality. While these may not seem logically connected categories, these performances demonstrate both a continuum of Enlightenment Thinking as it remakes the individual's relationship to the church, religion, and spirituality and a reaction to social and political philosophies such as Darwinism, Utilitarianism and Socialism. The influence of the Aesthetic Period is evident in each of the texts I've chosen through the aesthetic play of the monkeys in *The Jungle Book*; the poet Rat and aspiring aesthete Mole as well as the target for so much ridicule, Toad in *The Wind in the Willows*; Jeremy Fisher as blundering "dandy" in Potter's work; and the language games and all-male companionship in *Winnie the Pooh*. Aestheticism's rejection of moral as the purpose for art is certainly an underpinning in Milne's work where friendship ("nothing more noble or higher") exists as a primary reason for existence and a performance of masculinity that challenges individualist impulses inherited from the adventure novel tradition.

Spirituality, as I see it, is a connection characters have to forces higher than themselves, which propel and establish an identity to the characters, setting, and self. Wilde's Christianity and Kipling's evidenced use of Hinduism and Islam both exist and reflect a performance of masculinity that seeks to understand itself and its place in the social universe and the geographical present recalled, whether it is the Irish folktales of Wilde's youth and the intersections of those tales with Christianity and paganism or if it is the childhood of Kipling and his embrace of aspects of Hinduism and Islam.[2] Though a character like Mowgli is raised in the jungle, it is a "social" jungle with relationships to be worked out with force and philosophy beyond singular identity. Perhaps Beatrix Potter, whose stern Unitarianism and practicality dominate most of her stories, could be said to be the least concerned author with spiritualism. Though her very rejection of such elements may constitute a rebellion to organized religion and certainly the pervading patriarchal systems that sought to control females and social systems where females had little agency. Sentimental spiritualism, as tied to Romantic conceptions of nature and an individual's relationship to nature, pervade *The Wind in the Willows*, and this philosophical stance could be said to represent a feeling of loss as felt by Edwardians in their conception of the countryside and the "real" England. And, finally, Milne's spiritualism is almost a return to Barrie's reverence for youth: in youth is our beginning, middle and end. Though Christopher Robin ages, Pooh remains the same: the "uncarved block" to Benjamin Hoff in *The Tao of Pooh* and one character in, as Allison Lurie claims, a "loosely organized society of unemployed artists and eccentrics, each quietly doing his own thing ... the perfect commune [counterculture types] are always seeking" (*Don't Tell the Grown-Ups*, 155).

Chapter Three, "Reputation, Hierarchy, Masculine Logic, Law and Codes" proposes that masculinity can be observed in characters' relationships as to how reputation is used and how hierarchy is established, subverted, or defended through the use of language. Hierarchy is a key element in Kipling's world as groups and individuals seek to find, establish, and defend their place in the order. Kipling's "Law of the Jungle" relies on knowledge of languages (various animal calls and responses) as well as knowing the hierarchal order. Certainly, rebellion is an element that all of the books I examine possess.

And nowhere is this more evident that in Mowgli's killing of Shere Khan (noticeably done in collaboration with other animals). Wilde and Milne frequently undermine ideas of hierarchy as they present order as unstable and frequently don't center either tales, in Wilde's case, or episodes, in Milne's work, around building or defending order. Most often they are undermining order. Grahame's book is the most problematic in examining hierarchy, most likely due to the structure of the novel. It begins by challenging some hierarchal notions and ends with the order restored. Potter's hierarchies are curiously arranged to challenge masculine hegemony, in business and in isolated adventurist schemes, through reward/punishment systems she employs: those who know the order and follow it are rewarded. Women who follow acceptable social patterns are rewarded; those who don't are punished. Boys are frequently punished in Potter's work for failing to recognize hierarchal modes of social order that center around the home. Finally, Wilde's work reveals that codes of masculinity and hierarchy are a source of humor and satire, on one hand, and a source of critique, most noticeably in how beauty and emotional effusion are forwarded as masculine virtues, destabilizing notions of "uniformity" in masculinity.

In Chapter Four, "Collaboration, Compromise, Group Performances," I examine how masculinity is expressed in collaborations and compromise. In contrast to the individualism that is rampant in escape and rebellion, when characters perform in groups often heteronormative power and power arrangements are modified. Frequently, the "muscular Christianity" we come to associate with Victorian masculinity is transformed into displays of affection, compassion, recognition of weakness and vulnerability, and companionship, which often doesn't result in power or movement in hierarchy.

But many of the collaborations, even same-sex homosocial/homoerotic couplings, demonstrate that males need an audience (a collaboration of sorts) and the reinvestment in patriarchal masculinity is evident. There are also performances, as in *The Jungle Book* and in *The Wind in the Willows*, where collaborations do reinforce schemes of power and authority that favor traditional male hierarchal patterns. The only female author in my study, Beatrix Potter, scripts heterosexual couplings, often with family, that rewrite the script for marriage. Her couples share duties, perform collectively (to ensure homes for children and to secure food), as well as demonstrate that anger and play are a facet of these unions.

I contend that as the influence of socialism, emancipation movements, and war affected society, we see these influences on the characterization of anthropomorphic characters in these children's tales as they behave in groups. Where Kipling represents community in *The Jungle Book* and *The Just So Stories*, we see the influence of the Englishman abroad. Where Potter represents collaborations, she frequently rewrites marriages and family units in her stories where power is more equal, though the representations often seem formal and traditional.

Chapter Four also examines compromise, and nowhere is this more visible than in *The Wind in the Willows* and the Pooh stories. Both Milne and Grahame script masculinity that encourages male-male companionship but, more importantly, also males who must compromise with individualist, escapist impulses. While certainly nostalgia permeates the settings of both novels, characters find mutual benefit and assurance in compromises where a character sacrifices personal gain in order for another or for the group to prosper, even to reinscribe "gentry masculinity" (*The Wind in the Willows*).

Finally, I need to clarify the selection of the characters who are studied in this book. Both male and female characters are examined, particularly in Potter and Grahame's works. I felt this was necessary due to the complex ways both writers characterize certain females through their actions and speech. Also, I consider Mowgli as a character in the anthropomorphic tradition: he can represent human as much as he is human. His characterization, like Toad, Mole, Winnie the Pooh, and Peter Rabbit, demonstrates his position as the child ready for a process of masculinization.

ONE

Adventures, Escapes and Violence

A primary representation of masculinity in the works I examine is in active posture: by this, I mean where boys, men, girls and women resort to the body and active representations usually associated with boys. This chapter will investigate reactions to the adventure story tradition as configured in these anthropomorphic tales. Robert MacDonald, in *The Language of Empire: Myths and Metaphors of Popular Imperialism, 1880–1918*, summarizes the genre as follows:

> Typically, the adventure story sets its narrative at the beginning of the imperial enterprise. Its heroes enter terra incognita over a desert, across a mountain, up a river, down a tunnel, wrecked at sea; the land is "new," forgotten, closed off from civilization, preserved from "progress," ripe for change. The heroes — and in the imperial novels they frequently travel in company — are seeking treasure of one kind or another, diamonds, gold, animals unknown to science. The heroic task is often sexualized: the metaphor of entry is penetration, peaceful if possible, violent if necessary. The unknown land will be subdued, and its treasures stolen. With the male "natives" overcome, the females, decorative auxiliaries, will submit to or fall in love with the heroes. The conquest over, the land will be set in order [210–211].

As the empire expanded from the early nineteenth century, stories in *The Union Jack: Tales for British Boys, The Halfpenny Marvel,* and the *Boy's Own Paper*, reflected the expectations of British society:

> Many Victorian children, particularly boys, shared their parents' interests in the empire, expecting to work there when they left school, in commerce, the armed forces, or as public servants. (Girls would expect to become the loyal companions and helpmates of their husbands according to the conventions of the age, of course) [Butts, 328].

This chapter will demonstrate reactions to these depictions of masculinity as described by MacDonald and Butts. On one hand we have the colonialist impulses of Mowgli and on the other the use of doubles/doubling by a writer like Wilde and Grahame when they use (Wilde) or resurrect (Grahame) the adventure story tradition. That the adventure story tradition was (is) a dominant genre in children's literature is firmly established; how these writers from the late nineteenth century and early twentieth century encounter its legacy reveals a range of "manly" performances and reactions to such performances.

The heroes in Wilde, Grahame, and Kipling don't emerge as untarnished British models of manliness. Wilde's adventurers reveal a preference for same-sex unions, which question the depiction of the individualistic hero. Grahame's heroes problematize the adventure story genre and the notion of myth, legend, and history. Kipling's Mowgli, a model of the boy at the edge of empire, is a troubled, individualistic youth who shuns the society and "law" that Kipling goes to great lengths to build. These are but a few of the ways that masculinity is not a unified identity, and this variance in masculine depictions illustrates how important an investigation of gender depictions becomes when we examine these works.

Consistent with the adventure story tradition is the notion of escapism, particularly for boys/men. As many of the male characters in these works seek to escape home, domesticity, work, station/class, or even hegemonic notions of self, they reveal the locus of power they seek to escape, frequently patriarchal figures or systems of power. Though in Potter's work, escape of the domestic center frequently occurs when a boy seeks to escape the home with only a mother. The power and lure of escape is inherent in much of children's literature and not simply a masculine representation (*Alice in Wonderland*, *Pippi Longstocking*, *Harriet the Spy*, among others). Where escape is different in these works is that it often is directed specifically at the power structure, which is named or made evident (the Law of the Jungle, the animal villages of Potter's stories, the Riverbank, the Hundred Acre Wood). As Michel Foucault contends in *The History of Sexuality*, "There is no power that is exercised without a series of aims and objectives" (95). And these "aims" and "objectives" are precisely what the children/boys in these stories seek to escape, most noticeably, control.

Frequently, escapist schemes in the works I examine end in repression or return to the hegemonic norm: domestic center (Potter), Jungle hierarchy (Kipling), or squirearchy (Grahame). In fact, for the corrective to escapist fantasies, one need look no further than Beatrix Potter and Rudyard Kipling who traumatize, kill, and terrorize characters who seek to escape hegemony. But the escapes frequently make comic material of the adventure tradition and boy's perceptions of heroism (Grahame, Milne). What escape teaches us is that mis-performance occurs as often as performance in heroic vein and that by the end of the Victorian era and the beginning of the new Edwardian era, children's literature was shifting away from the attempts to mythologize the Victorian boy as a miniature, heroic Victorian man.

This chapter also includes an investigation of invasions, rebellions and depictions of trickster figures. As the "active" boys (and girls) rebel, they reveal the power structures they attempt to subvert, as well as the class, race, and sexual biases of their authors. Conditional rebellions occur in Potter and Kipling's works, revealing their essential conservatism. A character's motivation makes all the difference in their works.

Finally, I examine violence in this chapter and how violence is used to reveal different problems with class, gender, and character behavior. We witness threats and boasts of violence in Wilde, Grahame, and Kipling. Perhaps most unique is the manner in which Wilde links aestheticism and Gothicism in how violence brings distinct and overt pleasure to a character. Class violence attends Grahame and Potter's work, the two most decidedly Edwardian writers in this study. As the empire fell apart, perhaps one's place became a matter even children's authors — using anthropomorphism — felt obliged to characterize. Curiously, the range of violence situates Potter as one pole, who uses violence to correct escapist schemes, to re-establish home as the center of children's worlds, and to reveal problematic relationships in class dynamics. The other pole or end of the spectrum is Milne, who uses almost no violence in his idyllic Hundred Acre Woods.

Adventure Story and Complications

One wouldn't normally categorize Wilde as an adventure story writer, but his tales reveal the influence and reaction to the genre. In "The Fisherman and His Soul," the Soul functions as a traditional adventure story hero, replete with characteristics of the masculine colonialist. He visits exotic places, subdues potential non–English captors, and demonstrates intellectual and physical superiority over indigenous tribes in final contests of skill, cunning, or martial arts. The fictitious tribes the Soul encounters — the Magadae, Laktroi, Kriminians, and Agazonbae — add to the exoticism Wilde employs and provide the enticing "otherness" that appeal to Victorian audiences and would be recognizable as the threat to the heteronormative hero.

In addition to the exoticism, Wilde scripts the soul as a traditional hero in its use of the body and superior physical prowess. When the Soul does battle with an emperor, he demonstrates the same attributes we have come to associate with a hero from a Stevenson or Haggard novel: "The emperor leapt to his feet, and taking a lance from a stand of arms, he threw it at me. I caught it in its flight, and brake the shaft into two pieces. He shot at me with an arrow, but I held up my hands and it stopped in midair" (290). These physical tests establish the superiority of the Soul specifically as it is pitted against the exotic others.

Grahame also scripts his hero's retaking of Toad Hall in the language of manly adventure:

> in the panic of that terrible moment when the four Heroes strode wrathfully into the room! The mighty Badger, his whiskers bristling, his great cudgel whistling through the air; Mole, black and grim, brandishing his stick and shouting his awful war cry, "A Mole! A Mole!" Rat, desperate and determined, his belt bulging with weapons of every age and every variety; Toad, frenzied with excitement and injured pride, swollen to twice his ordinary size, leaping into the air and emitting Toad-whoops that chilled them to the marrow! [239].

And this isn't the only incident where weapons and fighting are centerpieces to both the action and to character's masculinity. Earlier in the novel, Rat goes into the Wild Wood to save Mole. It may be worth remembering that Rat's pistol and cudgel become his hero accoutrements in the "The Wild Wood" chapter and actually comfort Mole enough to physically stop his shivering. Both Wilde and Grahame's descriptions show how much the adventure story (itself spawned from epic, myth, sensational news, and popular entertainment) had become part of a formula for success in publishing a children's book. But both Wilde and Grahame also draw on "darker" sides to the adventure story tradition: doubling.

Much like *The Picture of Dorian Gray*, *The Importance of Being Earnest*, and other works, Wilde employs the use of doubles or doppelgangers. That our essence, body and soul ... could be comprised of a variety of gender experiences gains a curious representation in "The Fisherman and His Soul" where the fisherman cuts his Soul free from body. The allure of the adventuring Soul, though nongendered grammatically, is due to its representation as the adventuring male side of the Fisherman's overall identity. The Soul literally calls the Fisherman from "the deep," away from the mermaid (and his Self as distinct from his Soul) to regale him with stories, alternate lives, and possible fulfillment of fantasies; all unavailable to him while loving in heteronormative union (albeit with a mermaid) under the sea. Certainly much has been written about dichotomies and dualities in Wilde's work (see Carroll, Wood, Sedgwick) and the coded nature of his works where heteronormativity hides a more "essential self." But, in terms of the artistry, these dualities aren't paradoxes but are complimentary:

> Wilde simultaneously aestheticizes the gothic and Gothicizes the aesthetic. The merger is possible, and inevitable, because of the tendency of Gothic writing to present a fantastic world of indulgence and boundary-crossing and the tendency of the aesthetic, in Pater, to press beyond conventional boundaries and to recognize terror within beauty [Riquelme, 610].

With art as its own reward and morality as a secondary consideration, the use of doubles functions with adventuring representations of masculinity to counter the domestic influence of the mermaid and to fetishize the colonialist subtext in "The Fisherman and His Soul."

This doubling is evident in *The Wind in the Willows* as well. Rat and the Sea Rat are not only linguistically categorized together in species naming, but the Sea Rat is the "Soul" of Wilde's tale, enticing Rat and functioning as an alter-ego who acts out the fantasies of the insulated Briton who, while happy in rural Arcadia, is still susceptible to what the commercial publishing industry has told him he must revere to be a man: colonialist adventure and the unattached, nonfamilial life of the adventurer. When the Sea Rat regales him with tales of Constantinople, Venice, Palermo and the Mediterranean, he functions as the largely reporting adventurer we see in Toad's stories of escape. He even teases Water Rat to join him:

> Take the adventure, heed the call, now ere the irrevocable moment passes! Then some day, some day long hence, jog home here if you will, when the cup has been drained and the play has been played, and sit down by your quiet river with a store of goodly memories for your company [180].

But not all characters fall victim to this most masculine of schemes. Water Rat does become spellbound, literally walking like a zombie towards the door with travel goods when Mole intervenes. What Water Rat reveals in his desire is the need for legacy in the reported adventure:

> Tell me ... what sort of harvest an animal of spirit might hope to bring home from it [a life of coasting from port to port] to warm his latter days with gallant memories by the fireside; for my life, I confess to you, feels to me today somewhat narrow and circumscribed [172].

Domestic life is too small for the Water Rat as he compares himself to the Sea Rat. Rat, like Mole in his escape from home, yearns for something more than what his provincial English countryside, Arcadian life has provided — friendships, messy loyalties with characters like Toad, and drab, domestic life with no real adventure. With "harvest," it appears that Ratty desires the stories of the adventures afterwards rather than the actual process or life that such adventure would involve. Masculinity relies on the storytelling, the epic making that storytelling grants. This gains additional momentum, this idea of epic masculinity through adventure in exotic realms, even if it is reported adventure.

Grahame constructs this psychological dimension to masculinity as natural. Ratty watches birds flying south, speaks to them and begins to understand or feel the influence of the escape and imagination: "In himself [Rat], too, he knew it [call of the South] was vibrating at last, that chord hitherto dormant and unsuspecting" (167). Grahame constructs impulses that affect the body of the male characters as they develop their identities, the same war between the loco-specific love of home and the mysterious calling for adventure (Water Rat) and escape (Mole). The resolution for both characters is to compromise as if these are midlife crises.[1] Rat's realizations of an antithesis to these callings is an equivalent to guilt: "With closed eyes he dared to dream a moment in full abandonment, and when he looked again the river seemed steely and chill, the green fields gray and lightless. Then his loyal heart seemed to cry out on his weaker self for its treachery" (167). To stay at home is "loyal," while travel and adventure is "treachery."

Conflicts between home and adventure are central to the adventure story tradition. Such dilemmas and doubling occur in that most famous adventure story novel, *Treasure Island*. The conniving, quick thinking, and flexible Long John Silver is a perfect foil to the loyal, professional, and honorable Dr. Livesey. In Stevenson's development tale, Jim Hawkins' morality, as well as his life, are at stake. In *The Wind in the Willows*, Rat's conception of himself, his use of fantasy in his creative arts, and masculinity are at stake. Rat's eventual rejection of the Sea Rat's life (saved by his friend Mole), mirrors the eventual resolution of *Treasure Island*: Jim ends the novel writing his memories, withdrawn from "real" life, like the Rat. But, for both Wilde and Grahame, the adventuring side of the double relationship allows for the repressed self to travel and experience the fantasy space of sensual adventure and show the dangers, physically and psychologically, that these fantasies entail.[2]

The adventure story tradition relies on repeated stories to establish the myth qualities that surround recounted stories. Fantasy is constructed in the imagination, so when a character is retelling a back story before the main story is taking place, both reader and intended listener (another character in the story) are constructing both story and self in relation to the story. This can also occur in illustration, most famously in Beatrix Potter's *The Tale of Peter Rabbit*, where Peter's father is insinuated (and illustrated) to be in pie cooked by Mrs. McGregor.

In Wilde's work, the Soul is representing himself to the Fisherman through his storytelling; this is a recounted experience and not directly experienced by the reader or the Fisherman. But the Soul is part of the Fisherman, so he is constructing the Fisherman in absentia, as in "this could all be yours." Wilde demonstrates the allure of the adventure story in that his Soul entertains both the Fisherman and the child reader/listener with his resourcefulness against overwhelming odds.

Uniquely among the authors I examine in this chapter, Wilde buried the Soul's encounters with the Fisherman in the pronoun "it." Wilde never ascribes gender to the Soul, and this genderlessness parallels the mythological, fantastical world of the story. It is important to remember that the human character in this story asks *not* to be human so that he can love a mermaid. He has to be summoned from his body's desires from a quasi-heterosexual coupling, out of domesticity by the Soul, tricked or teased back to the magic of fantastical living the Fisherman first chose. As he is enticed or tricked by this genderless part of himself, he is lured into a mode of adventurous masculinity by reconstituted adventure stories used as a model for masculinity.

And when a same-sex companionship results in a story, such as *The*

Masculinity in Children's Animal Stories, 1888–1928

Happy Prince, we still see the influence of the adventure story. In *The Happy Prince*, a swallow, intent on fulfilling a motivation for fantastical flight, escapes to the docks, dreaming and shouting of his trip to Egypt with the other swallows. He recounts in each of his conversations with the Prince the different exotic activities his brothers experience in this exotic locale: flying into the tombs of the Pharaohs, visiting the Sphinx, and listening to the roaring God Memnon. This may be considered an initial masculinized plot: adventure awaits. Naomi Wood categorizes the swallow's cataloguing of his travels and adventures as part of Wilde's aesthetic concern, but with a deeper connection to "love [that] is rarely depicted as heterosexual, never domestic, and most likely to culminate in death" (165). But the context of this story reflects the adventure story tradition in the accretive piling of actions, sights, sounds, and imagery in this story as a foil or, we could imagine, a double for the swallow who, in real story time, invests his emotional energy in same-sex companionship.

At the very least, Wilde demonstrates a knowledge of the publishing industry and its marketing of stories for boys, while subverting the tradition with the transformation of the swallow and this same-sex union. Wilde's tales were published five years after Stevenson's *Treasure Island* (1883) and one year after Henry Rider Haggard's *Allan Quatermain* (1887). In this context, the exoticness of both the Soul and the swallow (both reported adventure) reveal the fundamental attraction that the mid-nineteenth century had for the traveling, adventurous male and the need for the legacy that only storytelling and mythmaking provides. Where Wilde differs from Stevenson and Haggard is how companionship, framed next to this adventure story tradition, could be subverted to illustrate transformation from a boy/child to a man, resulting in same-sex unions and in masculinity, which is less centered on recalled adventure and more centered on displays of affection and "brotherly love." In Wilde's imagining, adventurous masculinity is contextually reworked in imaginatively differentiated gender: one storyteller whose gender is neutral (*The Fisherman and His Soul*) and the other who undergoes a transformation (*The Happy Prince*).

Grahame's reported adventuring episodes are more picaresque than Wilde's. Similarly to Wilde, Toad relies on storytelling for self-aggrandizement. Toad is thrown from the boat by the barge woman after he escapes from jail, and then steals her horse. He then trades the horse, fills up with food and some money and begins walking home. But he can't

One • *Adventures, Escapes and Violence*

resist his egotistical self: "I snap my fingers, I walk out, I swim to shore, I seize her horse." He then proceeds to sing a song about himself in the third person: "The world has held great Heroes,/ as history books have showed;/ But never a name to go down to fame/ Compared with that of Toad" (200–201). And it is in the related adventure escapades that we see both this humorous and controlling side of Toad's characterization. His reporting of the escape from jail to Rat and Mole reveals the same insecurity: "I've been through such times since I saw you last, and you can't think! Such trials, such sufferings ... made 'em all do exactly what I wanted! Oh, I *am* a smart Toad, and make no mistake!" (210). Toad proceeds from sympathy to conceit. His masculine performances in this adventuring mode reveal a fundamental privilege afforded to the middle-class male gentry.

Grahame also reveals, in more direct fashion than Wilde, that adventurous masculinity needs an audience.[3] But Grahame invites us to question this type of masculinity, as the narrator deconstructs the entire genre:

> Toad, with no one to check his statements or to criticize in an unfriendly spirit, rather let himself go. Indeed, much that he related belonged more properly to the thought-of-in-time-instead-of-ten-minutes-after-wards. Those are always the best and raciest adventures; and why should they not be truly ours, as much as the somewhat inadequate things that really come off? [233].

Are we led to believe that stories, myths, and legends should be questioned? That the British adventure story genre, with its famous narrators recounting their adventures — Jim Hawkins, Allan Quatermain, Robinson Crusoe — is only a fantasy based on events which never occurred? That British masculinity has been influenced by fictions that are fabricated with episodes that are full of "inadequate things" and imagined conquests, victories, and superiorities of "native pluck" and character? As Grahame subversively entitles Toad's homecoming as "The Return of Ulysses," aren't we to think that classic never really told us the truth? And why not use animals in a children's story to make one's subversive critiques? Toad demonstrates, through Grahame's comedic scripting, that adventuring behavior and even epics may have been falsely created, transmitted, and preserved.

The seriousness with which writers like Kipling and Haggard took the empire and the notion of manliness tested in adventure story setting is reflected in works like *King Solomon's Mines* and *The Jungle Book*. But their work is more evidence of mid–Victorian values and conceptions of masculinity, as well as the publishing houses' capitalization on audiences at home for exoticism abroad. Writers like Wilde, Grahame, and Milne — arguably comic writers, in many ways — all too frequently subvert the ideals of the adventure story tradition to mock a stable notion of masculinity and to subtly mock the process of becoming male.

The comic tones of the reported adventure story abound in Grahame for plot reasons, to satirize middle-class pretensions at heroism, and to reveal escapist tendencies in the masculinizing process.[4] Grahame's allusions to Ulysses may be in a mock tone, but Toad's adventuring spirit is both serious and escapist. His equipment for such masculine performance begins with a caravan:

> There's the real life for you, embodied in that little cart. The open road, the dusty highway, the heath, the common, the hedgerows, the rolling downs! Camps, villages, towns, cities! Here today, up and off to somewhere else tomorrow! Travel, change, interest, excitement! The whole world before you, and a horizon that's always changing! [34].

Too busy to speak in complete sentences, too busy to restrain himself from excessive exclamation points, Toad accumulates language and imagined visuals in many of his speeches. But we must remember Toad is free of a father figure, represented by the boathouse in the beginning of the novel: "The place [boathouse] had an unused and deserted air" (34). Son Toad, like so many late Victorian boys, wishes to leave, travel, and experience in a more hedonistic fashion and doesn't have the censoring influence of a father figure. Peter Green, author of *Kenneth Grahame, 1859–1932: A Study of His Life, Work and Times*, contends that Toad's fetish over automobiles — another vehicle for his escapist fantasies — is like a mid-life crisis: "What goes on in his [Toad's] mind as he tears along the highway suggests the kind of compensation ... fast cars (now as then) symbolize unattained power, potency, or pure irresponsible authority..." (283). Deceased Father Toad may be a reason for Toad's desire to flee home as he screams down the highway to create himself far from Toad Hall and Victorian patriarchy.

In this way, like Jack Hawkins or Ralph Rover in *Treasure Island* and *The Coral Island*, respectively, Toad fights to become an individualized boy/man. His fight is to gain self-control over these adventuring and escapist fantasies. One may reason that he fails to do this; he continues to imagine himself in self-aggrandized fashion, despite the humbling retaking of Toad Hall. This failure is framed and even supported by the "rightness" of the British class system, which restores "harmony and justice" to both the River Bank and to Toad: a "harmony and justice" that takes precedence over his development (Butts, 332).

It is important to see Grahame's novel as a mock-heroic work, with specific humorous reversals mocking the adventure story tradition. But Toad's humorous episodes are frequently depicted in both violent and hierarchal ways. As he becomes intoxicated with the automobile, he expresses his desires in narcissistic and egotistical speech: "What dust clouds shall spring behind me as I speed on my reckless way! What carts I shall fling carelessly into the ditch in the wake of my magnificent onset!" (42). His "careless" control of the road and privilege as middle-class boy of leisure incite more and richer imaginative leaps into adventure when he drives the automobile: "Toad once more, Toad at his best and highest, Toad the terror, the traffic-queller, the Lord of the lone trail, before who all must give way or be smitten into nothingness and everlasting night" (120). The lingering influence of violence from the adventure story tradition now mingles with satire.

Too often we have continued our analyses of gender to submit points of categorization as finite. In this case, Grahame uses an outrageous character to mock the class of character, revealing the very "unfitness" that a character like Badger condemns. Masculine performance required imagination, perhaps molded by adventure stories for boys. John Tosh, in *A Man's Place: Masculinity and the Middle Class Home in Victorian England*, posits that fiction followed factual circumstance (and publishing houses marketing towards this normalized gender expectation): "Men were supported in their choice by a vigorous bachelor society in the major towns and cities, and by a new genre of adventure fiction which glamorized their condition" (194). In Grahame's "Arcadian" countryside, Toad's imagination becomes both a performance and a realization of violence and hierarchal privilege enacted far away from colonial ambition. Grahame reveals class privilege in Toad's humorous behavior, but he is subtly critiquing the genre of the adventure story through this hyperbolic behavior.

And Grahame isn't the only one to critique the genre. Milne's critique not only extends the satiric tendencies he loved in Grahame's work, it also gave him an opportunity to employ the linguistic tradition of nonsense in the Pooh books. Ann Thwaite, in her biography, *A. A. Milne: The Man Behind Winnie-the-Pooh*, concludes that Milne was a fan of Stevenson,

Masculinity in Children's Animal Stories, 1888–1928

Marryat and Weiss: "What these books gave him, rather than a taste for exploration was a feeling for the joy of being your own master" (16). As the central character, Pooh does perform in various adventure modes (physically, through boasts, even in his imagination/dreams). The book, in essence, is even structured around episodic mini-adventures with Pooh as the central hero: he saves Piglet from the flood, grabs a pole and saves Roo from drowning, and even finds Eeyore's tail. True, the episodes are scripted with the humor intended for adults and children, but Milne's depictions of absent-minded bravery and "happenstantial" courage subvert the adventure story tradition more than reinforce it.

Heroic masculinity is frequently mis-performed in Milne's work. For example, in the episode where he tries to find Eeyore's tail, Pooh declares: "Eeyore ... I, Winnie-the-Pooh, will find your tail for you" (47). This epic boast, a verbal performance of masculinity, focuses the humor on expectations of heroism, which are undercut by Pooh's actual discovery of the tail. He "barely" discovers it, and the discovery is framed by Owl's fauxsage position in the episode. In another example of this mis-performance, we find luck as the primary agent in establishing the hero Pooh. In the "Expotition to the North Pole," Pooh inadvertently finds a pole, saves Roo's life, and is credited with discovering the North Pole. Following the 1909 Peary claim of discovering the North Pole, Milne couldn't have picked a greater ironic, yet fitting model. Peary's claim to have landed at the North Pole remains problematic today, a performance so seriously taken (possibly needed by the British public as the empire waned) that it could be, finally, fabricated. Milne doesn't mock as savagely as Wilde or Grahame. While Wilde skewers patriarchal masculinity, particularly male vanity and lack of individuality, Grahame's critique of Toad's masculinity encourages individuality but centers the mockery on vanity as it is mis-performed. In this way, we may remember that heroic masculinity needs an audience and, in Milne, this heroic masculinity is mocked and results in a mis-performance.

Clearly Milne was not as susceptible to the adventure story genre as Kipling and Grahame were. But Milne did script performances of adventure, which use the same physicality we associate with such heroes. But Milne does so problematically. Baby Roo and Pooh frequently demonstrate their masculinity through the use of their bodies. When Roo falls into the water on the "expotition," he can only call attention to his swimming. He appeals to all of the male characters to acknowledge his swimming performance:

> Pooh, did you see me swimming? That's called swimming, what I was doing. Rabbit, did you see what I was doing? Swimming. Hallo, Piglet! I say, Piglet! What do you think I was doing! Swimming! Christopher Robin, Did you see me... [125].

We see the same active body performances with Roo when he "practice[es] very small jumps in the sand, falling down mouse holes and climbing out of them" (98). Roo's performance is much the same, demonstrating his jumping for the males (Rabbit, Pooh, and Piglet) while his mother watches him, but the transgressive nature of Milne's scripting is evident.

What makes the performance transgressive is that Roo is actually taught how to jump by his mother; she is his model for adventure through the use of the body. Though Pooh will jump with him, we learn that Pooh is not only jealous of Kanga's jumping, he goes for lessons by the end of the story. Complicating this use of the body in gendered description is Milne's use of grammar. After Roo is abducted by the group, Pooh "practice[s] jumps" and "decide[s] to be a Kanga" (105, 109). This is certainly a more liberated use of the body: a male pretends to be a female who represents the whole species. This demonstration, both in performance and in verbal depiction, is one reason Carol Stanger in "Winnie the Pooh Through a Feminist Lens" gives for feminists responding to Pooh with more acceptance: "...Pooh's 'embodiment' of the physical side ... vs. a phallocentric value on the intellectual side..." (46–47). Stranger sees a physicality in Pooh that is more playful and less demonstrative or controlling. Kanga's use of the body is a model for adventure and physicality normally associated with the male-dominated field of the adventure story. Kanga doesn't serve merely as a domestic guide or mother (neither of which she is for Pooh) but as a model for a type of play, in physical dimension, that doesn't assert hierarchy or an extension of power.

Escape

If we reason that place, domestic place, is a source of identity for the feminine, then an escape from that place could be a source of strengthened identity for characters whose sense of place requires an escape from that place. Escape, particularly from the domestic setting/scene, is prevalent in many of the works in this book. Mole, in *The Wind in the Willows*, has a continuing process of conflict between home and escape that is only resolved by his eventual co-habitation of Rat's water home. When Mole leaves his hole, he leaves behind one steady and unchanging identity: housecleaner. Mole's escape rambles, linguistically, as much as it does physically: "Hither and thither through the meadows he rambled busily, along the hedgerows, across the copses, finding everywhere birds building, flowers budding, leaves thrusting — everything happy, and progressive, and occupied" (11). Mole is freed from the domestic underground into a self that is free and expressive. He becomes a natural rambler and open spaces traveler. The urgency with which Mole performs is reminiscent of Toad's expressive adventuring (though Mole's escapist expression occurs earlier): "Hang spring cleaning!" [Mole exclaims] and bolted out of the house without even waiting to put on his coat. Something up above was calling him imperiously" (9). This escape is an escape from domesticity and an isolated bachelorhood.

The force holding Mole back may seem as if centered on his "little" home. But Mole also escapes narrowly defined masculinity. Masculinity was being redefined in the Edwardian Age; in this children's novel, Mole is the best example of the paradoxes, contradictions, and societal inscriptions that might occur. While Grahame frames part of Mole's desire in the seasonal and in the biological (Mole "bolts" in the spring), the locus of the conflict is identified early: domestic space/life vs. adventure, isolation vs. camaraderie.

External forces summon Mole from his boyish bachelorhood, and friends and adventures will shape him into an Edwardian gentleman. Grahame even frames Mole's escape as a quest for freedom; the narrator describes Mole as "emancipated" as he converses and picnics with Rat in the beginning of the novel. We could read part of the novel as a mini-bildungsroman for Mole. In fact, Neil Philips remarks in "The Wind in the Willows: The Vitality of a Classic" that the first five chapters feature Mole as a central character and that Grahame's original title was *Mr. Mole and His Mates*.

But this escape of Mole's finds him emancipated with another male/boy character. Just after Mole's initial escape of his home, he finds Rat and freedom in a picnic with Rat. This type of freedom and its representation of masculinity is quite different from Toad's. One part of his masculinizing process is framed in escape, yet Grahame refrains from overtly throwing him into adventure like Toad. Grahame maintains that escape from the domestic towards male/male companionship is an "emancipation." This freedom could be certainly connected to the limitations that marriage placed on a male. Lois Kuznets remarked in "Kenneth Grahame and Father Nature, or Whither Blows *The Wind in the Willows*" that Grahame dramatizes "woman's dangerous power to limit man's freedom" (175), and that we can read Grahame's disastrous marriage and stunted development in terms of interacting with the opposite sex in how he characterizes Mole and Rat's "ideal" companionship. It may not be any wonder that Mole and his "mates" successfully "escape" marriage along the River Bank when we consider the biographical influences. After all, the book has been classified as a "fantasy." Perhaps its classification demonstrates that the heteronormative idea of marriage is so dominant that only in fantasy can one escape it.

But escaping the heteronormative spaces, like marriage, isn't reserved for male writers. Masculinity, in Potter's work, includes the performance of escaping domestic spaces. Central to these escapes is the feeling of confinement among both male and female characters. Certainly Potter herself felt this confinement in her sequestered life in Kensington and may have even autobiographically written an escapist fantasy of her own in *The Tale of Hunca Munca*. But escape, as a performance of masculinity, may be tied to the absence of father figures in her work as the absence of a patriarch haunts *The Fierce Bad Rabbit*, *The Tale of Peter Rabbit*, *The Tale of Tom Kitten*, *The Tale of Jemima Puddle-Duck*, and *The Roly-Poly Pudding*.[5] Without the patriarchal force of a Badger or a Bagheera, as we see in Grahame and Kipling's work, the lessons learned in development seem more "natural" in Potter's work (rather than culturally inscribed).

Yet, male characters don't prosper in the vacuum Potter creates in her work. Following in the footsteps of his father, Peter Rabbit risks the same death that befell his father in his garden adventures. And once is not enough, as we witness Peter return to the garden after his near-death experience with his cousin, Benjamin Bunny. Like Toad in *The Wind in the Willows*, Peter remains ignorant of his own father's legacy. A major change between Potter and Grahame is the responsibility Peter demonstrates with his own garden in *The Tale of the Flopsy Bunnies*. It takes two stories, both laced with tragedy, before Peter can grow up from his escapist fantasies.[6]

In Potter's work, escape is paired with curiosity. Potter punishes curiosity, particularly as it is rendered outside of female control. Or we may ascertain that Potter punishes the distancing from the domestic site of family and power. For example, in *The Tale of Peter Rabbit*, Peter stands away from his mother at the beginning of the story, reinforcing the distance between male and female, illuminating the desire for escape from family and home. His back is to his mother as she speaks to the children. In fact, his eyes slope downward as if in consternation or anger (his sisters' eyes focus upward or on the mother).

Peter's anger and rebellion are evident in his illustrated posture. Potter also frames Peter's lost father in this initial rendering and sets Peter off on a performance of masculinity that has endured for centuries according to Alice Byrne: "Peter follows the pattern of the archetypal hero who sets out in quest of his lost father" (Mackey, *Beatrix Potter's Peter Rabbit: A Children's Classic at 100*, 140). And the escape must take place, in the mythical sense, where domesticity can't intrude ... where the father was lost. While this analysis may seem a bit too Freudian for some readers, Potter's concern with the natural cycles of nature intersects with one of the core structural elements of the adventure story: a boy without a father faced with a world that is neutral to his plight. Potter seems to insinuate that it isn't worth the search, that happiness is more English than exotic, that it is more domestic bound and integrated with a large family than in individualist schemes of escape and adventure. And, if we end where we begin, the anger that prompts the journey leads to an ill-suited adventure resolved only by a subsequent escape from the dangerous, exotic garden.

We witness the same resistance to domesticity in *The Tale of Benjamin Bunny*, as well as some of the same elements of storytelling. Benjamin, though "little," escapes both his father and his aunt (Peter's mother) when he finds Peter alone at the beginning of the story. Benjamin is active in his avoidance of the domestic power: "Little Benjamin did not very much want to see his Aunt" and persuades Peter to go back to the garden (18). Both boy bunnies, Peter and Benjamin, perform their escape into a space noticeably absent of adult eyes. And to correct this escape, Potter uses realism as an antidote. Both a violent father, old Benjamin Bunny and death in waiting, the cat, provide an all too realistic battle where escape consistently has the same ending: correction from the adult.

Boyish escape is depicted not only as dangerous but deserving of the terror and trauma Potter uses as a punishment. Peter Hollindale, in "Humans are So Rabbit," sees the boys' play in *The Tale of Benjamin Bunny* reflecting a male desire to resist authority, to break the law: "This second expedition is at Benjamin's instigation. Peter is merely a reluctant and bemused accessory. Benjamin does not forage on the spot, as Peter did; he loots the onions" (in Mackey, *Beatrix Potter's Peter Rabbit: A Children's Classic at 100*, 168). Benjamin's instigation resists the domestic center of power (his aunt, Peter's mother) and the patriarch (Benjamin's father). Because he also breaks the code (looting the onions), he must be corrected. Both *The Wind in the Willows* and *Winnie the Pooh* have companioned play as well, but neither is accompanied with such patriarchal violence or framing, which places the domestic site so closely to the punishment.

Potter, a Unitarian, was raised on a moral and political diet of utilitarianism and conservative politics. She scripts anti-fairy tales whose central message seems to be communality over individuality. Alice Byrne contends the opposite: "Peter's experience [in *The Tale of Peter Rabbit*] resembles the perennial theme of the fairy tales in which the youngster wanders into the primeval forest" (Mackey, 140). While I agree that Potter creates spaces for her characters to wander, particularly dangerous places where death is waiting, the central message or moral to her stories isn't transformation (as it is in so many fairy tales). In fact, we may read more of the influence of John Locke, Sarah Trimmer, and the mid–eighteenth century's embrace of reason over fantasy.

The problem with Byrne's analysis, besides the autobiographical evidence, is that Potter's plotting of *The Tale of Peter Rabbit* is initiated by the mother's orders not to go into the garden. Peter's escape is a rebellion that ends disastrously, with negative reinforcement as the tool for moral instruction; there is no transformation.[7]

Ironically, escape is rendered in costumes in many of these anthropomorphic tales. Though not a transformation, characters don costumes and remove costumes, which reveals (rather than the costumes that reveal) escapist tendencies in masculine representation. In Grahame's work, escape is a charade-like performance, particularly for Toad. In English literature, cross dressing has long been a tradition in comedy and satire. In *The Wind in the Willows*, Toad's flight from jail is assured only when he dresses up in women's clothes and makes his way home. He even poses as a washerwoman, only shedding his costume when he confronts the feminine model of the servant class — the washerwoman. He uses the costume to escape, though his class and sexual prejudice are proudly on display as he makes his way home.

The same cross dressing occurs in Beatrix Potter's *The Tale of Tom Kitten* where Tom, punished with his sisters for losing their clothes, is sent upstairs. Mocking his mother, he dresses up in her clothes (in illustration). While this may be an example of anti-authoritarianism rather than misogyny, the behavior still demonstrates the comedic effect of cross dressing, its satiric nature, and its mocking of female authority.[8]

As in Grahame, in Potter's work costumes are made to escape. Largely because of her exquisite illustrations, costumes add not only to the aesthetic effect of the stories, but can become part of the plotting and the gender depictions. In *The Tale of Tom Kitten*, not only does the mother dress Tom in "all sorts of elegant uncomfortable clothes" (151), but he loses buttons and escapes these clothes as soon as he is out of sight of his mother. Tom discards his clothes as soon as he can in an effort to escape societal circumcision. Kutzer claims that "he [Tom] ... sheds both his clothing and civility upon the garden wall" (207). Carole Scott, in "Between Me and the World: Clothes as Mediator between Self and Society in the Work of Beatrix Potter," sees this conflict as a "clash between the children's animal spirits and their restrictive, socially acceptable covering" (195). She goes further to claim that in many of Potter's stories costumes are prohibitive:

> It is clear that Potter's resentments against the social conventions and constraints that are senseless and galling to children (and to others that retain an unspoiled vision) are being expressed in her characters' clothes-related adventures [196].

But as characters are made naked, in Potter's works, they are punished. When Tom's jacket is pulled off, he is then rolled into a sandwich. Peter Rabbit's loss of clothes is attenuated with his near death in McGregor's garden. For Potter, resistance to costuming is funny and necessary as long as the domestic center is maintained. When the authority of the home is challenged, as in *The Tale of Peter Rabbit*, shedding one's clothes is the beginning of a disaster.

One • *Adventures, Escapes and Violence*

In this study of masculinity, I contend escape from the domestic is a masculine performance. But this isn't restricted to male characters. Several female characters in Potter's work escape the "clutches" of domesticity. Perhaps the most famous is Jemima Puddle-duck. Potter, even at the beginning of the story, doesn't sentimentalize domesticity and motherhood. Jemima's sister-in-law, Rebeccah Puddle-duck, claims that she is "perfectly willing to leave the hatching to someone else — I have not the patience to sit on a nest for twenty-eight days..." (161). So when Jemima Puddle-duck "escapes" to go lay eggs without disturbance, she is, paradoxically, fleeing to become a mother. Her escape is not "boyish," but still involves unaccompanied adventure and fleeing a site of domesticity (the farmyard). Self-discovery is an impulse that Wilde, Kipling, Grahame and Milne all script for their characters. But in Potter's mind, self-discovery is not as valuable as knowing a center or place of commitment and social belonging. In other words, Jemima's escape is doomed from the beginning because she doesn't accept her place: the farmyard.

Jemima's escape is even configured in unnatural description by Potter: "Jemima Puddle-duck was not much in the habit of flying. She ran downhill a few yards flapping her shawl, and then she jumped off into the air" (163). She bravely goes where no farm girl has gone before: out into the great wide open to become a single mother without extended domesticity to surround her. Potter's eye towards naturalism depicts the flight of a goose as accurate — awkward and clumsy lift off but steady and "beautiful" once in the air. But when a woman behaves transgressively, she is punished by Potter in the same ways she punishes boys (Peter, Benjamin, Tom Kitten) who attempt to flee domestic sites. In Jemima's case, dogs sent to find her kill the fox who was a tempter and eat all of her precious, newly laid eggs.

Many escapes, especially ill-planned ones, are framed with trauma afterwards in Potter's works. But in Wilde's work, he rarely scripted escape plots in both *The House of Pomegranates* and *The Happy Prince and Other Stories*. A possible exception may be *The Fisherman and His Soul*: the Soul ventures forth each year after being cut out by the Fisherman, but it's [Soul's] journeys, exciting as they may be, always bring it back with the yearning to be reunited with the Fisherman's heart. Wilde thwarts the escape/adventure plot of the swallow in "The Happy Prince" through love; he introduces a quasi-adventure plot in "The Star-Child," but that is begun only by the principal character to search out his mother — almost a reversal of the archetypal search of the son for the father.

In Grahame and Potter's work, adventure and escape are framed with psychological trauma afterwards. There is an insular quality to their work: if you leave the domestic setting, for which you should be glad and appreciative, you will suffer a psychological trauma. Mole and Rat both enact psychological breakdowns: Mole when he can't find a home and desperately needs to reconnect with his own home, and Rat when he encounters the Sea Rat and rashly tries to run away from the riverbank. Peter Rabbit, Benjamin Bunny, Tom Kitten, and Jemima Puddle-duck all bear the psychological scars of their ill-conceived escape plots. What Potter and Grahame reveal in their representation of masculinity is that escaping the domestic site (whether that site be female-dominated, as in Potter, or male-dominated, as in Grahame) is not to be rewarded and, seemingly, contradicts the adventure story tradition, which blessed the colonialist ambitions and dominated the establishment of "true" masculinity for the late eighteenth century in the pages of Victorian periodicals for boys such as *The Halfpenny Marvel*, *The Union Jack*, and *Pluck*.

Invasions/Rebellions/Trickster Figures

Potter frequently enacts rebellions in her stories that take the form of characters "invading" home spaces or domestic sites frequently controlled by females. In *The Tale of Mrs. Tittlemouse*, Mrs. Tittlemouse lives alone and frequently has to battle intrusion into her space: bees, spiders and Mr. Jackson, a toad. Potter clearly separates gender in this story: cleanliness, female vs. invasiveness/dirtiness, masculine. While in other stories, such as *The Story of Two Bad Mice*, homes are also invaded, Potter makes it clear that invading males (acting in self-centered ways) have no place in the female-dominated home.

When masculine privilege, the assumption of a hierarchal position based on one's gender, is the cause, Potter scripts an initial rebellion by male characters (think Peter Rabbit, Benjamin Bunny, etc.); a counter rebellion or resistance may also occur from female characters. Mr. Jackson, in *The Tale of Mrs. Tittlemouse*, performs in heteronormative fashion, offering to rid the house of attackers while Mrs. Tittlemouse can clean up afterward. He even presumes she will offer him dinner for such services. But invasive masculinity is not rewarded in Potter's work as Mrs. Tittlemouse makes a door too small for Mr. Jackson to enter her house (though she does allow him to attend the party at the end of the story as he reaches through the window for refreshments). More importantly, Potter's cardinal solution to conflicts involving female characters in heteronormative spaces is invoked; male characters are thwarted and working-class domesticity is upheld as a paradigm of virtue.

Similarly, Milne depicts Pooh's invasion of Rabbit's house as one based on privilege. Because Pooh wants honey, can't control himself, and even carries a reputation for both characteristics, he demonstrates the same characteristics as Mr. Jackson in Potter's work. Pooh's inability to self-regulate his eating and curb his impulsivity lead him into a fixed position as he tries to leave Rabbit's hole. It may be remembered that Rabbit lies to Pooh about being home — Pooh has a reputation for this masculine privilege he exerts. We may not see this as a rebellion, but Pooh does invade domestic spaces, as if he is privileged to placate his desires without recourse.[9]

The Jungle Book has a curious example of a male figure invading domestic space. As Shere Khan hunts Mowgli into the wolf den, violating the rules by hunting humans and hunting into the wolf's home, it is Raksha who offers the resistance to his intrusion. While she is ostensibly resisting his form of hunting, the location of the scene at the cave mouth and Raksha's defense makes Shere Khan's invasion similar to that depicted by Potter. Though Shere Khan's invasion is more aggressive than the bumbling Mr. Jackson, in both Potter and Kipling's work initial male rebellion is countered with female resistance. In Kipling's Darwinian jungle, invasions of homes can be deadly and become sites where masculinity is contested with death lurking behind the door. Even as Shere Khan retorts to Raksha's defense: "Each dog barks in his own yard!" (9), he frames his invasion in acknowledgment of hierarchy and privilege: "We will see what the Pack will say to this fostering of man-cubs" (9). He clearly indicates that Raksha's rebellion will become a matter of legal workings in the male-dominated jungle legal system. Kipling's script calls for rebellion from both a male, dominant character and a female, mother character. Both these characters violate the law and both shirk male-centered places of authority such as the Pack meeting rock. Though female resistance and rebellion is intrinsic to literature and how we understand rebellion and its relationship to power, in children's works, Potter and Kipling stand out (Potter in many of her works, Kipling in this particular work) for framing rebellion — to domestic sites by males and counter resistance by females so closely.

Another form of rebellion to entertain is that of trickster figures. Trickster figures are often male characters in the works I examine. And we may, wrongly, assume that trickster behavior is only masculine. But in the works I've examined, tricksters are mostly male and their behavior presents the rebellion we see with many young males' initial characterizations. For example, in *The Tale of Squirrel Nutkin*, Nutkin jests and teases Old Mr. Brown, the patriarchal figure of the story, with rhymes and songs while other characters pay their respect by giving sacrifices of food. He is "excessively impertinent" with "no respect" (25, 27) while the other squirrels march in unison with minnows in their uniform paws. The "rebel" Nutkin stands alone to the side, free and chaotic with his ears perked up and his full, bushy tail in the air. This rebellion is more a part of the folktale tradition than the psychological imbued tales of Peter Rabbit and Benjamin Bunny. We may consider Nutkin's actions childish, strange, even pagan as he attempts to personify nature: "Nutkin danced up and down like a sunbeam ... [he] made a whirring noise to sound like the wind" (33–34). Potter's scripting of his rebellion in elemental and natural language suggests a cyclical quality to resisting hierarchs.

Theoretically, rebellion could be linked to the Bakhtin and the carnivalesque. While Bakhtin wrote primarily about "carnival festivities" and "comic spectacles" (5), we may consider some of his findings in relation to play and performance in these texts. The liberating impulse to rebel against authority may find credence in psychological sources (Freud, Erikson, and others), but as it is expressed in these works, the trickster or rebel figure challenges, often humorously, an adult figure. In this vein, masculine rebellion can serve as a challenge to authority, with all the violence that ensues — a safety valve for the dominant discourse (Foucault), or a comic inversion of hierarchy and a revelation of a more "true" identity (Bakhtin). As we examine these texts, the reversals inherent in the carnivalesque (character of lower stature satirizing those of higher stature; parodic laughter and representation; and challenges to hierarchy through revelation of more "true identity") will become more evident as an integral part to the performance of masculinity in these texts.

One • *Adventures, Escapes and Violence*

The idea that rebellion can serve as a safety valve for resistance to a dominant ideology works well in an analysis of Potter's stories. In *The Tale of Two Bad Mice*, as Tom Thumb and Hunca Munca invade a house of dolls (static and plastic females), they are also invading a manifestation of Victorian hierarchy, heteronormative marriage, and its links to class positions. Her parents opposed Potter's engagement to Norman Warne and the story of the two rebellious mice, a couple, is thought to be an autobiographical, literary depiction of that rebellion. M. Daphne Kutzer has observed, "The novel is in some sense, a foreshadowing of Potter's life to come, in which she gradually cut the ties to home in favor of Hill Top and Sawrey, and ultimately marries Mr. Heelis of Hawkshead" (210). And certainly rebellion as it is configured in carnivalesque terms is both subversive and productive; Potter and her famous mice eventually unite outside the scripted bonds of society.

Class rebellion is evident in the monkeys' behavior as well. Kipling frames the dangerousness of the monkeys next to Mowgli's training. Mowgli is being trained in the laws and languages of the jungle, and the lawless monkeys kidnap him when Mowgli is resisting Baloo's instruction. The monkeys' transgressive play and performances are at odds with the hunting/heteronormative behavior Kipling's Baloo and Bagheera are in charge of providing the "man cub."

These monkeys function in a Bahktinian sense as trickster figures as they challenge the norms of jungle society due to their play and irresponsibility. These characters sing songs, swing from tree to tree, steal Mowgli, and further incriminate themselves against the societal norm by taking up residence in the abandoned human village. This sort of rebellion seems to be normal though. After all, Mowgli likes the monkeys and is taken with their play and free spiritedness, so much so that he is physically punished by Baloo. Kipling takes Mowgli's initial fascination with the monkeys and ends this fascination with the monkeys' slaughter by Kaa.

This rebellion is no different than the rebellion of the stoats, weasels, and ferrets in *The Wind in the Willows*. They not only ambush Mole and Badger and take Toad Hall for their own, but their laughter/songs/celebrations mock the police and the courts — the social and political system of the riverbank. Their rebellion, much like the Bandar-log (monkey), is a rebellion framed in class performances. In fact, Peter Green and others have seen the autobiographical incidents of Grahame's life contributing to this scene. In 1903, Grahame was serving as the secretary for the Bank of England and successfully thwarted an assassination attempt by the Socialist agitator, George Robinson, which included gunshots and police action against the supposed Socialist. The threat of socialism is evident in Rat's report of the rebellion when Toad returns from jail:

> The Wild Wooders have been living in Toad Hall ... Lying in bed half the day, and breakfast at all hours, and the place in such a mess ... Eating your grub, and drinking your drink, and making bad jokes about you, and singing vulgar songs, about ... prisons, magistrates, and policemen; horrid personal songs, with no humor in them [216].

This savage rebellion enacts a form of lower-class socialism that represented precisely the fears of the English middle class. Grahame depicts the lawlessness and anarchic Wild Wooders but also their humor. As Bahktin has noted, this form of class rebellion in the carnivalesque includes mimicry (of the upper class) and humor (oral, costumed, etc.). And this is mirrored in the "lower class" behavior of the stoats and weasels.

But laughter and comic jest is part of the rebellion of all the riverbank denizens. And the rebellion can be problematic. Certainly the most famous case of rebellion is Toad's adventures. Viewed as a rebellion, Toad's behavior reveals a psychological rebellion against the absent patriarch. When Toad is at Toad Hall, he is taken care of. He spends the beginning of the novel trying to escape Toad Hall by caravan or car. This rebellion would seem psychologically appropriate as Toad eventually opts to "fit" his social milieu and assumes his rightful place — heir to Victorian wealth, social class, and landowning bachelor.

But his rebellion betrays the "solid" values of a middle-class gentleman, revealing the hypocrisy and failings of the late Victorian and Edwardian society to continue the values so esteemed from the nineteenth century. What Grahame reveals, no less, is that the values as attributed to blood or family name were a sham. The carnivalesque nature of Toad's rebellion reveals that the codes were a hypocrisy and that the real "English" virtue lay somewhere in between the stoats/weasels and Toad/Badger. If the corrective to episodic humor and carnivalesque humor is to be found in *The Wind in the Willows*, it is evident in the companionship and loyalty of Mole and Rat.

Grahame may differentiate in his rebellions based on class, but Kipling and Potter differentiate based on purpose and plotting. Both Kipling and

One • Adventures, Escapes and Violence

Potter were conservatives who believed that the development of one's character is reflected in action. Rebellion is conditional for these two writers, where some rebellion is rewarded (if appropriate, i.e., harmless and in good fun or with an eye towards mocking social conventions deemed to be obsolete) and some rebellion is punished (genderless monkeys are too anarchic, little boy bunnies wandering off from home are too unlicensed). This differentiation of rebellion reveals as much about composition strategies in children's literature as it does about consistency in rebellion.

But Kipling's characterization of masculinity in this trickster vein are varied. In the beginning of the novel, for instance, Tabaqui, the hyena, functions as a "coarse" jester. He is despised "because he runs about making mischief, and telling tales, and eating rags and pieces of leather from the village rubbish-heaps" (2). But, in Kipling's hands, there are positions of power for so many males in this text. In Tabaqui's case, his jester status is combined with "dewanee-the madness," where he goes mad and "forgets that he was ever afraid of anything, and runs through the forest biting everything in his way" (2). But his trickster status is also tied to speech:

> "All thanks for this good meal," he said, licking his lips. "How beautiful are the noble children! How large are their eyes! And so young too! Indeed, indeed, I might have remembered that the children of Kings are men from the beginning." Now, Tabaqui knew as well as anyone else there is nothing so unlucky as to compliment children to their faces; and it pleased him to see Mother and Father Wolf look uncomfortable [2–3].

Tabaqui is rebelling in more active masculine fashion through his speech and his challenge to the norm, but he is challenging the only heteronormative couple in the jungle. While Kipling may be advancing the plot with an element of foreshadowing as to Mowgli's survival trials, there appear to be different levels of tricksters and what society will tolerate.[10]

But not all rebellion is male dominated. Potter scripts what seems to be a masculine performance of rebellion in her female characters. Sometimes it is punished (Jemima Puddle-duck); sometimes it is rewarded (Hunca Munca). Bahktin proposes that material bodily images can tend toward objectifying "parts of private life, the goal of egotistical lust and possession" (25). But the rebellion in *The Tale of Two Bad Mice* is a rebellion against mouse traps and guarding policeman — the plastic Victorian life embodied in the story and the house. In this rebellion, anger isn't reserved for male characters: "there was no end to the rage and disappointment of

Tom Thumb and Hunca Munca" (77). Hunca Munca tears apart the kitchen — her rebellion couched in third-person plural pronouns — yet returns with Tom Thumb to their family of mice. The two rebel to create and not in "egotistical lust and possession" but to fulfill heteronormative family rearing. The story ends with Hunca Munca rocking the child while Tom Thumb lectures the children on a mousetrap.

While we use terms like *liminality* to mark a character who straddles many identities, places or representations, Bakhtin's investigation of clowns and fools and how they straddle "the borderline between life and art" (8) allows us to frame Potter's rebellion to marriage. She rewrites heteronormative unions to ease the class restrictions (the story takes place in a doll's house with plastic dolls as representatives of the Victorian norm). In addition, Potter may have used objects that signify possession and materiality, but the behaviors, even the illustrations, promote the idea of family in its actions (provision, comfort) as worthy of rebellion, even against the upper class.

We may classify Mowgli's usurpation of power in the last section of *The Jungle Book* as rebellion, like Potter's, against the norm of the society. He participates in the socially organized gatherings of the jungle where leadership and groups are carefully delineated by Shere Khan, Akela (lead wolf), and other older, parent figures. This leadership is all-male and hierarchal. While the human presence may be privileged by the end of the novel, the norm of society — the wolf pack — retains its age old hegemony.

When Mowgli both plans and executes his plan to kill Shere Khan, he violates the rules and norms of the jungle code. He effectively "rises" as he eliminates his rival. In fact, he uses buffaloes — human property — to divert Shere Khan into the stampede, thus violating his own species' organizational structure by using another's property for personal gain. It may be noted that Shere Khan does shirk codes of behavior in the jungle as well, but his punishment is rendered justified, while Mowgli is not punished. And Mowgli is looked at by the wolves as a natural leader following this coup. He may not be a trickster figure, but Mowgli's rebellion is violent and usurps class position. His rebellion reconfigures the order of jungle hierarchy.

Kipling differs from Potter in that despite a well-motivated rebellion (Mowgli's hunting and killing of Shere Khan), Mowgli doesn't fare well by the end of the novel. He has become angry and distant, ending the novel by refusing leadership of the pack and leaving them behind. It seems as if heteronormative leadership isn't the fit for Kipling's Darwinian subject and, with no domestic site to return to, Mowgli's rebellion is but a temporal exercise, without lasting connection for the "man cub." Revenge, as modeled in Mowgli's rebellion, isn't ultimately satisfying (though the display of Shere Khan's skin and Mowgli's speech may seem otherwise).

Violence

Milne's work easily is the least violent of the writers I examine in this book. In Milne's work, violence has little place in the masculinizing of a character. Characters do not even imaginatively opt for violence, though Piglet has fears of violence or physical imagery due to his reduced size. Milne's experiences in World War One (the only soldier of the authors I have examined), particularly at the Battle of the Somme, may have informed his decisions in characterizing the nonviolent toys in the Hundred Acre Wood. We may imagine Kipling and Lord Baden-Powell, founder of the Boy Scouts, shaking their heads at such characterizations or even laughing, as so many have, at the mis-adventures.

But Kipling fetishized violence (ever the voyeuristic reporter) and Powell never served in a "modern" military capacity. Milne's service at the Battle of the Somme brought him face to face with carnage and death. A result of this experience and the subsequent realization of the war profiteers during the First World War was Milne's poem, "O.B.E" (Order of the British Empire), a bitterly sarcastic poem about war profiteering and class privilege as well as the play, *The Boy Comes Home* where a soldier/boy returns and confronts his war-profiteering uncle with a revolver. In *Winnie the Pooh*, Milne may have dramatized other aspects of masculinity, but it would appear that the modern war traumatized Milne to such an extent that he found it impossible to inscribe violence upon his humorous animals in their English forest.

Violence does occur in Wilde's work, but it is limited and relies on threats for the most part. His use of violence isn't inherited from the adventure story tradition, nor is it used to inscribe Victorian codes of conduct on his characters. For example, the Wolf in "The Star-Child" threatens to eat the turtledoves if they don't believe him. The water rat in "The Devoted

Friend" proposes that the baby ducks in the story should be drowned (Grahame mirrors this scene in *The Wind in the Willows* when Rat holds the ducks underwater, torturing them). But these threats and actions are intended to be humorous rather than establish the masculinity of their characters, due in no small part to the length of the stories and the small amount of time devoted to character development, particularly to minor characters in Wilde's stories.

Grahame also use threats of violence in his novel, particularly in developing Toad. As I posited earlier, though Toad is largely a comic character, he does threaten the citizenry with violence through his domineering of the road, his verbal abuse of the bargewoman and his maniacal driving episode at the end of his escape from jail. Where Grahame differs from Wilde is that Toad's character development demonstrates a repetitiveness that the longer novel form can accommodate. But Toad's threats, because of their repetitiveness and the specificity of his class and position, reveal masculinity as embracing violence in terms of social control.

Badger and Otter use threats of violence in the same manner: to keep society in line. Both characters differentiate themselves from the Wild Wooders and suggest violence as a way to keep them under control. So, though Toad's characterization is comic, violence as a corrective device in Grahame's hands is consistent with Kipling and Potter. Violence as a corrective device is the basis of the "The Retaking of Toad Hall" chapter when the Riverbankers use a sneak attack (hardly heroic?) and reinstall the princely Toad.

In contrast with Grahame is Wilde's uses of violence. Wilde seems to disdain violence, despite his threats of it in some of his stories (again, largely in humorous vein). In fact, he often "writes it out." In "The Fisherman and His Soul," the Fisherman cuts away his Soul who returns three times to tempt him and eventually entices the Fisherman to join it on a journey. But the Soul never actually uses violence. The closest it comes is through passive defense against violence of other rulers (all men) by catching arrows and deflecting blows. But his evilness is like the Star-Child's: both characters act like minor gods. The Soul, without a heart, only knows instincts and uses these to tempt the Fisherman: riches, sex, and finally guilt. Wilde doesn't need violence to equate overly sensualized masculinity with evil; he has human pathos, at least in "The Fisherman and his Soul."

Violence has a curious intersection with aestheticism in Wilde's "The Star-Child." In this story, cruelty and beauty are constituent parts of

One • *Adventures, Escapes and Violence*

Wilde's main character, "Yet did his [Star-Child's] beauty work him evil. For he grew proud, and cruel, and selfish" (306). In this case, Wilde's use of violence reinforces beauty as a source of cruelty against the more modest "swarthy and black-haired" village children (305). Wilde is famous for his use of dualities and foils, but this use of violence connects aestheticism to how beauty and violence merge in many gothic settings (Riquelme).

In "The Star-Child," masculinity retains its links to hierarchy through the depiction of aesthetic beauty and the violent actions as generative of and sustaining to the initial power scheme. Wilde's Star-Child tortures animals and the other village children. His beauty and pride masculinize him and permit him the violence he uses to sustain his hierarchal position. And, very different from Kipling, for Potter and Grahame it is the pleasure violence brings. This pleasure is consistent with the dualistic beauty/evil personality Wilde uses in his adult tales and is consistent with the Gothic or Aesthetic tradition, but violence still remains a tool for social control, despite the reversal that occurs by the end of the story.

While Wilde joins beauty and cruelty in his violent depiction of masculinity, Kipling uses violence as a "natural" aspect of gender formation and as a corrective to behavior outside the masculine norm. For example, Shere Khan's stalking of Mowgli adds a level of danger that reinforces the "Law" as right in jungle society and posits hunting and the violence animals commit against other animals as "natural."

We see violence as a corrective in many instances in the novel, but the best example is in regards to Mowgli's "education." First, Baloo beats Mowgli for his natural resistance to authority. Baloo uses violence to punish Mowgli and, when Mowgli mentions how the monkeys comforted him following a physical punishment, Baloo throws Mowgli to the ground and pins him with his claw. True, Bagheera does chastise Baloo for his corporal punishment saying," His face [Mowgli's] is all bruised today by thy [Baloo's]—softness. Ugh!" (33). Bagheera's sarcasm reveals a distaste for violence as a corrective, at least when violence becomes excessive. Perhaps Kipling didn't forget the incidents of bullying in his own life at Westward Ho! Devon, recounted in *Stalky and Co.* While he may have admired how violence, strength, and the physical use of the body can be constructive in the formation of a male, in this instance, he scripts an argument between the chief father figures in the story over the use of violence.[11]

But Kipling serves up many problematic and paradoxical takes on the use of violence as a corrective. Though this "Law" exists (with all of its nuance), it is frequently broken, framed with violence, and not completely settled as the best performance of masculinity. For example, at the beginning of the story, Shere Khan has broken the code by hunting in the village and eating man flesh. He follows Mowgli's escape and is only rebuked by violence, or the implied threat of violence: "Shere Khan might have faced Father Wolf, but he could not stand up against Mother Wolf, for he knew that where he was she had all the advantage of the ground, and would fight to the death" (9). The "unnatural" Shere Khan, hunter of cattle and men (both forbidden by the Law of the Jungle), is corrected by the "natural" Raksha performing as mother and violent protector of Mowgli as a child. In the second case, Baloo may have been chastised for the violence he uses in training Mowgli, but even Bagheera isn't prepared for the slaughter of the monkeys that Mowgli witnesses when Kaa joins the rescue party. Mowgli is put front and center in the use of violence as a corrective force for lawless parody and genderless play. Finally, Mowgli also breaks the law when he hunts Shere Khan using the cattle from the village. But for Kipling, violence seems to be a nuance performance of masculinity: when it is called for, it is appropriate. But, when we consider Mowgli's malaise at the end of the novel, it is apparent that violence costs a character, perhaps in communality and in ways of being male that transcend even Kipling's colonialist Victorianism.

Kipling's use of violence is consistent with Potter's uses in many ways. Potter's summer holidays and study of the natural world brought her into contact with the forces of death and decay that many women of her time were shielded from. As Margaret Lane has attested,

> Beatrix Potter was deeply aware of the realities of nature ... and the laws of nature (especially those of pursuit and prey, with which the life of most wild animals is endlessly concerned) are nowhere softened or sentimentalized in any of her stories [124].

The motive to perform violence directs the consequences of Potter's stories. The sex of a character performing violence is important to the outcome as well. Males use violence to establish and reinforce hierarchy and are punished or rewarded depending on whether the motivation is to keep order or to subjugate females, while females use violence and are rewarded for their transgressive performances as killers and, more often as mothers to maintain the centrality of the domestic center in the tale.

One • Adventures, Escapes and Violence

This isn't to say that Potter doesn't follow the size/age hierarchy matrix in her configuration of violence. In *The Story of a Fierce Bad Rabbit* (1906), the bad rabbit uses his size and aggression to dominate the smaller rabbit. In *The Tale of Benjamin Bunny*, the older Mr. Benjamin uses corporal punishment on the boys (son Benjamin and nephew Peter), and the accompanying illustrations show the boys crying as he holds them by the head and whips them.

In *The Tale of Benjamin Bunny*, Potter not only enacts the performance of violence in verbal/linguistic mode — a violent patriarch in the action of controlling younger males through violence — she illustrates the violence: Mr. Benjamin's eyes wide and dark, his body stretched out, ears perked up straight. As a model of performance, the Rabbit boys witness a life or death scenario with the menacing cat, and like Mowgli in *The Jungle Book*, they become inscribed with violence in both sight and in scene as a way to manhood and a way to have escapist impulses corrected.

Clearly another use of violence in Potter's work is in how male hierarchy is preserved. For example, in *The Tale of Squirrel Nutkin*, Potter relies on illustration and innuendo as Old Mr. Brown, the owl, buzzard like, beak open and head profiled, attacks the jesting Squirrel Nutkin. Nutkin escapes, but the violent masculinity of Old Mr. Brown and the subsequent off-page dismemberment of Nutkin's tail reveals the lesson: respect for an older male is enforced through violence and violence can be a corrective for overly masculinized performances of the younger male.

Like Kipling, Potter also scripts violence as a tool for female characters. The settings may be different, but females can threaten and enact violence to keep order in their houses. For example, Mrs. Tabitha, in *The Tale of Tom Kitten*, beats her kittens for losing their clothes. In the accompanying illustrations, she has one kitten by the neck with her arm ready to smack the other on the head; the last kitten covers its head and ear with a paw. And much like Raksha in *The Jungle Book*, Cousin Ribby, in *The Roly-Poly Pudding*, threatens both male and female, stranger and family: "I'm not afraid of rats; I will help ... find him [Samuel Whiskers] and whip him too!" (178). Kipling explicitly assures the reading audience that hunting is not exclusively reserved for males, while Potter portrays motherhood as a profession that almost demands a taste for violence.

True, the violence performed by women in this story is always directed at rats, but it is consistent with the female characters. And like Kipling's Raksha, reputation and boasts attend female use of violence. Tabitha, the mother, boasts, almost as if to equal her cousin: "I caught seven young ones out of one hole in the back kitchen, and we had them for dinner last Saturday" (179). And the two sisters in the story, Moppet and Mittens, demonstrate that violence, reputation, and business can coalesce in gender depiction. By the end of the story, the two girls have "grown up into very good rat catchers ... and go out rat-catching in the village, and they find plenty of employment. They charge so much a dozen and earn their living very comfortably" (195). The curiously ignored sisters in the beginning of the story "blossom" into killers.[12]

Margaret Mackey, reviewing M. Daphne's *Beatrix Potter: Writing in Code*, identifies their actions as rebellious: "His sisters, whose rebellion has been quieter and who have been willing to bide their time, take on as adults some of the masculine attributes of aggression and entrepreneurship that one would more commonly expect from Tom" (209). Except that the "dynamic duo" had a mother and aunt as role models who boast of their kills. Granted, their enacting of previously considered masculine violence is centered on killing for good and for food, not for individualist, male curiosity. And like their mother and aunt, they keep score, hanging the tails of the dead rats on the barn door.

And it should be noted that Potter uses violence as a corrective to boyish adventure schemes. As noted earlier in this chapter, escape plots, especially those initiated by boys (Peter Rabbit, Benjamin Bunny, and Tom Kitten, in two stories), include violence as a warning, corrective, or legitimized outcome to these escapist plots. Mothers and potential prey look to enforce both a Darwinian code and a social code to regulate this masculine behavior, and this behavior differs in Potter's stories because it usually involves "mini adventures"— the localized exploration that ends in the corrective use of violence as the necessary outcome.

There is a difference between the boys' escapist adventures and a story that uses older male characters. For example, in *The Tale of Mr. Jeremy Fisher*, Jeremy Fisher's urbanity and improper preparation for the task of catching dinner results in a more Darwinian depiction of violence as he is almost eaten. While both the boys' tales and this tale use violence as a corrective for ill-conceived behavior, boys are corrected and brought back to the domestic home with mother at center while the adult Jeremy, Edwardian bachelor, eats vegetarian and is depicted as "less than" masculine by Potter at the story's end.

Perhaps the most startling use of violence as a corrective occurs in *The Tale of Jemima Puddle-Duck*. Jemima lays her eggs in the questionable secret location far away from the farmyard where they are always collected. But it seems as if Potter punishes her for her rebellion as Jemima watches as "the puppies rush[ed] in and gobbled up all the eggs before he [Kep, the collie] could stop them" (170). The puppies are rewarded for violence with the eggs (eating them) while the transgressive behavior of Jemima is punished. Daphne Kutzer has remarked that the dogs are still in training as hunters and that their excitement is to blame (206). But it isn't the violence she condemns, just their training. Jemima does go on to lay eggs in the barnyard, but this is only after Potter depicts her as emotionally scarred.[13]

This story has many similarities to fairy tales, especially if we consider how hegemonic notions of motherhood are vindicated over more liberated, feminist notions of motherhood. Margaret Lane asserts that Potter saw *The Tale of Jemima Puddle-Duck* as a parallel story to *Little Red Riding Hood* and that a "pursuit and prey theme runs undisguised through many of the tales.... In dwelling on this theme Beatrix Potter was following, more or less consciously, the simple traditional pattern of the fairy tale" (125–126). The danger of masculinity certainly lurks in the "foxy gentleman" who is eventually slaughtered by the dogs, but Potter may have been trying to shock herself, her parents, and her readers — protecting domesticity as it was more hegemonically conceived — through this use of corrective, masculine violence as represented by the guardian collie-dog, Kep, and the fox hound puppies.

Elements of class bias emerge in Potter's depictions of violence as well. In *The Tale of Timmy Tiptoes*, Chippy Hackee is bestial to his wife. She won't go down the tree to get Chippy because of his violent performances in the past: "my husband, Chippy Hackee, bites" (245). Compared to Timmy and Goody Tiptoes, their neighbors and Potter's foil/couple in the story, Chippy and wife fight and bicker and even threaten a bird with an umbrella — Chippy waiting to pounce. This violence is contrasted with Timmy and his wife walking home under an umbrella, gathering nuts together, and "playing house" the right, English, middle-class way.

Yet Potter revolted against this conservative picture of marriage and consolidation of identity based on pre-determined pattern. She even scripted a rebellion to this manner of living through the story, *The Story of Two Bad Mice*. Hunca Munca and her husband, Tom Thumb, ransack the house, taking what they need back to their children. Their anger and violence, literally, rips through the middle-class dollhouse as they provide for their own children and home. That Potter would surreptitiously script her own allusive rebellion in such violent terms may suggest that even late-Victorian women, regardless of politics, had a reservoir of violence that superseded allegiance to class.

We may see class violence as it is represented in *The Wind in the Willows*. At the beginning of the story, when Mole and Rat are in the forest, Rat's gun is intended to protect them from the Wild Wooders who are depicted as "other" characters as placed against the River Bankers. This is really a foreshadowing of the class violence and bias that will follow. As the stoats and weasels use violence to take Toad Hall, displaying the violent and dangerous side of the lower and working class, Mole, Rat, Toad, and Badger return violence with violence as they spring from their secret tunnel to retake Toad Hall. The heretofore passive Mole (arguably the character who is undergoing the most visible transformation in the novel) becomes the fiercest warrior, demonstrating that masculine violence is both infectious and normed as a way to keep "the order," particularly against the lower classes.

Conclusion

Claudia Nelson, in her essay "Sex and the Single Boy: Ideals of Manliness and Sexuality in Victorian Literature for Boys," finds that representations of masculinity shifted in the nineteenth century from a "sexuality generally judged as male/strong/regrettable against an asexuality that is female/weak/laudable ... [to] natural/heterosexual/good versus unnatural/homosexual/despicable [by the end of the nineteenth century]" (545–546). My own examination of how animals represent masculinity demonstrates that elements of the adventure story surely affected and influenced how masculinity was represented by these various authors (Wilde, Kipling, Grahame, Potter, and Milne). But a conclusive picture of masculinity as it is performed in these works more often shows difference, whether that be from the Englishman abroad (Kipling) or the conservative feminist at home (Potter).

Escape and rebellion seem almost necessary performances of masculinity as hierarchy is contested. Frequently, the hierarchy or order is the family structure, though we see evidence of heteronormative groups being challenged in the works of Grahame and Kipling, most specifically. The Edwardian Era certainly was full of class awareness, particularly as class, empire, and society (transportation, work, technology, economics) were shifting in the late Victorian and early decade of the twentieth century. We witness such rebellions to the "established" law, pattern, or organization of society in some of these children's works as both normal (Peter Rabbit) and as dangerously subversive and requiring violence to correct it (Grahame).

Finally, violence can be a humorous scripting of masculinity in action or in jest. Milne, Grahame, and Wilde use threats of violence and language shadowed in violence that mirrors children testing others (and themselves). But violence can also be a performance used to control, punish, and kill those who challenge the order of a society, be it jungle or riverbank. Perhaps what can most clearly be ascertained in this examination is that violence is a tool used by characters to control other characters and when linked to play, it still mirrors physically what society does in its wars, its institutions, and its laws. The use of anthropomorphism liberates authors to use violence in ways they wouldn't dream of if they had employed specifically human characters.

Two

Aestheticism, Christianity and Spirituality: Masculinity in Flux

An aspect of masculinity rarely touched upon in criticism of anthropomorphic tales is spirituality and religion. By spirituality, I mean the affections inherent in and the uses of nonphysical relationships a character entertains and endures to investigate, develop and understand their existence: who am I, where do I belong? My investigation into the various performances of masculinity has led me to consider spiritual representations of masculinity as well as the forces behind what these representations look like and how they are constructed. In addition to the nonmaterial relationships characters have with other characters, the influence of religious doctrines, frameworks, and influence emerge from the characterizations of animals acting human and problematize the representations of gender these authors propose.

As mentioned earlier, the influence of "muscular Christianity," particularly on children's works is hard to ignore. Perhaps the biggest influence on the animal tales included in this study is Charles Kingsley's *Water Babies* (1863). Indeed the monkeys in Kingsley's work provide the model for Kipling's aesthete-like monkeys. While many writers had to contend with Darwin's *Origin of Species* (1863), Kingsley's work absorbed Darwin's evolutionary thoughts into a "muscular Christianity" marked by "the promotion of physical strength, courage and health, the importance of family life and married love, the elements of duty and service to mankind and the scientific study of the natural world to discover the divine pattern of the moral universe" (Vance, quoted in Managan 103). How writers expressed a continuation of, argument with, and surpassing of Kingsley's influence, both in literature and in theology, forms the basis of this chapter.

The influence of medievalism and the debates within the Anglican church form no small part of stylistic choices of writers like Wilde and Kenneth Grahame. We witness this in their use of exotic myths and leg-

Two • *Aestheticism, Christianity and Spirituality: Masculinity in Flux*

ends, pagan characters and settings, and an interest in "brotherly love" over the individual in a moral development tale such as Kingsley's *Water Babies*. But what became more important in the continuing development of the anthropomorphic tale were the more literary and less moral aspects of texts like "The Happy Prince," *The Wind in the Willows*, and *Winnie the Pooh*. Wilde, Grahame, Kipling, Potter and Milne reveal that spirituality and the influence of aestheticism are concerns for the late Victorian and early twentieth-century children's writer of anthropomorphic stories. Whether critiqued or resuscitated, spirituality remains an aspect of manliness that these writers respond to in their scripting of masculinity.

In the case of Oscar Wilde, his combination of Catholicism, Hellenism, paganism, and aestheticism form a sometimes radical notion of spirituality, specifically as it is expressed in his children's works. His early Catholic upbringing, under the guiding hand of Jane Esperanza Wilde, combined with her love of folklore and radical political support of an independent Ireland. Indeed, in Wilde's work we see the historical forces at work in Ireland, which helped form the worldview we see in Wilde's children's works:

> The first form of Catholicism [prevalent in the nineteenth century] was a version of folk-Catholicism, predominant in rural areas of the country, such as the west coast and the south. This was a form of Catholicism with strong connections to pre–Christian traditions, and which blended belief in fairies, magical healing, holy wells, popular prophecies and divination with more "orthodox" Catholicism such as Transubstantiation, Marianism and the sacraments [Killeen, 18–19].

One part of this chapter will examine how Wilde represents gender and masculinity, specifically, how Wilde's masculine performances run contradictory to the legacy of muscular Christianity, as evidenced in the works and legacy of children's writers from Jean-Jacques Rousseau to Thomas Hughes. Wilde's rewriting of Christianity in his work demonstrates a rebellion to more utilitarian (Potter) and Imperial (Kipling) notions of English masculinity.

Examining Grahame's *The Wind in the Willows* provides a resuscitation of Wilde and a re-envisioned aesthetic masculinity. Neither Grahame's Scots Calvinist background nor his "social Anglicanism" (Carpenter) structured his writing for children, though religion in its social aspects could arguably be said to have helped him prosper at the Bank of England rather than to have liberated him to engage in a full-time literary career. In fact, writing out of a repression of sorts made the author of *The Pagan Papers* (1893), *The Golden Age* (1895), and *Dream Days* (1898) a perfect mouthpiece for a mixture of transgressive gender performances embodied in narratives predominantly centered on identity quests.

In the various adventures of *The Wind in the Willows*, Grahame critiques aestheticism while also resuscitating it. The slippery and inconsistent representations of masculinity that Grahame employs in his character's desires and spiritual fulfillment make a clear picture of what masculinity should finally look like — spiritually impossible. What is evident, however, is that Protestant manliness and muscular Christianity are not the centerpiece of Grahame's masculinity or even his novel; the chapter, "The Piper at the Gates of Dawn" exhibits his blend of paganism, Romanticism, and resuscitated aestheticism.

Perhaps the most controversial and less insular writer in this study, in terms of spirituality, is Rudyard Kipling. Born in Bombay, Kipling's identity and allegiance to nation would always be complicated. Even more complex are his ideas on religion and spirituality. Though nominally Anglican, he embraced the Masonic order in his early days in Lahore, Pakistan. This idea of universal brotherhood — promoting social good through order and works — proves a foundation for *The Jungle Book*'s "Law of the Jungle." Even Kipling attributed the creation of *The Jungle Book* to early memories of the Mason's influence:

> ... of the winter of '92 some memory of the Masonic Lions of my childhood's magazine, and a phrase in Haggard's *Nada the Lily*, combined with the echo of this tale. After blocking out the main idea in my head, the pen took charge, and I watched it begin to write stories about Mowgli and animals, which later grew into the two *Jungle Books* [67–68].

We will find that the influence of brotherhood may have formed some part of the foundations of Kipling's spiritual sense of Mowgli, but this brotherhood gives way to individualism in Mowgli's development from a boy to an adolescent. But not before we witness Kipling's distaste for symbolically aesthetic characters like the monkeys, who not only are censured in the jungle's caste system, but are exterminated because of their nonutilitarian, artful play in this system, which values hunting and group solidarity.

Beatrix Potter's spirituality is perhaps the most consistent feature of

Two • *Aestheticism, Christianity and Spirituality: Masculinity in Flux*

her stories. Raised in a dissenting household, Potter's Unitarianism is on display throughout her stories, where common sense, caution, reason and responsibility dominate the outcomes of protagonists and supporting characters. We've seen in the previous chapter where Potter's own rebelliousness, another spiritual characteristic Potter inherited from her own religious upbringing, may have been channeled in female characters who act transgressively, in terms of violence. In this chapter, I will, however, be examining how Potter responds to aestheticism and the idea of the decadent city in her Edwardian Era animal tales and what that may demonstrate in terms of how masculinity is represented.

As for A. A. Milne, his views of spirituality and how they are represented in *Winnie the Pooh* are a mix of Potter's belief in action, the jarring personal effects Milne underwent from his experience in World War One, an inheritance of aesthetic discourse and representations in both Grahame and Wilde, and a modernist stance in terms of his use of nonsense and performance. Milne's pacifism and criticism of organized Christianity form the basis for his stories where sentimental Arcadia takes the place of church, where masculinity is more comical, performed in songs and speeches, and largely concerned with the construction and exploration of the self (as opposed for the common good: Potter, Kipling, Grahame). Milne's debt to Wilde hasn't been fully explored and it is hoped that this chapter will more effectively link Wilde to Milne, in terms of the influence of aestheticism. In Ann Thwaite's biography of Milne, the relationship with Barrie, Shaw, and other prominent critics and authors of his time is articulated. But she makes the case that Wilde's drama is directly an influence on Milne's works for the theater.[1] Whereas Grahame's work is more closely aligned with the pagan and Hellenistic roots of Aestheticism, Milne's relationship with aestheticism is more evidenced in the humorous performances and modernist use of puns, wordplay, and nonsense.

While this chapter does not explore the various shifts in religious philosophies, particularly between the Low Church, Broad Church, and the Oxford Movement, these shifts in Anglican England are important in their relationship to literature. Certainly, Wilde's Catholicism is an important part of his stories for children, particularly "The Selfish Giant." But the rejection of Anglican Christianity is what permeates these tales more than its acceptance. And in terms of how this affects representations of masculinity — the key theme of this book — spirituality is as important if not more important than violence, collaboration, and legal codes and rules. Because the "soul" is at stake, particularly when adults write for children, spirituality emerges as a dominant concern for these authors, though how they express this concern varies.

Paganism

Early critics like James Frazer and Edmund Chambers provided Victorians and Edwardians with readings of paganism in the natural and medieval worlds (see *The Golden Bough* and *The Mediaeval Stage*). And recent critics have contextualized literature and the influence of paganism like Darcy Jane in "The Representation of Nature in *The Wind in the Willows* and *The Secret Garden*" who has noted both the reverent and cruel sides of pagan myths and Margot Lois in "Gods and Mysteries: The Revival of Paganism and the Remaking of Mythography through the Nineteenth Century" who has traced Romantic Hellenism to late Victorian Era paganism.

In children's literature, the influence of paganism on Oscar Wilde serves as a touchstone for writers as various as Rudyard Kipling and Beatrix Potter. But it is the intersection of church debate, aestheticism, Romantic era Hellenism, Christianity and re-imagined gender representations that Wilde reveals in his scripting of manliness that is recognizable in the works of Grahame and Milne. In all, Wilde's "Irish folk-Catholicism, a religion of seasons and the senses, of the irrational and irreality, of performance and perversity" (Kileen, 188) influences his aesthetic philosophies and how those philosophies are displayed in spiritual masculinity.

Though not the first writer to employ anthropomorphism, Wilde's use of the format provides some interesting ways to investigate Celtic folklore, Catholicism, and their relationships to masculine representation. Pagan sensibilities are illustrated in Wilde's fiction for children in ways that celebrate their folk character. For example, in "The Birthday of the Infanta," the dwarf character has been brought to the court because of his very exoticism. But Wilde demonstrates (away from civilized eyes in the story) that the dwarf's exoticism is both traditionally masculine and subversive to the masculinity we might find in late nineteenth-century London. We learn that the dwarf

Two • Aestheticism, Christianity and Spirituality: Masculinity in Flux

> knew the trail of every animal, and could track the hare by its delicate footprints, and the boar by the trampled leaves. All the wild-dances he knew, the mad dance in red raiment with the autumn, the light dance in blue sandals over the corn, the dance with white snow wreaths in winter and the blossom-dance, through the orchards, in spring [267].

What begins in knowledge, ends in a mystical binding of art (dance) and science (weather, seasonal chance). There is a utilitarianism in the description Wilde offers, not unlike the description Kipling renders of Mowgli's training or the household rulers in Potter's stories. In Wilde's text, Pagan sensibility is both practical, as tied to custom, and concerned with aesthetics, as visible in their illustration for the sake of beauty.

It might be said that paganism is a mainstay in both Wilde's work and in the subsequent works this chapter will explore. References to Pan color both Wilde's and Grahame's work. In "The Birthday of the Infanta," the dwarf "could make little cages out of rushes for the grasshoppers to sing in, and fashion the long-jointed bamboo into the pipe that Pan loves to hear" (267). Another example of Hellinism occurs in "The Fisherman and His Soul," where paganism is more nautically set as the mermaid sings to the fisherman

> of the Sirens who tell of such wonderful things that the merchants have to stop their ears with wax..., of the nautilus who has a boat of her own that is carved out of an opal and steered with a silken sail; of the happy mermen who play upon harps and can charm the great Kraken to sleep... [276].

In Wilde's hands, many of these scenes are rich in color and sound, but also consistently framed in kaleidoscopic artistic production: piped song from Dwarf, songs of mermaids about songs of Sirens, and mermen on harps — all contained inside a story for children. Masculinity, it would appear, is both vulnerable to the pagan sensibilities of art as reproducing history and intertwined with the production and performance of art, particularly as it is expressed through Greek myths and legends.[2]

Blurring Christianity and Paganism

But in Wilde's creation, pagan and Christian symbols and settings blur. It is a curious spirituality with no clear path for the child reader to follow in Wilde's "The Fisherman and His Soul." On the one hand, the fisherman (our closest young man character) bargains with a witch who repeats her taunting question like a street barker in late 1800s London: "What d'ye lack? What d'ye lack?" (279). And what is the fisherman bargaining for? Love. But according to the dominant religious system on land, Catholicism, the fisherman can't have "what he lacks." That Wilde would employ Christian motifs in his work is no surprise. As Jarlath Killeen has noted,

> Irish folk-Catholicism was Wilde's way of interpreting the world. Both religion and nationality were bequeathed to him by his parents, and his life was spent exploiting the Irish tensions they personified, tensions between elite and popular culture, England and Ireland, Protestantism and Catholicism, orthodoxy and subversion [188].

When the fisherman asks about sending his soul away for his love, the priest pontificates,

> As for the seafolk, they are lost, and they who would traffic with them are lost also. They are the beasts of the field and know not good from evil, and for them the Lord has not died.... The love of the body is vile ... and vile and evil are the pagan things God suffers to wander through His world. Accursed be the fauns of the woodland, and accursed be the singers of the sea! [277–278].

Like much of Wilde's work, again we have his construction of paradoxes that have to be worked out, or suffered through. The spiritual sensibility the fisherman seeks to satisfy will find no succor in late nineteenth-century religious dogma. Christianity can't permit love, particularly love of the body, and restrictions on who God loves are firmly in place. In this case, a man clearly has choices to make, which are lined with danger in any case: to succumb to a witch's desire and experience the spiritual and carnal love one desires, or resist dominant urges inside oneself and categorize the world and its population according to the will of God as set forth by his representative on earth — an unmarried man installed in a hierarchal system of social control. It becomes clear that the dominant spiritual strain Wilde proposes is not the painful inscription of the church, but the human-animal bonding between man and mermaid: love over scripture.

Wilde also blurs the two worlds of pagan and Catholic sensibilities in "The Selfish Giant." In this story, the giant doesn't want to share his garden or castle and scares away children from his lawn. There are elemental forces personified: the North Wind as a bearded man, Snow as a woman in "her great white cloak," and Hail as a rambunctious breaker of slate roofs. More importantly, Wilde personifies Autumn as an woman who "gave golden fruit to every garden, but to the giant's garden she gave none. 'He is too selfish,' she said'" (336). Nature may be anthropomorphosized for the delight of children, but anthropomorphosized characters, in pagan characterizations, can reveal matriarchal sources of power alongside patriarchal ones.

But Wilde's depiction of masculinity mingles pagan symbolism and characterizations with Christian allusions. The little boy who the Giant puts in the tree, with arms flung out wide, returns after many years and "on the palms of the child's hands were the prints of two nails, and the prints of two nails were on the little feet" (337). This Christ figure takes the giant character to heaven saying "You let me play once in your garden, to-day you shall come with me to my garden, which is Paradise" (337). This story presents us with more human characters, a more naked form of masculinity without fins or feathers, but the subversiveness remains. Jack Zipes sees the union at the end of the story as a liberating portrait of Wilde's homosexuality, but also, perhaps more important for this chapter's focus, as a

> type of human compassion which Wilde felt was necessary for the building of socialism [and that] the giant's pursuit and union with Christ is the pursuit of the Christ within us, and as we know from his essay *The Soul of Man Under Socialism*, this type of joyous individualism which can only flower the progress made toward utopia [Zipes, 120].

Important in both Zipes' assessment and in Wilde's story is the power of the individual guided by compassion, without the anxieties of political and religious dogma, which informed Anglican Christianity of mid-nineteenth-century England. The Christ figures in Wilde's work are too numerous to be accidental and demonstrate a variety of ways he saw the spirit of Christianity: whether it was as a boyhood innocent in "The Selfish Giant," a dying leader/companion of men in exhorting the value of giving and sacrifice in "The Happy Prince," or a female artist figure (the Nightingale) sacrificing for the possibility of romantic love in "The Rose and the Nightingale." One reads Wilde's aestheticism and is exposed to a variety of manifestations of pagan, Christian, and aesthetic masculinities. Each synthesizes artistic and moral concerns evident at the fin-de-siècle.

Paganism in Grahame

The lure of paganism and its influence on a character is also clearly evident in *The Wind in the Willows*. Both Wilde and the Aesthetic Period had an influence on Grahame, particularly on how Grahame represented masculinity and expectations of masculinity in a pagan setting. For Wilde, the fin-de-siècle included an embrace of alternate spiritualities and paradoxical embraces of nature along with pre–Modernist sympathies in regards to the influence of urban life. For Grahame, through his dalliance with publishing in the *Yellow Book* and its cadre of aesthetes (Beardsley, Wilde, Symons, Dowson), paganism formed both an alternative to "muscular Christianity" as well as a re-embrace of the rural qualities of Englishness a pre–Modernist writer like Wilde found ripe for satire. In other words, paganism is a fixture in both writers' works, but with different motivations.

Nowhere in the novel is paganism as visible as in the "Piper at the Gates of Dawn" chapter. As Rat and Mole try to find Portly, Otter's lost son, they stumble upon Pan who is watching over Portly. The inclusion of Pan certainly could be read as a reminder of the Aesthetic Movement in England, which had ended, in many ways, after Wilde's conviction. But pagan spirituality is evident in the text before and after this chapter. What makes this chapter so illustrative is the language Grahame employs. Rat is bewildered, almost maddened by the music as they approach Pan:

> Rapt, transported, trembling, he was possessed in all his senses by this new divine thing that caught up his helpless soul and swung and dandled it, a powerless but happy infant, in a strong sustaining grasp [132].

That Grahame "typified" characters has been discussed by other critics (Hunt, Philip, Green) and Rat's "poet" character clearly emerges as vulnerable to pagan and romantic influences. And this vulnerability to Pan and his spell reveals the lingering influence of Wilde and the continuing fad of paganism evidenced in the work of Saki, Forster, Barrie during the Edwardian Era. As Annie Gauger has chronicled, Grahame himself used Pan in essays, stories, and fiction. Grahame's characterizations in this chapter propose masculinities that undergo transformations that don't result in final and heteronormative masculinity (as we see in Mowgli or in Potter's reformed Peter and Benjamin of *The Tale of the Flopsy Bunnies*).

Most importantly, Grahame doesn't just ascribe the influence of Pan on the "poet/aesthete" character, Rat. Mole also is "under the influence"

Two • *Aestheticism, Christianity and Spirituality: Masculinity in Flux*

of Pan's spell. He feels "a great Awe" and knows it can "only mean that some august Presence" is about him (134) . But his conditioned recognition of Pan is not rendered in the psychological language that reveals Rat's experiences as a mixture of terror, religious epiphany, fear and awe:

> Though the piping was now hushed, the call and the summons seemed still dominant and imperious. He [Mole] might not refuse, were Death himself waiting to strike him instantly, once he had looked with mortal eye on things rightly kept hidden. Trembling, he obeyed, and raised his humble head; and then, in that utter clearness of the imminent dawn, while Nature, flushed with fullness of incredible color, seemed to hold her breath for the event, he looked in the very eyes of the Friend and Helper [134].

In terms of masculinity, hierarchy is still evident in Rat and Mole's subservience to a male Greek god. The irony is hard to miss: two animals with human characteristics would fall into a religious trance under the spell of another anthropomorphic/theriomorphic character, Pan. But again, as in Wilde's two stories, music is the calling force. And though Grahame's work is framed in more melancholy and ecstasy than Wilde's tales (as a whole), Grahame provides a blurring of pagan sensibilities and hierarchical spirituality, which seems less equivocal. After all, the spell the two characters are under renders them powerless, subservient, and spiritually satiated.

Grahame's pagan vision differs from Christianity in at least two important ways. First, Pan never speaks and his presence is rendered in the effects nature has on the characters. He is characterized as the helper and is a figure that represents nature's presence and supremacy. In fact, Pan disappears as does his memory, so that any lingering worship of a figure, god or man, is diminished:

> For this is the last best gift that the kindly demigod is careful to bestow on those to whom he has revealed himself in their helping: the fit of forgetfulness. Lest the awful remembrance should remain and grow, and overshadow mirth and pleasure, and the great haunting memory should spoil all the afterlives of little animals helped out of difficulties, in order that they should be happy and lighthearted as before [136].

This forgetfulness renders the experience less hierarchically consistent with Christianity and more liberating for Rat and Mole after the "spell" is over.

Second, the paganistic spirit of the Pan encounter is rendered in song, a song sung by the wind through the reeds:

> Lest the awe should dwell
> And turn your frolic to fret
> You shall look on my power at the helping hour
> But then you shall forget [140].

And after Rat's recitation of what he hears in the reed's song, the two characters forget. We see how important to Grahame the experience is as he renders it in song. But it is a song for song's sake or art for art's sake, as neither character can remember nor champion the experience: their "specialness" for undergoing the experience, even meeting Pan, is lost.

More importantly, as mentioned previously, Pan — the central figure of paganism — is a kindly figure, a helper and healer, with no lingering insistence on worship. The central figure of spirituality in the novel, then, is a figure who doesn't want characters beset with anxiety over worship and obedience; who helps and heals characters who are lost or hurt; and disappears behind or into natural landscape and into aesthetic representation or song. John David Moore has suggested that

> This is a Pan made safe for a middle-class Arcadia, where instinct is equivalent to decorum and custom. As the genius of Grahame's suburban, sexless garden, Pan appears as a castrated Priapus. He is the Pan of fin-de-siècle paganism, though much tamer than anything in Beardsley or even Swinburne. As an aesthetic version of the goat god, this Pan finally does fit into the middle-class menagerie of well-dressed animals; the ideal Arcadian aesthete is not merely half man, half animal, but half animal, half aging dandy [58].

Moore doesn't acknowledge that the Pan we see in the novel is filtered through Mole's consciousness. Thus Grahame "sanitizes" Pan for his middle-class reading audience who were all too aware of the dangers of a dandy like Wilde, but he also resuscitates Wilde, aestheticism, and a different sense of spiritual masculinity in his creation of Pan as more mystical than hedonistic.

Landscape and Aestheticism

One might see the merging of landscape with humans and "nature personified" as merely continuing a tradition in English literature, partic-

Two • Aestheticism, Christianity and Spirituality: Masculinity in Flux

ularly the Gothic and Romantic influences of writers such as Emily Bronte and Coleridge. But when amorous relationships are illustrated, some pagan sensibilities emerge. For instance, in Wilde's "The Birthday of the Infanta," Dwarf has fallen in love with the Infanta: she of Catholic/Spanish/civilized world, he of pagan/natural/uncivilized world. As the dwarf imagines some kind of relationship between himself and the princess, he visualizes taking her into the forest:

> And when she was tired he would find a soft bank of moss for her.... He would make her a necklace of red byrony berries.... He would bring her acorn-cups and dew-drenched anemones, and tiny glowworms to be stars in the pale gold of her hair [268].

In this story, the gothic sensibilities marry the pagan idea of earth as marriage bed and home. In another story, "The Star-Child," Wilde employs the same demonstration of pagan symbolism. In the beginning of the story, the earth is personified as she, and as it is winter and "she" is covered with snow, "she" is seen as both dressed in a "white shroud" (by the linnets) and in "her bridal dress" (by the doves) (304). Wilde's illustration of paganism would seem benign and liberating male characters (and authors) to display a masculinity embracing nature rather than conquering it.

His pagan brushstrokes take a different turn when the earth seems less like a virgin ready to marry or a crone ready to die and becomes a force of correction. In "The Star-Child," the cruel and violent title character is depicted in lush verbiage:

> His curls were like the rings of the daffodil. His lips, also, were like the petals of a red flower, and his eyes were like violets by a river of pure water, and his body like the narcissus of a field where the mower comes not [306].

As a supernatural child found in the woods, he emerges as villainous rather than good. But Wilde even subverts the dichotomy of good an evil, as the Star-Child will make a transformation. But only after encountering the power of nature, depicted as female:

> Wherever he went harsh briars and thorns shot up from the ground and encompassed him, and evil nettles stung him, and the thistle pierced him with her daggers [311].

A more divergent characterization of nature as a goddess force punishes the boy for his earlier cruelties, and eventually leads him out of the forest as he fulfills the quests he has been charged with. We may read a pagan sisterhood at work defending and revenging injustices inflicted upon female characters (including nature). The Star-Child is punished for his earlier excesses yet forgiven and shown the way out of the forest. Indeed, the boy's reformation is configured in quasi-religious language: "Nor would he suffer any to be cruel to bird or beast, but taught love and loving-kindness and charity" [314]. Wilde's fabled and feminized forest emerges as a character in her own right, one that offers herself as a instructive force, enduring civilized man's cruelties as the Pan-like figure of the Star-Child develops from child to man. Again we witness Wilde's paradoxical and conflicting dialectics at work: Catholic, symbolic, transformational through suffering vs. Pagan, vindictive, gothic, and without the restrictions of civilization.

Though distinctly not pagan, both Kipling and Potter use landscape to wreak vengeance on characters, to punish them specifically, for transgressing the "law" or the communal code (in Potter). Both Potter and Kipling punish aesthetic characters with Darwinian violence, though both use animals rather than flowers and fauna in anthropomorphic fashion. And in *The Wind in the Willows*, the "Terror of the Wild Wood" drives Mole into hiding and brings Rat "manfully" with his pistols and cudgel to save him. The differing use of landscape show a gothic side to Grahame (which we also witness in "The Piper at the Gates of Dawn" chapter) and as in Potter, Kipling and Wilde, landscape acts in a psychological and spiritual manner to punish individualistic and overly masculine characters, to correct behavior, and to reinforce social controls or, as in Wilde and Grahame, critique them. In *The Country and the City*, Raymond Williams comments on Nature in much the same way as these authors depict nature:

> There is nature as a principle of order, of which the ordering mind is part, and which human activity, by regulating principles, may then rearrange and control. But there is also nature as a principle of creation, of which the creative mind is part, and from which we may learn the truths of our own sympathetic nature [127].

All of the authors in this study contend with nature in creative and destructive ways, from rain storms that wash away houses (Milne) to the re-discovery of home and innocence (Grahame). The authors in this study read paganism as a destructive and creative force and read landscape as way of spurring, controlling, or thwarting identity and the development of masculine identity.

Two • *Aestheticism, Christianity and Spirituality: Masculinity in Flux*

Aesthetic Masculinity

Perhaps another aspect of masculinity to explore is aesthetic masculinity. The Aesthetic Movement has it roots in Enlightenment philosophy, more specifically in the freedom from authority thinkers like Hobbs and Locke espoused. English aestheticism combines elements of this thinking with the artistic revival that the Pre-Raphaelites (Morris, Rossetti, Ruskin) had begun. But the influence of French aestheticism (Gautier, Mallarme, Verlaine, and others) pushed the boundaries, particularly what was appropriate for poetry, stage, and page, for Victorian aesthetes.

In Wilde's works for children, his penchant for aestheticism is evident throughout. Whether he uses synaesthesia, as in "The Star-Child," with colors and sound corresponding to character and overall tone or in "The Fisherman and His Soul," where decadence and sin, anti-natural imagery such as mythological sea creatures and lavishly described jewelry and exotic characters dominate the story in its creation of plot and mood; Wilde's prose for children reveal the philosophical belief in art for its own sake, rather than morality, and in the anti-rationalist and anti-authoritarian stance he sought to illustrate for children.

Oscar Wilde wasn't the only Victorian aesthete, but was certainly a central figure, even part of the composite characters of Bunthorne and Grosvenor in *Patience* , the 1881 musical by Gilbert and Sullivan. English Romanticism, a revolt against stifling Victorian morality, and the aesthetic and philosophical influences of Walter Pater and John Ruskin combine in Wilde's luxurious prose as characters work out the dilemmas of existence without moral certainty or aesthetic finality.

For the purposes of this chapter, I will examine the influence of aestheticism as well as the critique of aestheticism because its resuscitation by Grahame and its production of reaction by Kipling and Potter attest to not only its influence, but to the liberating effects it has on representing masculinity as well as its perceived dangers. The influence of aestheticism can be traced from Wilde through Grahame, with reactions by Potter and Kipling, and can even be witnessed in Milne's more modernist tale.

Aestheticism can also demonstrate the spiritual aims of characters. At the very least, we have the self-expressiveness and self-reflexivity of the Remarkable Rocket, Toad, and Pooh. But I suggest a spiritual quality as well as a connection to gender because the Aesthetic Movement (emerging out of the Arts and Crafts Movement and its mixture of utilitarianism and beauty) positions the individual consciousness as central, not the church. Masculinity, under the influence of aesthetic writers and artists, is represented by suggestion and sensuality, in mysticism and beauty, and in Pater's credo "To burn always with [a] hard gemlike flame" (152).

Surely, such a movement, with its challenges to heteronormative representations of masculinity; its associations with drugs, prostitution, and the theater; and the historical context of the Cleveland Street Scandals (1889–1890) and Oscar Wilde's trial in 1895 would be short lived. But its influence was great. And this influence has spiritual and artistic representations in children's works.

Aestheticism in Grahame

Grahame revives the spirit of aestheticism in *The Wind in the Willows*. But this revival is conditional: the pair of companions — Mole and Rat — still have to conform to the social hierarchy at the end of the story and help to retake Toad Hall, but their adventures and Grahame's characterization reveal an aspect of masculinity inherited from Wilde and a masculinity that would conflict with the militaristic Kipling and utilitarian Potter.

Grahame's aesthetic touch begins the novel as witnessed in Mole's characterization. Mole rejects the utilitarianism of cleaning his house for the physical, tactile sensuousness of nature. He rejects the code of masculinity, which connects work with being a man, a masculinity reckoned by "accumulation and action, self-denial and foresight" (Livesey 109). Mole trades the "dark and lowly little house with its spirit of divine discontent and longing" (9) for the "soft breezes [which] caressed his heat brow, and ... the carol of happy birds [which] fell on his duller hearing almost like a shout" (10) as well as the more general "glints, gleams and sparkles, rustle and swirl, chatter and bubble" (11). Mole's initial characterization reveals a revitalized aesthetic nature.

But Grahame's revitalized aestheticism is problematic. Mole's home reveals the conflict a working-class figure faces with the more elitist nuance of the aesthete. While Mole's house has "sleeping-bunks in the wall" (93) and "little wooden tables with rings that hinted at beer mugs" (94), he also has "a small round pond containing goldfish ... surrounded by a cockleshell border" (94) and "a fanciful erection clothed in more cockleshells and topped by a large silvered glass ball" (94) in the center of the pond. This combination of working-class décor and aesthetic excess reveals the very same conflict Mole undergoes in the course of the novel. But Grahame's purpose is also evident here: a boy/man can have more than one identity; in fact, he can transform and retain elements of both identities — working-class bachelor and companion/burgeoning aesthete. In many ways, Grahame's Mole is the realization of the aesthetic man imagined by William Morris, Edward Carpenter, and Oscar Wilde, particularly as envisioned by Wilde in "The Soul of Man Under Socialism": "the true personality of man ... will grow naturally and simply, flowerlike.... It will not be at discord.... Its value will not be measured by material things" (1046). I am not proposing that Grahame is referring to this essay with Mole's description, but the psychological landscape Grahame creates and which Wilde proposes in his essay include living in another house without thinking of material things, "being" vs. "accumulating," and a harmonious relationship and understanding of nature (rather than a positing of symbols in nature for the human dilemma).

The aesthetic identity that Mole entertains parallels Grahame's own development. In fact, the description of Mole's house closely mirrors the bachelor lodgings Peter Green reveals in his biography of Kenneth Grahame (163). Dichotomy was one of the major themes of Grahame's life and he seems to have invested his principal characters — indeed both Rat and Toad as well — with ongoing conflict in their establishment of identity. It is little wonder that the former Secretary of the Bank of England, also became a member of the Shelley society and acted in its controversial production of Cenci or wrote for both the *National Observer* (edited by W.E. Henley) and for the *Yellow Book* (a journal associated with Henry Harland and Aubrey Beardsley): his life was completely torn between responsibility and the pretensions of an aesthetic life.

Less submerged aestheticism is visible in the characterization of Rat in *The Wind in the Willows*. George Landow has identified several characteristics of aestheticism and we witness these in Rat: self-reflexive mockery, the use of paradox, challenging bourgeois values, and the use of epiphany. ("Aesthetes and Decadents of the 1890s — Points of Departure"). Rat's song and sentiments when playing with the ducks and creating the

"Duck's Ditty," demonstrate his "art for art's sake," his refusal to view them in sentimental ways, and provide a particularly rich scene to examine in light of aestheticism.

Grahame bases this scene off of Wilde's "The Devoted Friend." In Wilde's story, the old water-rat claims:

> I know nothing about the feelings of parents.... I am not a family man. In fact, I have never been married, and I never intend to be. Love is all very well in its way, but friendship is much higher. Indeed, I know of nothing in the world that is either nobler or rarer than a devoted friendship [341].

In Grahame's revisiting of Wilde's work, Rat imagines the ducks as seeing both himself and Mole as intruders on their play, even as he creates the line "Everyone for what he likes!" (28). More importantly, both the old water-rat and Rat act as teachers or mentors as they philosophize different aspects of the aesthetic credo.

Pederasty and Aesthetic links

In both Wilde and Grahame's scenes, we may remember the influence of an older man on a younger man. While Wilde would defend himself using examples of pederasty (Socrates, Shakespeare and Michelangelo) at his infamous trial, Grahame most certainly wasn't establishing this kind of relationship between Mole and Rat. But he was placing one aspect of their relationship, the mentoring of a less experienced male character with a more experienced male character, at the center of the novel, particularly in the beginning of the novel. The "Duck's Ditty" scene demonstrates Mole's resistance to some of Rat's artistic ideas, but the lingering echo of male-male companionship framed in aesthetic discourse is hard to ignore.

Though I will address collaboration and companionship more in the final chapter of the book, it is worthwhile investigating male-male companions for the sake of fully illustrating the influence of aestheticism. The most public exhibition of a male-male companionship could be the Prince and the swallow in Wilde's "The Happy Prince." The Prince teaches the swallow about compassion and charity. Similarly, Rat teaches Mole, and Pooh "teaches" Piglet about the values of such a pairing and, indeed, these pairings function as a mentorship and have erotic possibilities. In both Grahame's and Milne's tales, the principal male couples dominate the plot

Two • Aestheticism, Christianity and Spirituality: Masculinity in Flux

of both novels. For contextualization purposes, it may be useful to investigate someone like Edward Carpenter. This early socialist and sexual studies pioneer modeled the very life Mole/Rat and Pooh/Piglet have in their novels: a man in love with nature and long rambles, but who has a companion (George Merrill in Carpenter's life); a writer/artist demonstrating that same-sex companionship can work across the class system (if we think Rat and Pooh as "higher" in class than Mole and Piglet). Potter's work doesn't have examples of same-sex couples in the same structure of physical, emotional, and psychological support that these other writers employ. In her work, companionship is limited to heteronormative couplings.[3] Though Kipling would never claim it, his scripting of Mowgli's relationship with Bagheera and Baloo is reminiscent of the pederasty Wilde justified at his trial. "Greek love," the codified name of homosexual coupling in the late 1800s, demonstrates two particular philosophical and political nuances that are associated with aestheticism: first, the roots of aesthetic and philosophic basis for these same-sex companionships found in Victorian Hellenism; second, the aesthetic movement, due to its historical moment, was bound to be seen as a liberation movement against class, sexual politics, and the production and value of art in opposition to the creeds of Matthew Arnold and criticism of John Ruskin. This intersection of fin-de-siècle politics and history with the Romantic Era ideas of children and innocence produce a fascinating anthropomorphism, which can code these male-male relationships for a reader.

The "innocence" associated with child characters shadows much of how Grahame writes Rat's experiences in the "Piper at the Gates of Dawn" chapter. But there are other links to English Romanticism in this chapter as well. Richard Gillin has assessed the influence of Keats, Wordsworth and Shelley on Grahame's language, particularly his dialogue as pertains to Rat.[4] But these "Romantic echoes" also serve as a reminder of the connection Romanticism has with aestheticism. Rat becomes "transported ... possessed in all his sense by this new divine thing that caught up his helpless soul and swung and dangled it, a powerless but happy infant, in a strong sustaining grasp" (132). Rat's artistic sensibilities mingle with this new knowledge in language that reflects a transformation, on the verge of an epiphany. This is not a middle-class luncheon on the banks of the river with Toad, but an intense experience that is reminiscent of the "art ... [that] belongs to the realm of dreams, nightmares, and other phantasms of diseased imagination" (qtd. in Lambourne 92). Grahame revives this aesthetic sensibility because in order for his characters to develop (Mole, Rat and Toad), they must undergo transformations. Rat's transformations (including the lure of the Sea Rat and the encounter with Pan) most clearly indicate the influence of Romanticism, with its demonstration of the "natural innocence" of a child character, and the Gothic/Aesthetic influence of Wilde as it is illustrated in Grahame's work.

Critiques of Aestheticism

Lest we devote too much time to Rat and the "seriousness" of aestheticism, an examination of Toad demonstrates the excesses Grahame saw in the Aesthetic Movement. What Grahame continues is the self-referentiality we see in aesthetic art and in works intended for children, which would seem to increase its subversiveness, calling attention to the façade of adulthood masculinity. For example, Wilde's Remarkable Rocket claims, "I like hearing myself talk. It is one of my greatest pleasures. I often have long conversations all by myself, and I am so clever that sometimes I don't understand a single word of what I am saying" (379). In terms of critiquing aestheticism, Wilde may have been his funniest and most cutting critic.

In Grahame's *The Wind in the Willows*, he continues this sort of self-referentiality with Toad, but Grahame's critique, like Wilde's, is multifaceted. The flamboyant, privileged Toad not only serves as an anthropomorphisized, Wildean character, he allowed Grahame to criticize the landed class who had little connection with the "real" England. As much as critics have linked Grahame's aesthetic and artistic aims with a sentimentalized and Arcadian England, there hasn't been an assertion that Grahame uses Toad for comedic effect to chastise the landed class and to resuscitate the philosophical vein both the Pre-Raphaelite and Aesthetic Movements espoused for the working class.

The connection between Wilde and Grahame in critiquing the aesthetic figure are also evident in Toad's relationship to nature. In Wilde's "The Decay of Lying," the quintessential aesthetic stance on nature is rendered: " At twilight nature becomes a wonderfully suggestive effect, and is not without loveliness, though perhaps its chief use is to illustrate quotations from the poets" (943). Toad's poetic waxings on nature in the caravan scene concentrate on how nature affects him, but his behavior during the caravanning episode of the novel suggest that his kinship with nature is more aligned with Keats and Wilde than Clare and Hardy. Surely, Grahame was satirizing the urban aesthete in the countryside and the dismissive nature aestheticism took of nature, but in building his Arcadia, in many ways, Grahame creates the perfect conflicting characters: overly romantic-influenced Rat and utterly modern and dismissive Toad. And it is in this vain that the caravanning episode reveals the consumption of nature by a character like Toad (and by extension the British public). For Toad does no chores nor actually interacts with nature; nature is a background for his musings.

Even something as simple as clothing reveals a subtle critique of manliness and aestheticism. The loose and flowing clothing of the aesthetes was a direct flouting of the stiff, contained outfits of Victorian England. While the aesthetes philosophized about the healthy effects of looser clothing, the associations made by the general public were not concerned with the arguments for a healthier, more beautiful body. The general public had been sold on the benefits of social control by both tradition and in terms of the spirit of the age: loose clothing meant loose morals.

Toad's clothing should certainly not be taken as overtly sexual, but his aesthetic identity based on excess and masks is called into question. His "play" as a motorist is a critique of both modernism and industrialization: " A good deal of his [Toad's] blustering spirit seemed to have evaporated with the removal of his fine panoply. Now ... he was merely Toad, and no longer the Terror of the Highway..." (109). Without a costume, Toad's performance of masculinity is more anxious and confused. We could contrast this comment on clothing with Rat's compliment to Mole on his attire: "'I like your clothes awfully, old chap.... I'm going to get a black velvet smoking suit myself one day" (15). While this scene occurs early in the novel and helps establish the companionship between Mole and Rat, clothing as a mask and a performance is evident: Mole is an infant aesthete, while Toad's clothing is a pretension towards modernism Grahame won't tolerate. As a dreamer and poet, amateur naturalist and River Banker, Rat's flirtation with aestheticism is sanctioned. But Toad's flirtation with aestheticism is too dangerous.[5] Middle-class censure in Grahame's novel will harshly judge both aestheticism (masculinity, roles) and modernism (in dress, gender and machinery), as if only the Edwardian Era with its sentimentality, retrograde recognition of class structure, and escape to the countryside was correct, particularly at novel's end, in its estimation of character.

Clothing linked to character is evident in Potter's work as well. In *The Tale of Jeremy Fisher*, Potter's painstakingly focused eye illustrates the downfall of a dandy. She, unlike Grahame, doesn't revive aestheticism; she condemns the artful male as ineffective and vulnerable in her world of prey and predator. Jeremy Fisher's fishing trip ends without his bachelor clothes and fishing accessories, as he barely escapes his ill-conceived expedition, declaring: "I have lost my rod and basket; but it does not much matter, for I am sure I should never have dared to go fishing again!" (128). He is the paradigm of aesthetic dandy at the beginning of the story, reading a paper in the window, artfully dressed. Potter almost kills him in the story, as she certainly does kill the Fox in *The Tale of Jemima Puddle-Duck*. We may not see the fox as a model of aesthetic manhood, but his links to the city and life outside the farmyard (reading papers, dressed in stylish clothing) are firmly established. The reason I consider him worthy of contextualization here is because of his urban nature. As Carole Scott has pointed out,

> In Jemima Puddle-duck, the fox's wily nature ... is metamorphosed into the suave urbanity of "the ginger whiskered gentleman" whose clever talk and seductive persuasiveness lead to Jemima's initial trust and ultimate betrayal. His rather caddish sophistication is expressed not only in his first presentation — he is reading a newspaper — but in his dress, the plus-fours suit of a country gentleman, complete with scarlet waistcoat; he is, as Jemima perceives, "elegantly dressed," his costume contrasting with Jemima's country shawl and dated poke bonnet [193].

Certainly, this story is thematically concerned with seduction, serving as a warning tale for an overly curious young women. But, despite the focus on the fox's naked and bestial nature as the plot progresses, his initial characterization reveals the prejudice Potter, indeed many Edwardians, felt towards the corruption and decadence of the city vs. the more "normal" environment of the countryside. These ideas, as Raymond Williams contends, are embedded in "the contrast of the country and city [as] one of the major forms in which we become conscious of a central part of our experience and of the crises of our society" (*The Country and the City*, 289). In Potter's case, aesthetic dress is condemned and reveals a fundamental prejudice of a transplanted urbanite towards both art and characters who can't perform functionally in the countryside.[6] By extension, Toad, Jeremy Fisher and the fox are also critiqued (by Grahame and Potter) as ill-equipped to be masculine and utilitarian (Toad and Jeremy Fisher) and dangerous and subversive to real "English" family and heteronormative union (fox).

Another aspect of critiquing aestheticism is the critiquing of its performance. Kipling's critique of aestheticism lies largely in his portrayal of the monkeys in *The Jungle Book*. The monkeys do, after all, sing and play all day, creating nothing. Curiously, Kipling does script a song for the monkeys, "The Road-Song of the Bandar-Log." In this song, the monkey's praise their "pranceful bands," "tails ... Curved in the shape of Cupid's bow," and "Thinking of beautiful things" (68). These aesthetic stand-ins are the very model of manliness Kipling abhorred. This could also be the critique Mole launches at Rat's "Duck's Ditty" in *The Wind in the Willows*: "'I don't know that I think so *very* much of that little song, Rat,'" observed the Mole cautiously. He was no poet himself and didn't care who knew it; and he had a candid nature" (29). For both, Mole and Kipling can't embrace a masculinity they can't understand.

Kipling's distaste for England's aesthetic culture and overly radical literary society were chronicled in his other works. In "Tomlinson" (1891), he expressed his "distaste for young London aesthetes who so burden themselves with received, bookish opinions that they manage to lose their souls" (Lycett, 328). In fact, Kipling's appeal in this poem is to a Christian audience with the setting of judgment with Tomlinson saying he got his opinions from a "Belgian book" from a "dead French Lord," while the devil proclaims "There's sore decline in Adam's line if this be spawn of Earth" ("Tomlinson"). In obvious reference to Wilde's play *The Importance of Being Earnest*, Kipling's remarks on the domestic theater scene are revealing: "Earnestness ... means an infinite capacity for boring the other man with details of your own work" (Lycett, 164). In other words, call it Kipling's racial prejudice or belief in Imperial British manliness, but his scripting of the monkeys reveals a belief in degeneration. As Jopi Nyman concludes: "These [monkeys] are a bunch despised by the proper animals of the jungle. The monkeys do not respect law, and their irrational behavior violates the gendered codes of colonialist masculinity" ("Re-Reading Rudyard Kipling's 'English' Heroism: Narrating Nation in *The Jungle Book*,"

210). As in Potter's structuring of male performances, Kipling's monkeys are condemned for their uselessness and punished accordingly.

Curiously, a critique of aestheticism seems to rear its donkeylike head in *Winnie the Pooh*. As we have seen in other works in my study, aesthetic characters are paired with foils that neither value the expressions of aestheticism nor are comfortable with aesthetic performances themselves (who needs artists in an empire?). In *Winnie the Pooh*, that character is frequently Eeyore. He is both cynical and sarcastic. He denigrates aestheticism as subjective and as superfluous: "We can't all, and some of us don't.... Gaiety. Song-and-dance. Here we go round the mulberry bush" (74). While Eeyore does engage in "gaiety" earlier, he regresses to a masculinity that is performed in one dimension: defensive. More importantly, he performs his masculinity in opposition to the central character's optimism, song and dance, and nonjudgmental behavior, a performance celebrated by feminists according to Carol Stanger, particularly as it is focused on community and ridicules the judgmental and exclusionary performances of those like Owl and Eeyore ("*Winnie the Pooh* Through a Feminist Lens").

Aesthetic performances might not appear as liberated in *Winnie the Pooh* as they are in *The Wind in the Willows*. The characters in the "Hundred Acre Wood" aren't as obviously repressed as Toad, Water Rat, and Mole. Milne constructs performances that allow characters to question their existence and express their desires in their aesthetic utterances and expressions. But these expressions also include deceit and vulnerability as well as denunciations and regressive masculine performances in characters like Eeyore. While Pooh is the primary song creator and performer, his performances are not consistent. Either way, aesthetic performances in *Winnie the Pooh* demonstrate that the psychological burden of Victorian masculinity we see in aesthetic releases for characters in *The Wind in the Willows* have given way to aesthetic performances that reveal modernist apprehensions and anxieties: reaching forward in existential angst and backward in traditional masculine epic self-aggrandizement, semiotic word play, and nonsense songs.

Performance in Aesthetic Mode

Many instances of performance demonstrate the aesthetic character in many of these tales. The lingering influence of the Aesthetic period is visible in the songs, self-reflexivity, and loosening of content in favor of frivolity over overly moralistic plotlines. For example, Toad's self-reflexivity and the narrator's estimation of Toad's storytelling seem to be a resurrection of Wilde in *The Wind in the Willows*. When we remember the tour Wilde made in support of Gilbert and Sullivan's *Patience*, we might remember one of the key elements of aesthetic representation: self-reflexive mockery. Toad's songs and excessive boastings may have links to his animal construction (bufo regularis) and his too easily puffed out cheeks and chest, but his "buffoonish" nature includes some rather telling associations with aestheticism, indeed, storytelling as an art. In one instance he claims "I've been told I ought to have a salon, whatever that may be" (226). Wilde claimed that "Life should imitate art" (Wilde, "Decay" 943), and Toad's characterization is certainly art, and in metafictional references reveals the influence of aestheticism as well. As the novel approaches the end, the narrator asks us:

> Toad, with no one to check his statements or to criticize in an unfriendly spirit, rather let himself go. Indeed, much that he related belonged more properly to the category of what-might-have-happened-had-I-only-thought-of-it-in-time-instead-of-ten-minute-afterwards. Those are always the best and raciest adventures; and why should they not be truly ours as much as the somewhat inadequate things that really come off? [233].

This meditation on storytelling and the artificiality that propels a narrative forward in more interesting ways for the reader is more consistent with Wilde's Socratic dialogue, "The Decay of Lying." In Wilde's essay, art trumps truth and lying is necessary for the greatest art. In this way, Grahame is rehearsing Wilde's poetics through Toad's method of storytelling.

Winnie-the-Pooh reveals the influence of the Aesthetic Movement as well. Pooh frequently performs, aesthetically, for his own amusement and edification. Published in 1926, but taken from stories published earlier in magazines as varied as *Vanity Fair, St. Nicholas Magazine,* and *Punch, Winnie the Pooh* could be taken to be a text that ushers in a modernist form of storytelling with some roots in aestheticism, while also retaining the sentimentality (Arcadian setting, childhood as time of innocence, absence of sexuality and violence) that many associate with the "Golden Age" of children's literature. While Pooh looks for honey he sings a song, albeit with no audience, and, more importantly, with no overt moral. In the vein of self-reflexive mockery discussed earlier in reference to Toad, we witness the same type of performance in Pooh. He makes up songs about himself in his quest for honey, discovering the North Pole, and the "Anxious Pooh Song" in the chapter, "We Say Goodbye." His performances are for self-satisfaction, refuting the Edwardian hangover of moralism still prevalent in the middle classes, yet demonstrating a metafictionality about them that is one of the hallmarks of modernism.

Before investigating individualism and its ties to aestheticism in *Winnie the Pooh*, it is helpful to contextualize Milne's religious beliefs. His two pamphlets, *The Norman Church* and *The Ascent of Man* demonstrate that Milne's spirituality was not without mystery but was certainly without dogma. In a series of public letters between T. S. Eliot and Milne, Milne defended peace as an option before Britain's entry into World War Two. Milne linked the church with excesses of Imperialism and tied warfare to the state building. Eliot turned out to be right in his opinion about the necessity of fighting Hitler, but his motivation was different than Milne's. Milne's beliefs weren't framed in terms of "Christian peace" [Eliot's words], and secular arguments removed the Christian manliness that one like Eliot would have preferred. We can see the Enlightenment and its connection to religion and aesthetics in Milne's own words:

> All life came from the Sun, scientists tell us; all life is sustained by the Sun. I do not think of him as the Sun, for my mind is not large enough to conceive him at all; but when I think of the might and majesty and the dominion of the Sun, and then turn my thoughts upon myself, I feel that I am in less danger of losing my sense of proportion than are those who think of him in human terms [Thwaite, 344].

Milne's secularism even extended to his son, Christopher, who was neither baptized nor confirmed in the church.

We witness the aesthetic manliness, devoid of "muscular Christianity" in Pooh's songs and his actions. Whereas Toad sings in epic boast, Pooh sings for pleasure and for self-examination in various episodes of *Winnie the Pooh*. One might read Milne's construction of Pooh as a critique of the egotistical child, but if Pooh resembles Toad in places, we can extend this critique to aestheticism. For when Pooh's episodes are most absurd there is usually a song or performance attached. And frequently Pooh exhibits the influence of the nonsense tradition in his song constructions. As Carol Stanger has suggested: "Pooh unknowingly describes himself as of semiotic disposition, being open to his instinctual drives as they affect language making" (44). For example, as Pooh walks towards Rabbit's house on a leisurely, bachelor stroll, he hums his made-up song to himself. The illustration by Shepherd depicts Pooh with hands behind his back, casually looking up to the sky. He sings the song and walks "along gaily, wondering what everybody else was doing, and what it felt like, being somebody else" (24). His aesthetic performance reveal an existential stance and self-referentiality we witnessed in Wilde and Grahame.

But it isn't just Pooh who searches for himself in song. Even minor characters do in *Winnie the Pooh*. In the last chapter of the book, "Christopher Robin Gives Pooh a Party," and "We Say Goodbye," Milne builds his sentimental and idyllic forest scene in a long, fourteen-line, run-on sentence. Buried in the middle of this sentence is a male performance: "the cuckoo was trying over his voice carefully and listening to see if he liked it" (147). Both Grahame and Milne's tales reveal a different sensibility from earlier children's works, notably in the aesthetic characterizations of Toad and Pooh. Both of these characters demonstrate that, spiritually, one is the center of their own universe. Singing, one type of aesthetic performance, is a dominant mode of aesthetic performance in Milne's work.

Individualism is clearly celebrated in *Winnie the Pooh* (though there are many adventures where groups are assembled by Milne). But the self as subject almost contests the mythologizing of epic models of literature because of the comedic aspect of self-reflexivity and self-referentiality, which is obviously being performed in Milne's novel. Because of the highly performative nature of masculinity in both Grahame and Milne's texts, the highly performative nature of masculinity, in general, is more clearly illustrated. In this vein we can certainly see Toad's and Pooh's frequent performances and their egocentrism as reflections of the aesthetic influence. While this type of male mythologizing has links to the oaths and swears of Celtic literature and Anglo-Saxon representations of heroism (particularly when we think of boys and heroes), the difference is the comedic aspect of these performances in *The Wind in the Willows* and *Winnie the Pooh*. One of comedy's functions is to deflate previously held conceptions that society uses for control and, in these books (as well as in Potter's works, paternal control is at stake.

While aesthetic performances are certainly used for comic effect by both Grahame and Milne, there is a deliberateness in these characterizations. Still largely chauvinistic in many ways, both novels still anticipate the modernist movement, albeit on the edge of sentimental River Banks and Hundred Acre Forests, but the borders of identity and masculinity are undergoing transformations. In large part, these transformations, both in characterization and in sentence style, owe a large debt to the Aesthetic Movement.

Visions of Multicultural Masculinity in Spiritual Framework

While Wilde was influenced by both Catholicism and Irish folklore in his stories for children, other spiritual influences can be detected in the curious case of Rudyard Kipling. In action, his characters reveal spiritual and religious ideas that resulted from his unique biography. Spiritually, his work demonstrates a revolt against Anglicanism as practiced and debated in England in the late 1800s. Andrew Lycett claims that Kipling's views on religion were a "cerebral mixture of polytheism, agnosticism, and Christianity" (601). But we must remember Kipling was raised in a non-believer family and went on to find a home in the Masonic Order, albeit a temporary one. Lycett claims that this home served as a framework for Kipling and demonstrates the expatriate's liminal status as insider and outsider:

> The reason [Kipling chose Masonry was] its ethical and metaphysical elements, provided the nearest equivalent to a coherent belief system for a young man who, for all his knowingness, was still floundering to make sense of India's mass of conflicting creeds [176].

Though we could contend that Kipling never really found a spiritual home, the Masonic "order" was well suited for his early philosophical template as regards spirituality and, by extension, his view of the Imperial mission as a brotherhood of men, working towards the maintenance of order and control.

We witness the intersection of Kipling's spiritual and religious ideas when we confront the monkeys in *The Jungle Book*. Critics have seen the monkeys representing America (from Kipling's travels and stay in Vermont where he wrote the stories) as well as racialized others (see Lycett, Nyman, and McBratney). But the monkeys may just as well be inherited from

Two • *Aestheticism, Christianity and Spirituality: Masculinity in Flux*

Charles Kingsley's *The Water Babies*. In both books, the inaction of the monkeys is suspect. In Kingsley's novel, the fairy explains that the "doasyoulikes" have turned into apes as a result of doing only what they like. This rendering of the common populace in Kingsley's novel parallels the frivolous monkeys in Kipling's tale. The "muscular Christianity" we see in Kingsley's tale coincides with Kipling's own ideas of spirituality and religion, recalling the utilitarian ideas of mid–Victorian Anglicanism in conflict with the softer, more effeminate Oxford Movement spirituality one reads in Wilde and other aesthetes.[7]

Utilitarianism seems to be the basis for Potter's construction of male characters as well. Potter's spiritualism is more closely aligned with Kipling's than Wilde's or Grahame's. And the influence of Potter's Dissenter background is a fertile place for scholarly investigation. As Leslie Linder has asserted: "The influence of Unitarianism on Potter's intellectual outlook has been neglected by scholars, but its cultural influence is central to her emotional and intellectual perspective" (Lear, 461). Potter's spiritualism is evident in her punishment/reward system for characters who adhere to the lessons and the power of the maternal center of each story, usually the home. Despite the settings for her stories and the abundance of animals, Potter's stories function like parables more attuned to Kingsley than Wilde and Grahame. Her Unitarianism is evident in the lack of pagan or religious symbolism, the absence of nature in romantic descriptions where the characters undergo some kind of transformation, and little word play, punning, or wit.[8]

Action may be an integral part to both Kipling and Potter's formation of character, but a distinct difference is Kipling's position that in order to counter spiritual, emotional and psychological decay, the male child needs brotherhood. Many critics and scholars have pointed to Kipling's association with the Masons as informing this world view (see Lycett, Allen, and Islam). Freemasonry, as a fraternal order of men, necessarily excludes females, though all races and nationalities may join, as the Masons claim to embrace the fundamental aspects of religion that these various male-dominated systems share. Shamsul Islam claims, in *Kipling's Law: A Study of his Philosophy of Life*, that Kipling "naturally came to respect all religions, whether Christian, Muslim, Hindus, Sikhs, and members of the Arya and Brahmo Smaj at the Masonic Lodge" (25). Though I hold with Allen that Kipling critiques Hinduism in his works, and specifically the idea of passivity in *The Jungle Book*, for the purposes of illustrating the spiritual dimension, it is helpful to examine the text for representations of Freemasonry.

In many instances, Mowgli is called "Little Brother" by the "wisemen" figures: Baloo and Bagheera. Their fraternity is a bond that replaces Mowgli's family bonds, emotionally and psychologically. When the Bandar-log steal Mowgli, Baloo writhes on the jungle floor at the loss, while Bagheera admonishes him for his display of emotion: "What would the Jungle think if I, the Black Panther, curled myself up like Ikki the Porcupine, and howled?" (43). Baloo's manliness is called into question by Bagheera, but Baloo responds by claiming, "What do I care what the Jungle thinks?" (43). And later Baloo explains to Kaa why Bagheera and Baloo are trying to rescue Mowgli, "I — we — love him" (48). A hallmark of Kipling's work is the inconsistencies of one characterization posited next to another. In *The Jungle Book*, emotional excess is framed next to the more formal hierarchy of this fraternity of male characters.

The frailty of fraternity is evident as the novel progresses, giving way to a "dark hero" scheme when Mowgli takes over in his revenge scheme. Mowgli must reconcile his identity without the brotherhood he once celebrated. As the wolves descend on Akela, who is older and his leadership sabotaged by Shere Khan, Akela reminds them that Mowgli "is our brother in all but blood" (25). But the damage has been done; Mowgli is given his chance to speak and the spiritual connection he has found in the Wolf Pack is broken:

> There is no need for this dog's jabber. Ye have told me so often tonight that I am a man (and indeed I would have been a wolf with you to my life's end), that I feel your words are true. So I do not call ye my brothers any more, but sag [dogs], as a man should. What ye will do, and what ye will not do, is not yours to say. That matter is with *me* [26].

This confrontation foreshadows the group hunting that eventually results in Shere Khan's death, mirroring the farewell scene at the end of the novel. But this particular ending to the illusory bonds of fraternity Mowgli once felt is heavy with emotional display on Mowgli's part:

> Something began to hurt Mowgli inside him, as he had never been hurt in his life before, and he caught his breath and sobbed, and the tears ran down his face.... Mowgli sat and cried as though his heart would break; and he had never cried in all his life before [28–29].

Two • Aestheticism, Christianity and Spirituality: Masculinity in Flux

He cries into Mother's Wolf's body when he says goodbye to his surrogate mother and father, and we see the beginnings of a children's tale turn adolescent, the beginnings of a "training tale" turn rebellious and more emotionally painful for Mowgli. The hero from Western civilization is more compatible with Imperial British masculinity, and is employed by Kipling to resolve the conflicts Mowgli has with the Wolf Pack and Shere Khan — an individualist hero rises above the weak masses to demonstrate the value of hierarchy in action rather than the common bonds of brotherhood Mowgli once celebrated.

What Kipling may reveal is that the initial brotherhood established in the novel is a spiritual connection the immigrant Mowgli needs in order to replace his loss of family. Kipling's life could be summarized as an outsider who searched for a home: not comfortable in England and not comfortable abroad. An individual in search of "home" and "family" is evident in other tales from *The Jungle Book*, such as "Rikki-Tikki-Tavi" and "Toomai of the Elephants." The surrogacy of home is also evident in Kipling's cruel and masculine *Stalky and Co.* (1899) where Beetle, based on Kipling himself, finds a family in Stalky, M'Turk, and Mr. King. Still, this all-male brotherhood Kipling continued to portray in his stories reveal a respect and adherence to religions and societies that have all-male patriarchal control at the root of both their moral and social orders.

Spiritual connection is valuable to Kipling in the children's tale (earlier part of the novel), but spirituality is discontinued as a worthwhile venture in the tale as the novel turns action oriented and increasingly psychological and violent. Charles Allen, in *Kipling Sahib: India and the Making of Rudyard Kipling*, claims that behind this idea of action is a critique of Hinduism: "Kipling seems to be saying that the Hindu creed of passivity and acceptance of fate, worthy as it is, is not enough; that in a crisis it is the Western notion of action and intervention that saves the day" (332). This critique seems especially poignant considering the human villagers are victimized by Shere Khan in *The Jungle Book*. It takes a hero to save them, one that the village cannot produce in human society.

The fight for spiritual dominion and one's soul is evident in Mowgli as it is in Wilde's "The Fisherman and His Soul." Mowgli is of two minds as he sings at the end of *The Jungle Book*: "These two things [village identity and jungle identity] fight together in me as the snakes fight in the spring.... I am two Mowglis.... My heart is heavy with the things that I do not understand" (98). Kipling's two-minded daemon (as a writer and thinker) is resurrected in Mowgli's tension between identities. As heavy as Kipling's "Law" is in the story, Mowgli's character is suspended, spiritually, between the devotion and obligation he feels for the Wolf Pack and the original birthplace, the village. Spiritually, transformation requires the killing of Shere Khan, but also the bitter exile from the pack.

Conclusion

In the works examined in this chapter, attempts to clarify and define masculinity and its relationship to spirituality have usually been defined through Christianity, and not unreasonably so due to the influence of the Bible on the writing styles of authors such as Kipling, Potter, and Wilde (see Lear, Lycett, Whitlark, Killeen). But the contradictions and paradoxes of an Anglo-Irish writer whose artistry combined affinities for the Oxford Movement, Irish folk-Catholicism, and a critique of middle-class Anglicanism; the multicultural influences on the Anglo-Indian writer with sympathies for the Masonic Order; the Dissenting Unitarian author whose tales reward and punish characters, particularly male characters, according to their actions in a "less than" Arcadian setting; the aesthetic-influenced children's writer resuscitating male friendships and backwards glances at paganism; and the humorist whose male friendships and sentimental Arcadia replace the church and morality as spiritual guides: these authors reflect not only the mid–Victorian divisions in the Anglican Church, but also the nascent agnosticism and distaste for moral children's tales couched in Christianity previous to the late Victorian period.

A. A. Milne once remarked, "goodbye to all that" (speaking of his children's works), and this could serve as a bookend to masculine characterizations of spirituality. Wilde's characterization of pagan and Catholic spirituality, in both cruel and benevolent terms, avails a reader/listener of alternatives to the "muscular Christianity" of children's writers before him like Thomas Hughes and Charles Kingsley. In many ways, we could say that Wilde, Grahame, and Milne's work reflect a Christian socialist view, though Grahame's revival of paganism and Milne's nonsense performances of egotism, deception, lying, and trickery make this statement problematic.

Finally, the influence of aestheticism is hard to ignore after Wilde. Whether critiqued by Kipling and Potter in their utilitarian view of masculinity, paired with Grahame's development theme of boys/animals into men of companionship and secular support for a class system, or continued in the disillusioned humor following World War One, aestheticism proves to be an influence on how authors construct manliness in their anthropomorphic tales, revealing a modernization of mid–Victorian expressions of spirituality in these works for children.

Three

Reputation, Hierarchy, Masculine Logic, Law and Codes

Authoritarianism could arguably be one of the key concepts of masculinity, especially for its connection to the "'authoritarian family' ... where reproductions of class society and hierarchy is accomplished" (Connell, 17). Various social scientists and psychologists have examined the idea of authoritarianism as a type of masculinity (Horkheimer, Fromm, Adorno, Reich). Perhaps the one influence that unites Wilde, Kipling, Grahame, Potter and Milne is that they all write under the heavy lidded gaze of the Industrial Revolution. The intersection of rationalized and mechanized production of goods, along with a capitalist business structure could easily be pointed to as producing reputation, hierarchy and social codes that reinforced the post–Artisan, post–Romantic Age. Threats to rational control, particularly in sexuality, reveal an era's ethos on sex, punishment, and resistance.

Tess Coslett has written about the complexities of writing for children, and perhaps there is also an intersection here that highlights the hierarchizing of Kipling, Potter, and Grahame's work:

> Writing for children provides a space of license and play, though paradoxically one which must be watched over and controlled by the adult narrator, as the necessary transgressions of the talking animal convention and the ambiguous valuation of the "child" always threaten to escape from control ["Child's Place in Nature: Talking Animals in Victorian Children's Fiction," 491].

Control seems to be at the heart of this chapter because identity — who am I, what does it mean to be British, and how am I supposed to act — dominates the reasons for social codes. While I employ the term "hegemonic masculinity," diverse manliness will be represented, particularly as it pertains to reputation and hierarchy. More intrinsic to the idea of codifying or sorting through characters for power relationships is the idea that

Three • Reputation, Hierarchy, Masculine Logic, Law and Codes

slippage attends each of these novels. Though we are reminded of the Law of the Jungle throughout Kipling's novel, we are also consistently reminded that characters break the law, violate social codes, act on their own behalves, and behave in ways that undermine their reputations.

According to Anthea Trodd, hierarchies were to be resisted in the literature of the early twentieth century:

> Generational revolt is a major theme in the literature of the Edwardian period. The insistence that a new age was establishing itself found expression in novels and plays which described a young protagonist's attempt to rebel against the heavy inheritance of Victorianism, and the patriarchs and matriarchs who represented it [Trodd, 47].

While there are adult figures that generate revolt in Wilde, Kipling, Grahame and Potter's works, there is an appreciable quality of revolt inside characters as well. The increased psychological dimensions to characters and their interior lives, creates hierarchies and codes that are unstable. Milne's virtual absence of hierarchy seems to speak to the culmination, in a way, of what Wilde and Grahame started: an aesthetic masculinity modeled on all-male communities where play and escape dominate the day-to-day lives of characters rather than the need to establish order and reason. Characters like Pooh, Piglet, Eeyore, and Christopher Robin demonstrate the fantastical elements of the story as positioned next to the realism (these are toys and Christopher Robin will grow up), yet their fantasy still illustrates a revolt. As Carol Stanger has written: "conflict over accepting gender is an expression of the major conflict in the story: the struggle against integration into patriarchy" (46). This doesn't mean that Pooh doesn't engage in privileges according to a bachelor male that aren't available to a character like Kanga. But it does continue the idea of control at the heart of hierarchy and the revolt it produced in the children's literature.

Ramon Hinojosa, in "Doing Hegemony: Military, Men, and Constructing a Hegemonic Masculinity" posited that hierarchies in gender coexist with gendered ideals that position subordinate and primary roles. His research continues to study what is evident in literature: control and preservation of control has produced not only literature, which uses hierarchies and social codes to regulate characters' sexualities, but also readers that look for the same regurgitation of hierarchies that are, at the best, ideals appreciated by that book's era. In this chapter, I hope to show that a variety of masculine representations occur, even when hierarchy and reputations are at stake. In addition, by examining social codes, laws, the use of reason and logic, and the very logic and language used by characters as they promulgate or question hegemonic codes, I hope the reader will see that inscriptions, re-inscriptions, and instability are consistent features of any order an author seeks to impose, and, in this era, demonstrate the "transgressions of the talking animal convention."

Reputation: A Variety of Uses

The variety of uses of reputation demonstrates, yet again, the multiple masculinities occurring during this time period. Whereas Wilde depicts sacrifice as an expression of masculine reputation, particularly in love plots, writers like Grahame and Kipling use warning plots to demonstrate that reputation needs to be protected and, often, requires violence to establish and re-establish reputation's use to maintain social order. Potter challenges the reputation males make for themselves, particularly as they stray from a domestic center. And both Grahame and Potter's use of reputation occur in more localized settings, which attempt to minimize upheaval and re-envision masculinity as a system of paradoxes to work out, escape, or grow out of (particularly as we consider Peter Rabbit and Benjamin Bunny). Kipling's use of reputation is so often at stake because, in many ways, a system of colonial control depends heavily on fear and overt recognition of hierarchy as a deterrent to rebellion. Kipling, like Grahame, frequently scripts reputation through the body, and also can blend gender associations as well as paternal and maternal roles. Reputation may be used by both authors, but the liminality expressed by Grahame underscores the depictions of Edwardian gentlemen with all of their "topsy turvy" characterizations.

Oscar Wilde depicts reputation, at least as it is connected to love, in scenarios where sacrifice is required. Reputation does not become a simplistic representation for the performance and construction of masculinity. For example, in "The Happy Prince," Wilde relies on a stereotype, the group council, to paradoxically arrange both reputation and the problematic interpretations we make with reputation. The prince is a statue admired for its beauty by that council. But the beauty is framed in jewels and gold leafing — a superficial reputation based on appearance. This reputation is undone, literally, as the prince sacrifices for various people in the story and the town no longer finds the statue worthy of its place when it is stripped down. The veneer of reputation is what the statue sacrifices, which is a sacrifice of what is deemed masculine (prominence, beauty, respect) by a group like the town council.

We might consider the reputation of the church in a story like "The Fisherman and His Soul," as problematic as well. In this story, the church prizes the soul more than money, seemingly enhancing its reputation. Wilde's use of reputation, as it concerns the soul, is undone as the unseen moves from reputation (belief, lore) to reality (character in the story). Moreover, the Soul becomes evil in its adventures and its functioning as a adventure story hero, replete with colonialist characterization. Wilde attacks the reputation of the church, as it is represented by the priest and his strict, unyielding adherence to dictum over passion. And the sacrifice that the fisherman makes enhances both his masculinity and his reputation.

In many ways, Wilde's use of reputation, as it concerns masculinity, most often centers on love. While there is humor (a swallow falling in love with a reed, a dwarf in love with a Spanish princess, a student who is played for a fool by a young lady), there is a myth-making agent at work in Wilde's use of folklore, satire, and morality play. In "The Nightingale and the Rose," "The Selfish Giant," "The Birthday of the Infanta," and "The Happy Prince" love is not only at stake but is mythologized. The reputation of love as a cleansing and changing agent in identity formation is strong in each of these stories. Systems of control (town councils, churches, religious dictates, selfishness) all conspire to block, prohibit or impede the love plots that each of these stories contains. Again, sacrifice becomes a masculine-making performance, many times exchanging one reputation (combative giant, golden statue) for another (reformed cynic, core foundation to God's city). In many ways, sacrifice is used in violence as a masculinizing agent in the authors I've examined and is needed to make reputation transform so as to "reformulate" as the new agent of masculinization for the late Victorian, pre–Edwardian child.

Sacrifice is a different agent of masculinization in *The Wind in the Willows*. In this story, the reputation that lingers as heavy as a ghost is Toad's dead father. Badger uses Toad's father's reputation to try to reform Toad. Through guilt and shame, Badger attempts to "restore" Toad to not only his socio-economic place, but his familial and obligatory place. In this sense, the Edwardian child needs to be cajoled and convinced of the Victorian past (manners, class system, self-discipline) as a worthwhile part of one's identity.

As in Wilde's stories, there has to be some sort of sacrifice for masculinization to take place, specifically as it is framed against reputation. Toad doesn't wish to be a stolid, largely off-screen landed gentleman, he wishes to be "the popular and handsome ... the rich and hospitable ... so free and careless and debonair" (141). But Toad also wishes to be the "Terror of the Highway" (109). Toad tries on different reputations because his identity is negotiable in the early stages of the novel. Because Grahame's novel is such a tale of transformations, Toad's process of becoming masculinized reveals the inconsistencies, paradoxes and ironies of such a development for an Edwardian gentleman. In other words, there isn't one way to become male (Grahame also uses a variety of male characters to demonstrate this) and there isn't one way to be male even in the same class (Mole and Rat). Reputation or myth-making is central to the need to retake Toad Hall, but the ties to traditional masculinity are visible earlier. We see this with the respect characters grant Badger, from the hedgehogs in the Wild Woods to the stoats and weasels at the end of the novel. The myth making Grahame endeavors in is more localized, as in Potter, but much more imbued with comedy, as in Wilde.

Potter, like Grahame, demonstrates that small, rural, English settings can act as arenas where reputation matters, and characters have to contend with not only their own establishment of reputation but with the reputation of others. As I've mentioned previously, in "The Tale of Samuel Whiskers," when Moppet and Mittens start killing rats and hanging their tails from the barn, we have an establishment of reputation that is transgendered, in many ways. But it is a reputation that is localized. In other stories, Potter scripts reputations where mothering, domestic provision, and shared heteronormative partnerships become the reputation or mythologized representation of an identity that the characters must negotiate. As it concerns masculinity, many of the reputations Potter constructs are reputations that must be undone to form a new, more domestic-centered male.

This transformatory plotting on Potter's part (and she is by no means alone) occurs in *The Tale of Peter Rabbit* and *The Tale of Benjamin Bunny*. The re-inscription of the death of the patriarch take place on Peter. Mr. McGregor, the agent of death, looms large in these stories as well as *The*

Three • *Reputation, Hierarchy, Masculine Logic, Law and Codes*

Tale of the Flopsy Bunnies. As I mentioned earlier, the corrective can be death or violence, but the reputation of punishment and death is an instigating, though often forgotten, reputation proceeding from the likes of Mr. McGregor and Old Mr. Benjamin Bunny.

Reputation, as it is used by Kipling in *The Jungle Book*, intersects with class. One's blood and one's name is an act in itself toward fulfilling the promise of epic masculinity, an act one doesn't always have control over, much like Toad in Grahame's novel. When Tabaqui addresses the Wolf family, he invokes the same sense of privilege according to Toad: "Indeed, indeed, I might have remembered that the children of Kings are men from the beginning" (2). While Grahame questions the notion of being born to power (requiring a transformation in Toad's case), Kipling supports the idea of a natural hierarchy it seems. As John McBratney claims,

> The boy enters the pack when he is abandoned by his parents, and like many orphans in Kipling (and in Victorian literature in general), he starts life with an advantage: the ability to fashion a self initially free of the constraints of his natural parents' caste [284].

It is no accident that Mowgli finds himself in the cave of Father Wolf and Raksha, two legendary members of the Wolf Pack, with reputations to match. And as Mowgli escapes an Indian upbringing for the jungle, Kipling's use of reputation as a masculine-making device becomes less localized and more universal. Framed next to Darwin and his *Origin of Species* (1859), it is hard not to see Kipling's aim for a larger setting — jungle — where *the* recipe for manhood is available in a more universal sense.

Kipling's use of reputation also includes a use of bias and class, particularly as it applies to the Indian village. Mowgli has no respect for the natives and Kipling's chauvinism is on full display in Mowgli's subsequent abandoning of the village to fulfill a destiny larger than the role inscribed with his initial birth. In much the same way, we may remember the denizens of the Wild Woods in Grahame's story, where the rabbits, stoats, and weasels are reputed by Otter, Rat, and Badger as disordered, chaotic, and needing control. In many ways, this is the setting used to allow a boy to demonstrate passage to manhood. Negative reputations of other characters allow a hero or heroes to become more masculine through actions used to punish these reputations. In the end, reputations are made while others are punished, and the hierarchy changes positions.

We see a changing hierarchy in *The Jungle Book* and the use of reputation when we consider Shere Khan. Tabaqui calls him "the Big One," certainly a reputation that enhances one's masculinity. But he is also called "Lungri," the lame one, so named by his mother (talk about emasculating a character!). With dubious reputation, Shere Khan begins the story. The deviant and disfigured Shere Khan has both a reputation, from birth, and a reputation, from actions — cattle killing, rule breaking — that marks him as the antithesis to "proper" masculinity, framed in epic, honorable tones, particularly as it concerns hunting.

For the villagers in the story, Shere Khan's reputation is mysterious but not as laden with the more aggressive and martial attributes commonly associated with masculinity. In the village, Shere Khan is reputed to be the resurrected spirit of a money-lender who was disabled. While Kipling may be mocking local supersitition, he is establishing that reputation should be considered next to action. Not only is Shere Khan a cattle killer, the tiger hunter is ineffective as a hunter of Shere Khan. Both of their reputations are troublesome and questioned in Kipling's novel.

Naming isn't the only way reputation is created in the novel. Kipling also uses the body, but in ways that may lead to a more liberated reading of gender roles and expectations. Both Baloo and Bagheera are first introduced through bodily descriptions: Baloo as "big, serious, old" (31) and Bagheera as "a black shadow" (12), denoting his stealth and quickness. But Bagheera's reputation, deeply intertwined with hierarchy, is revealed in both strength and in "softness":

> Everybody knew Bagheera, and nobody cared to cross his path; for he was as cunning as Tabaqui, as bold as the wild buffalo, and as reckless as the wounded elephant. But he had a voice as soft as wild honey dripping from a tree, and a skin softer than down [12–13].

The reputation Bagheera has isn't simplistic and allows Kipling to pair together masculine and feminine associations. Baloo becomes almost matronly in the manner Kipling uses to describe him, while Bagheera and Raksha become the mixed-gendered parents who hunt, caretake, and provide as developed in their reputations. Bagheera and Shere Khan testify to the power Mowgli has in his stare. Certainly there is good reason to see that Kipling's conception of gender was less clear and heteronormative (English, late Victorian) than conceptions of gender used by his contemporaries in stories with domestic settings.

Three • Reputation, Hierarchy, Masculine Logic, Law and Codes

But make no mistake about it, Kipling also enjoyed the use of violence in *The Jungle Book* as a way to cement reputation. Bagheera reminds the wolves that his "honour is something that he will perhaps fight for" (25), finishing his speech with "his white teeth bared under his lip" (25). Reputation based on killing and violence frames much of the novel (Shere Khan, Raksha, Bagheera, Kaa), but often times the use of the body with reputation and violence is quite noticeable. Bagheera's teeth assert a promise of violence, Mowgli's eyes as part of his reputation as "higher" than the wolves, Bagheera, and Shere Khan: both with a promise of violence. But no use of the body as a promise of violence establishes reputation or is as assertive as Mowgli's spreading of Shere Khan's skin in front of the Wolf Pack at the end of the novel. John McBratney sees the process of establishing reputation as progressive and ultimately, a reversing of hierarchy: "Even as a child, the weakest of the wolf-pack, Mowgli could always outstare the jungle creatures. And as he grew older, the strain between the fraternal and magisterial impulses in him increased" (286). The character Kipling has subjected to the most killings, threats, negotiation, and recognitions of reputation as centered on violence reinvents the hierarchy, fulfills his destiny, and establishes his reputation through the use of the body.

Perhaps the most noticeable use of the body as it is tied to reputation and performance is the scene where Kaa kills the monkeys. At stake is Kaa's reputation, when Baloo lies to him and says the monkeys have called him a "footless, yellow earthworm" (46). Kaa's pride is mingled with his reputation in the monkey community, revealing that his hunting is surreptitious as well as deadly:

> Generations of monkeys have been scared into good behavior by the stories their elders told of Kaa, the night-thief, who could slip among the branches as quietly as moss grows, and steal away the strongest monkey that ever lived; of old Kaa, who could make himself look so like a dead branch or a rotten stump that the wisest were deceived ... Kaa was everything the monkeys feared in the Jungle [59].

We see that power and reputation become a prophecy that needs a performance to re-inscribe the initial reputation. We also see that this lesson was done for Mowgli's benefit as much as it was done for Kaa and his need to re-establish his reputation.

We may remember that the monkey's reputation is one the whole jungle knows, and that this reputation serves as a "warning tale" for

Mowgli, much the same way that Kaa's reputation is used as a warning tale for the monkey community). While the hierarchy shifts in terms of Kipling's plotting, depending on which conflict arises, the social order is always at stake. Tess Coslett contends in "Child's Place in Nature: Talking Animals in Victorian Children's Fiction" that the Monkeys function as outsiders:

> The lawless, parodic behavior of the monkeys, who steal animal speech and mimic human actions is, of course, extremely carnivalesque. Their defeat and punishment places a limit on free-play, the inversion of hierarchy, that is allowed in Kipling's use of the talking animal convention [490].

The danger of the monkeys is their reputation; one can reason that their play is essentially harmless, though Baloo and Bagheera reason otherwise. That Mowgli's hierarchal rise won't be fulfilled is a challenge that must be negated. As Claudia Nelson has maintained: "The threat of a sterile and childish existence ... is forever ended [with the monkey's death]" (545). This liminal state is too much for the Imperial mind and requires, in a sense, genocide based on reputation.

We see more liminality in a character like Badger, who is frequently linked with the squierarchy and seems as if he is the source of power in the river bank. Certainly, many of the characters acknowledge Badger as a source of power in the community: the hedgehogs, Rat, even Toad (though he rebels against him constantly). But Badger's reputation is one that is superficial in some ways. For as martial and commanding as he is, he also takes in Mole and Rat during the storm, nurses Mole himself, and, with great humility, acknowledges to Mole that his house wasn't built entirely by him. In fact, Badger's conception of himself is that he is in a long line of badgers, and other underground dwellers (like Mole). Badger lives out the Edwardian bachelor with less aestheticism than Rat or Mole, but still he is a secret fan of children and friends (as we see at the end of the novel), can organize the "kids" (Toad, Rat, and Mole) and provides a model for Mole that, indeed, Mole adapts, in some measure, to his own identity.

We see this "topsy-turvy" establishment and subversion of reputation (as we see in much of Grahame's plotting) at the end of the novel. Like Kipling, reputation is used for societal control: the Wild Wooders are "successfully tamed" (253) and Toad, Mole, Rat and Badger are "respectfully ... greeted by the inhabitants" (254). So, at first glance, the hegemonic structure is restored. But, and we see this is many of these authors use of reputation, inconsistency lingers. Grahame has the mother weasels mythologize "the gallant Water Rat" as "a terrible fighter" (254). This is the same Rat that Badger doesn't trust as a soldier because he is a poet. We also learn that Badger is used as a warning tale to scare young children but that this is a "base libel on Mr. Badger" (254). With a child audience in mind, and for humor, the softening of reputation mirrors the shifting evaluation of reputation as an absolute value in establishing masculinity as we move from the Victorian Era to the Edwardian Era.

Reputation Oscillates Wildly

Reputation varies, certainly, among the authors I've examined, but it also vacillates in how it is represented and frequently subverted. How Kipling questions reputation reveals a distrust of group-based philosophies, how Potter legitimizes heteronormative uses of traditional reputations while punishing individual and escapist performances reveals a conservatism inherent in the English countryside, while Wilde and Grahame continually problematize masculinity, in terms of how reputation is used, with characters like the duck in "The Remarkable Rocket," the nightingale in "The Rose and the Nightingale," and Toad in *The Wind in the Willows*.

Wilde mocks traditional conceptions of masculinity at many turns, including subverting reputation in its ties to military prowess. For example, in "The Birthday of the Infanta" he has the "wizened apes play[ed] all kinds of amusing tricks ... fought with tiny swords, and fired off guns, and went through a regular soldier's drill just like the king's own bodyguards" (264). Wilde demonstrates that a child audience would find actors (in this case, anthropomorphic actors) "playing" soldiers as humorous, but the subversiveness is evident as well; not only is soldiery some kind of play that even apes could mimic, but they act like the king's bodyguard, a unit which should presumably be the best soldiers. Interestingly, reputation as the private guards for the king becomes a central piece of this satirical jab on Wilde's part. While he mimics masculinity in warlike guise, he doesn't mimic the reputation of pagan love and projection in the dwarf's fantasizing about the princess; this he takes seriously.

Another author who satirizes men and traditional, reputed roles of men is Beatrix Potter. In *The Tale of the Flopsy Bunnies*, we witness the instability of reputation as the father figure, Benjamin, can't provide for his family (we witness the same phenomena in other Potter stories: *The Tale of Mr. Jeremy Fisher*, *The Tale of Timmy Tiptoes*. In Benjamin's story, he not only is a poor representative of fatherhood as a provider; he is paired next to his cousin, Peter, who has become a reformed gardener, married, providing bunny. Benjamin, it may be remembered, also leads his children to Mr. McGregor's garden for the "soporific" lettuce ends that place them in such danger. Victorian fathers may be absent in Potter's stories, dead before the stories begin, but the now grown-up Edwardian fathers are both improvident and incompetent. In many ways, Potter's critique of manliness transforms from the ghostly presence of fathers to a more satirical and modern portrayal of fatherhood and manliness as the stories progress. In this way, Potter is not a merely sentimental children's story author but an author who participates in and is part of the literary tradition of modernism that sprung up around her.

Yet, Potter does provide examples where the reputation of a man as a provider is asserted. In *The Tale of Timmy Tiptoes*, Timmy provides as a soon-to-be-father as does Tom Thumb in *The Tale of Two Bad Mice*. Both of these characters provide examples of Potter's qualified scripting of masculinity: self-satisfaction, particularly in males, is a dangerous performance, whereas male characters who provide for families in heteronormative ways, with the female protected in the domestic center with children, are lauded. Adhering to the reputation of being a good provider provides safety in Potter's stories. Again, Potter positions characters as foils, almost options for the male reader/listener of her stories: Jeremy Fisher (bachelor, Edwardian gentleman, ineffectual hunter/gatherer) vs. provider for domestic, heteronormative union (Timmy Tiptoes, Tom Thumb). As much as she chronicles her times, she certainly positions dandy and stand-in aesthete characters as silly (and almost killed), framing their failures of manliness next to survival.

Oddly enough, a famous example of resistance to reputation is found in the least likely of authors, Rudyard Kipling. The power of reputation, as I've stated before, is certainly at stake in much of *The Jungle Book*, certainly in respect to a character's manliness. But when Baloo loses Mowgli, he cries "What do I care what the Jungle thinks?" (43). It must be remembered that this comment comes from the character responsible for inscrib-

Three • *Reputation, Hierarchy, Masculine Logic, Law and Codes*

ing the Law of the Jungle, the language of other animals, and the codes of hunting. That Baloo would posit such a rebellion is noteworthy, but it is also part of Kipling's method, similar to Wilde's, or working out dialectics and revealing the paradoxes and ironies of social communities. Love, paternal/maternal love is at stake here, and Kipling constructs perhaps his most emotional and intimate scene in the novel with Baloo's lament. Kipling is known for his resistance to both native superstitions and to urban and dandified English literary society. Is this resistance a reflection of the resistance Kipling himself felt for society? We aren't able to linger in this moment long enough, because, like Potter, Kipling brings the heteronormative censor to bear in closing out his scenes. In this case, Bagheera questions Baloo's manliness through his self-respect: "Baloo, thou has neither memory nor respect. What would the Jungle think if I, the Black Panther, curled myself up like Ikki the Porcupine, and howled?" (43). The community will be the judge for both of them, Bagheera asserts in his speech, though we know, by novel's end, that the respect Kipling demonstrates for the Wolf Pack is minimal.

Baloo's reputation as a "mothering" character might be at issue here. Reputation is not paramount when one has power or agency: the rules stick and reputation is secure (or, seems to be). When the balance is upset, a character feels the urge to challenge the code, like Baloo. A different instinct takes over that reveals the instability of reputation when reckoned with the bond between parent and child. But, in the end, reputation privileges power and punishes weakness, an important part of establishing a code when we consider the mission that must be impressed on the colonizer's mind.

Reputation can be, like gender itself, a fluid process as much as a final construction. While Baloo's reputation for teaching the wolf cubs how to hunt is static, in Kipling's Darwinian jungle, his performances towards that end can be gender blurring. He is a vegetarian bear and frequently performs in songs. One such song which begins "Kaa's Hunting" announces the self-perceived gender blurring role: "Oppress not the cubs of the stranger, but hail them as Sister and Brother,/ for though they are little and bubsy,/ It may be the Bear is their mother" (31). This self-perceived gender blurring is paired with the realizations that reputations are made and constantly remade. At stake is the threat of effeminacy in many cases. When Bagheera admonishes Mowgli following the slaughter of the monkeys, it is evident that one's own songs about oneself aren't nearly as important as reputation: "For, remember, Mowgli, I, who am the Black Panther, was forced to call upon Kaa for protection, and Baloo and I were both made stupid as little birds by the Hunger-Dance" (66). This fluidity in reputation is crucial to the shifting hierarchies in the story. Mowgli is able to resist Kaa's charm and surpasses his teachers, more human and more culturally inscribed. As Jopi Nyman claims, "Without Mowgli's intervention, Baloo and Bagheera would join the cult of Kaa, which would lead to their death (and being devoured by the python). for Mowgli, however, the hypnotic dance is a mere sign of native superstition" (211). Mowgli has to be taught a great deal in the jungle, but cultural prejudice seems to have been born inside him. More importantly, survival is at stake for Bagheera because Kipling has constructed a fate for Akela, leader of the Wolf Pack, where reputation and performance can lead to death for aging leaders.

But reputation can be a source of humor in a variety of veins, particularly when paired with identity and burgeoning sexuality. We see this in Wilde's tales for children. Wilde edited *The Woman's World* from 1887 to 1889 where he "systematically foregrounded women's intellectual issues, solicited famous contributors, and wrote a column reviewing relevant books" (Schaffer, 40). When we consider the phenomenon of the New Woman in British politics, it is surprising, in some ways, that Wilde's use of the mother duck in "The Remarkable Rocket," originates in the countryside. The reputation of both the New Woman figure and the Victorian gentleman becomes an intersection for Wilde that he decidedly exploits:

> I had thoughts of entering public life once myself ... there are so many things that need reforming. Indeed, I took the chair at a meeting some time ago, and we passed resolutions condemning everything we did not like. However, they did not seem to have much effect. Now, I go in for domesticity, and look after my family [360].

The reputation of politics as a man's endeavor is undermined, but more importantly, this man's endeavor is an arena full of failure. Surely Wilde has fun at the women's movement's expense, but the shifting gender roles is evident in this scene and demonstrates that reputations are targets for satire and also carry some burden of truth to them.

Wilde mocks reputation, particularly as it is expressed in Victorian expectations of men, in several stories. Perhaps nowhere is it so blatantly stated as in "The Nightingale and the Rose." The nightingale sings for the

Three • Reputation, Hierarchy, Masculine Logic, Law and Codes

lover, sacrifices for romantic love and dies. The student concludes, as Wilde critiques his mechanical and material age, "[love]s quite impractical, and, in this age to be practical is everything. I shall go back to philosophy and study metaphysics" (331). Love's reputation for unsettling manhood and reason are undermined as the student opts to return to his studies. Philosophy and metaphysics certainly wouldn't do for obtaining a job in Victorian London, but both the study and the rejection of love reminds us immediately of the man's privilege in obtaining an education. In addition, the reputation of love as undoing manliness has to be corrected. Naomi Wood has remarked of this last scene in the story that Wilde aims for timelessness: "the Student, frustrated with his object, throws that costly rose into the gutter and shits himself away with his books. Beauty creates its own meaning, whether or not it is transmitted to others" (161). Beauty cannot be transmitted to a male child who hides behind the reputation of books and study, reason and emotional control. We can see the foil of the nightingale against the student so clearly at the end of the story. Wilde criticizes how masculinity seeks to escape effeminacy and embrace a practical identity as a culturally acceptable way of resisting the forces of passion and love.

Of course what is most paradoxical is that the masculine performance that Wilde revives is the example of Christ. The nightingale's performance as a savior, dyed with blood and a puncture wound, is designed by Wilde to evoke a performance of masculinity that is far less "practical" and more "morally" centered. Wilde is so committed to this "other" aspect of reputation as a vehicle for transmission of gender that he uses a female character to perform this anthropomophosized version of aesthetic Christianity. The joke, as it were, is many faceted: moral sacrifice over practicality; the supposed guiding model of maleness in Christian England is transformed into a female (for look what males make of sacrifice); and the blend of aesthetic descriptions, song, and declarations require reason and avoidance, less the male child become as manly as Christ was.

Paradox and resistance to reputation are passed from Wilde down to Grahame, though the modernist era has its influences on Grahame. Resistance to reputation is more of a social critique and evident when we consider Toad in *The Wind in the Willows*. He consistently resists the roles that are prescribed to his class position. As he tries to repudiate the status quo, he flails around in identity crisis after identity crisis. In this manner,

Grahame's depiction of how reputation works in regards to development of manliness and identity is not unlike its place in the work of Saki or Evelyn Waugh.

Badger's frequent attempts to corral and control Toad represent the developing reputation Toad has created for himself and, at the same time, the hegemonic response to such a reputation from a caretaker for the group's norms. Grahame, perhaps more than any other novelist in the group I've studied, presents a central paradox in reputation: it is completely entertwined with the perceptions of the reader. Consider this: Toad is supposed to be converted and changed by the end of the novel, yet for most of the novel we have reveled in the consistent characterization of Toad as self-concerned, adventure addicted, and relishing escape fantasies. His reputation, I believe, far surpasses Grahame's constricting conclusion and provides the best example of reputation as oscillating wildly beyond an author's creation as we consider masculinity.

Hierarchy

Hierarchy may be one aspect of social grouping that is particularly appealing to the male mind. Alongside social scientists and psychologists study of masculinity and its links to hierarchy, as readers and students of literature we read hierarchy and can tease out connections to social history, literary history, autobiographical studies, and literary theory. As the titular leadership of England passed from Victoria to Edward, the literature began to demonstrate a plasticity that encompasses folktales, fairy tales, modernist satire, colonialist critique, and young adult themes. Examining the stories of Milne, Wilde, Potter, Grahame and Kipling reveals a remarkable uncertainty as to the efficacy of hierarchy as a model of leadership. A crucial question in this context is do we consider these authors to be writing for children? If so, then the resistance to hierarchy reflects a belief, in the British writer's mind, that some resistance is necessary. But after this initial question, how characters resist hierarchy, how hierarchy is unstable, and how hierarchy can come to be re-inscribed (despite its problematic representation in a text), the reader can see that hierarchy as an aspect of masculinity has a variety of representations but a consistent amount of resistance comes from authors as varied as Potter, Milne, and Wilde.

Three • Reputation, Hierarchy, Masculine Logic, Law and Codes

If we consider hierarchy in *Winnie the Pooh*, there is certainly a focus on Pooh and Piglet. And we could also posit that Rabbit and Owl are supposed to representative of adults, particularly Rabbit, as he provides explanations, leads expeditions and episodes, and even is called upon by Christopher Robin for leadership. The problem is that hierarchy isn't a stable feature of Milne's work because he stakes such great faith in the individualism and developing of the individual at the expense of hierarchy. But this is not the case with Milne's predecessors.

We see the use of hierarchy in Wilde, most notably in "The Star-Child." The beautiful protagonist leads other children into decadent, punitive, and self-serving behavior, all on account of his cruel beauty. He tortures other children, kills animals who are heteronormatively mated to others (doves, rabbits), and even teaches cruelty to the village children:

> His companions followed him for he was fair, and fleet of foot, and could dance and pipe, and make music. And wherever the Star-Child led them they followed, and whatever the Star-Child bade them do, that did they. And when he pierced with a sharp reed the dim eyes of the mole, they laughed, and when he cast stones at the leper they laughed also. And in all things he ruled them, and they became hard of heart even as he was [306].

Relying on the legend of the Pied Piper as well as following Keats' "beauty is truth, truth beauty," Wilde posits a hierarchy that children follow, even against the prevailing innocence of children and "natural goodness." The Star-Child eventually undergoes a transformation, but the underlying model of hierarchy is evident.

Wilde also uses hierarchy for humor and satire, especially in "The Birthday of the Infanta" and "The Happy Prince," where we see more stock use of characters of privilege as they are ridiculed next to the power of love, as Wilde expresses it. But there is a peculiar hierarchy, again linked with cruelty, in "The Fisherman and His Soul." Here, the seemingly "British" soul of the fisherman is able to control or demonstrate hierarchal power over the different societies it encounters, defeating them all. The soul certainly has a liminal position in the story, but the ghost of colonialism with the fetishizing of lands and people Wilde uses recall the adventure story, where native "pluck" triumphs over exotic incompetence.

Fearful about unmanly behavior, Kipling seems to have reveled in the process of hierarchy and ordering. The positions shift according to reputation, breaking the law, and the use of violence. The seemingly benevolent royalty of Akela is undone by the subversive Shere Khan as he helps the renegade wolves hunt cattle (forbidden by jungle law) and plots Akela's downfall with a missed hunting encounter. But Mowgli ascends into leadership with his pot of fire and promise of death. Generally, the characters know the hierarchy, and this hierarchy punishes characters at the bottom of the order (Tabaqui, monkeys).

In Kipling's jungle, imperialistic leadership replaces the native communalism of the Wolf Pack (though still headed by a male leader). Mowgli progresses upward from Baloo's training, Kaa's demonstration of slaughter, and his prodding by Bagheera to introduce fire into the Wolf Pack's gathering after Akela's failed hunt. His masculinity is firmly established in accumulative, superlative adjectival modifiers: "the best and wisest and boldest of Man-cubs" (48). Kipling contrasts this positioning with the "commonality" of the unnamed wolves. In addition, Kipling goes to great lengths, through Baloo's songs, to demonstrate that there are different roles in the hunt. In this vein, we can see how Mowgli — both outside the Wolf Pack and human village — brings a twisted sense of progress to the jungle: a more colonial form of leadership. When he leaves the Wolf Pack, Mowgli leaves the social order he first joined in much disarray.

The ways Mowgli assumes his hierarchal position are varied. He learns the languages and Law of the Jungle, assimilating Kipling's penchant for the Free Masons. And much like the Free Masons abroad during the Victorian Era, brotherhood gives way to Imperial leadership. Mowgli assumes Tabaqui's power by laughing at him when called to the wolf council, co-opting the "madness" attributed to the lowest order. When the younger wolves threaten to give Mowgli to Shere Khan, making familial and fraternal bonds unstable, Mowgli constructs a new hierarchy by subverting the group law and brings the "red flower" (fire), his symbol of control, to the communal meeting. Mowgli burns Shere Khan and calls the wolves "dogs," illustrating that nobility, heroism, and unity aren't characteristics of power and hierarchal privilege. Killing, the threat of violence, and "natural selection" make a boy a man, and, by novel's end, the hierarchal leader.

Hierarchy is also evident in the English settings of Grahame and Potter's work. Grahame's Riverbank rewards the four main characters with entrenched positions of hierarchy over the working-class stoats and weasels. Annie Gauger has defined this relationship as a squirearchy: "a collective body of squires, landed proprietors, or country gentry; the class to which squires belong, regarding especially in respect of its political or social influence" (145). While subplots demonstrate a variety of identity crises (Mole's burgeoning self, Rat's traumatic encounters with wanderlust and Pan, Toad's resistance to efforts to curb his privileged excess), the underlying power structure is understood from the beginning of the novel and is frequently revisited, firmly entrenched by the end.

Where Potter differs in the establishment of power is her use of matriarchies and single female characters asserting control over both their domestic spaces and in public spheres (*The Tale of Two Bad Mice, The Tale of Samuel Whiskers,* and *The Tale of Mrs. Tiggy-Winkle,* being a few). These stories virtually ignore patriarchal authority as they script rural power structures centered on females in domestic partnerships or acting as models for other females in roles and identity. For example, the masculine world of business and the exclusivity of male-owned and dominated businesses are critiqued in *The Tale of Ginger and Pickles*. The two male shopkeepers mis-perform—eat their sellable goods, miscalculate ledgers—and are driven out of business by mis-performance. The only other male in the story, Mr. John Dormouse, stays in bed all day while his daughter seeks to sell defective candles. Potter casts a doubtful eye on belief in hierarchal practices, particularly business ones, in her fiction as well as in her life; she argued with Harold Warne about lost opportunities for licensing deals as well as conditioned her support of the Warne publishing firm with his noninvolvement in her affairs.

When Potter establishes male-dominated centers of power, individualistic male escape plots, or episodes where females battle males over space (*The Tale of Peter Rabbit, The Tale of Benjamin Bunny,* and *The Tale of Ginger and Pickles,* to mention a few), she undoes male characters' assumptions of privilege and hierarchy. And this isn't because she is launching a critique for the sake of philosophical complaint, though surely her characterizations reveal a philosophy of female empowerment. Potter became more knowledgeable about business because she entered the business world due to her nature. Both Alexander Grinstein and Linda Lear have traced one aspect of Potter's conservatism and knowledge of business as it pertains to Free Trade Laws of 1909–1910. Free trade laws seriously undermined her franchise, and "she undertook her own campaign for fair trade, or protectionism, ... in support of the Unionist campaign for tariffs" (232). Potter's resistance to these laws mirror her resistance to hierarchy in many of her stories; common sense, inherited from her Unitarian upbringing, dominates her view of roles, choices, and responsibilities that should be accorded to females, even at the expense of previous social codes and hierarchies.

Potter isn't the only writer to critique hierarchy. While Wilde's "aestheticism" demonstrates a belief in the individual and the sensations, experiences, and emotional responses as a primary reason for belief and action (as opposed to reason or logic), he consistently undermines figures of authority in his tales for children. The Town Council in "The Happy Prince," the aristocratic Remarkable Rocket, the cruelty of the Spanish royalty in "The Birthday of the Infanta"— all of these hierarchically positioned characters are made to demonstrate the need for resistance to masculinized society and its privileges. Wilde's resistance to heteronormativity is a critique of society where expressions of manly love in more open-ended ways weren't possible. And his belief in beauty (in action, motivation, and sensations) demonstrates both a highly individualistic nature to masculinity that can also coalesce with more humanistic, civic and social-minded goals.

As I mentioned earlier, Grahame's Riverbank isn't free of hierarchy, but the resistance to hierarchy bears some resemblance to Wilde's characterizations. Toad's resistance is more akin to the Star-Child, where the existing order suits his own needs and desires at the expense of others. Rat's resistance to hierarchy is evident as he demonstrates that individualism is a pathway to realization: a path that includes transformations that include both physical and psychological sensations reminiscent of Wilde's characterizations. Rat's resistance is evident in Badger's frequent admonishing of Rat and in Rat's tolerated position in the squirearchy. Though Grahame's conservatism coalesces in the ending of the novel around this particular social structure, eruptions of resistance are evident in both Toad and Rat.

Certainly Milne's work is an effective critique of hierarchy. With the legacy of a "playboy" king and World War One as a backdrop, Milne captured not only a return to innocence but a distrust that Modernist artists demonstrate in their work. The cartoonish portrayals of Owl are reinforced by his reputation, replete with misspellings, confusions, and mis-performance as the supposed hierarchal head. As Pooh observes "if anyone knows anything about anything ... it's Owl who knows something about some-

Three • Reputation, Hierarchy, Masculine Logic, Law and Codes

thing" (48). But it isn't only Owl who reveals Milne's careful subversiveness. When characters gather for the "Expotition to the North Pole," they are united behind the authority of Christopher Robin. But his leadership is tentative and questionable: "It's — I wondered — It's only — Rabbit, I suppose *you* don't know. What does the North Pole *look* like?" (122). While several writers such as Jackie Wullschlager and Ann Thwaite have remarked on Milne's use of Christopher Robin as the voice of reason in the Hundred Acre Wood, Carol Stanger has observed that "The desire for power exists in Milne's fictional world" and that characters can be made to look "ridiculous" when they attempt to express that desire (41). This "ridiculousness" extends to characters who would blindly believe in authority. For example, Piglet repeats what Christopher Robin tells him regarding Kanga, expresses his complete faith in the North Pole adventure because Christopher Robin is coming, and consistently listens to Pooh's explanations with a naiveté that marks both his character and the unreliability of masculine leaders.

The self-reliance in the face of hierarchy is evident in a character like Pooh, but also in a character like Mowgli. The hierarchy Kipling seeks to establish is not only unstable, it allows for the rise of individualism to undo hierarchy. It may be important to remember that the hierarchal position Mowgli attains is the one he rejects, possibly foreshadowed by Mowgli's admission to Baloo following his time with the monkeys: "I shall have a tribe of my own, and lead them through the branches all day long" (35). Mowgli does become a tribe of his own, but it doesn't have any of the play of the monkeys. Mowgli's resistance to the hierarchy in the jungle is the same resistance we witness in his time spent in the human village: the same resistance exercised by Toad in his operating outside the social conventions of society.

But for all of Mowgli's resistance, to both hierarchal settings, he is not "transformed" into a happy, now knowledgeable young adult. Sadness and isolation follow him as a cost to any changes in character he has experienced. His greatest loss seems to be his loss of faith in the communal Wolf Pack. Mowgli sings at the end of the novel, "The water comes out of my eyes; yet I laugh while it falls.... My heart is heavy with things I do not understand" (98). Claudia Nelson hypothesizes that this situation, this chasm produces estrangement: "To be a real man, then, is to be strong mentally and physically, with no inner doubts (soul searching undermines power) ... and the strongest personalities among humans and animals alike are loners and outcasts" (544). Except that Mowgli is more "real" by the end of the story, and this may be precisely the dilemma Kipling concludes: real men are brought into power struggles and have to "play the game," sometimes to their own detriment, but certainly with scars, physical and psychological, as reminders of the cost of this self-reliance and self-actualization. In this manner, similarities abound between Potter's characters (Peter Rabbit, Jemima Puddle-duck, Tom Kitten, Jeremy Fisher), Wilde's characters (the Fisherman, the Swallow, the Dwarf), and Grahame's characters (Mole, Rat, and Toad).

As we look at hierarchy as it is represented and critiqued by the various writers we examine in this study, we may remember that social context underlies how hierarchy becomes imagined in the various authors' minds. The ascension of Edward to the throne becomes a model for a character like Toad: both playboys in their own settings, both ill-suited for their hierarchal positions. The hierarchy that Kipling critiques is a hierarchy of chaos (Wolf Pack and influence of Shere Khan) vs. a society of order (Law of the Jungle). But Kipling's imagination and plotting can't make hierarchy congeal in his primeval jungle where man (if Mowgli is to be recognized as a man) can't reconcile the process of experience it takes to become a man with the native communalism that is so evidently fragile to the influences of evil. In fact, children's authors use critiques of hierarchy to interest both child listeners and readers as well as examine the societies they live in: colonially administered India or morally obsessed late Victorian London. These various landscapes (psychological and geographical) provide scholars with a spectrum of how masculinity is by no means a uniform or consolidated identity in late Victorian and early twenty-first-century Britain. We notice differences between Grahame and Potter who, though using similar landscapes, provide a re-assessment of power as it is dispersed, used, and re-inscribed, particularly when we assess rural identity, the supposed "heart" of England. Potter's critique of masculinity continues in this vein of hierarchal construction around matriarchies, while Grahame's initial exploration of a Riverbank where hierarchy, as an over-arching masculine representation of control, gives way to liberating performances by Mole and Rat. These liberating performances become models for A. A. Milne in *Winnie the Pooh*, but none of these would be possible without the influence of Wilde. Milne and Graham won't go as far as Wilde does in positioning subversive representations of manly love, and neither will they

Three • Reputation, Hierarchy, Masculine Logic, Law and Codes

embrace beauty as a value that supersedes hierarchal control as Wilde does. Wilde's use of individualized masculinity, in the face of hierarchal pressures and characters, demonstrates that beauty, especially as it concerns a character's motivation, can be more civic minded, less imperialistic, and less escapist than Kipling, Grahame, and Milne. And this may be a lesson to be drawn from the overall study of hierarchy in this chapter: a male character may want to re-examine escape as a way to handle hierarchy and re-examine the governing power structures in the landscape presented, whether one is a rabbit looking for a lost jacket, a feral child feeling abandoned by an adoptive tribe or family, or if one is a poet co-opted into a squirearchy.

Law, Logic, Rules, Masculine Reasoning

In many ways, the boy character has always been on his own, at least in how we are to recognize the characters of bildungsromans and epics. The Western idea of masculinity as a force that individually makes it way to reveal heroism and nobility appears in English literature, especially as inherited from the adventure story tradition, in plots where the individual boy makes his way through a series of tests that mold character, reinforce values deemed manly by society, and, occasionally, provide characters that challenge these values and the idea of manliness. In the first chapter, I posited that the adventure story provided a model of masculinity where a young man, in exotic settings, found himself pitted against challenges that reinforced a sense of masculinity that was stoic, physical, resourceful, and honorable. This "logic" of how to be manly is visible in Kipling's "Law of the Jungle," but it's masculine logic or reasoning is also visible in Wilde, Grahame, Potter, and Milne's work, despite the fact that the latter authors don't name it as formally as Kipling does. How each of these authors constructs the logic at work in their stories — rules, laws, power structures — reveals, yet again, a variety of ways to express masculinity.

Kipling uses the "Law of the Jungle," and its ties to lore, to reinforce a sense of epic, yet sad, masculinity. Inherited tradition becomes s source of power for masculine codes and language, quite simply, gives power in the story. Those who are allowed or who are sanctioned to speak have not only agency but function as a part of the jungle aristocracy. This is similar to Grahame's use of Badger and Rat as Badger relates the history of the underground dwellers to Mole and resurrects Toad's father through memory of their conversations, and Rat serves as Mole's guide through Mole's newly discovered country (both literally and metaphorically). Baloo, Bagheera, Badger, and Rat all act as the sanctioned voice, the loci of masculine logic, in their respective tales, who carry the lore and reinforces the inherited ideas of what it means to be a man, who has power, and how power is to be used.[1]

If we think of Butler and Foucault's work on gender where metaphors of writing and the body are highlighted as the work society does to keep power structures in tact and, in this case, support masculinity that operates within a recognizable and traceable power structure, we may see how *The Jungle Book* requires frequent "re-signings" to enforce these power structures and their ties to masculinity. Masculine characters perform as epic tellers through speech (Baloo, Bagheera) and as punishers sanctioned by the Law of the Jungle (Kaa); they suppress desire due with an appeal to the logic of power.

But the initial stable characterization of the law, tied as it is to Mowgli's more "childlike" years, gives way to the more "young adult" nature of Mowgli and of the plotting in the story where law becomes fluid and able to be manipulated by individuals. Subversions to the law reinforce personal aims and desires (a revenge plot in Mowgli's case), and, as the novel progresses, consistently undermine the notion of a stability in this law. In other words, characters subversive to the law through aesthetic or gender-blurring behaviors, trickster figures, for example (monkeys, Tabaqui) are marginalized and punished. It may be noted that the purposeless and genderless monkeys "fight, play, cry, explore, rush, and pretend to be men" (52). While Disney will write in the King Louie character with swing music insinuating deviance with the monkeys, Kipling frames the monkeys, front and center, as the challengers to masculine law: "They have no Law, no Hunting Call, and no leaders" (53). Nyman sees the "otherness" of the monkeys in a postcolonial view: "Whereas trustworthy wolves ... rational brown bears ... obey naturalized hierarchies and social contracts ... degenerate monkeys seek hedonistic pleasure and self-gratification in denying the authority of colonial rule" (208). The "dewanee" or madness of Tabaqui is theorized by Jopi Nyman as having a "maddening effect [that] is emphasized in the text and shown as belonging to the sphere of nature, not of culture, its is part of the world of myth rather than reason" (210). What Nyman reinforces is the fluidity of this law, even though its intention is to align masculinity, normal, hierarchy, and law as correct. By using these "othered" characters, Kipling philosophizes, in some measure, about foreign settings where native customs, rules, and social codes were inadequate, at least in Kipling's mind.

In Kipling's novel, the logic of power suggests that communalism of the wolves is suspect. The law functions as an antidote to the excesses of freedom, even democracy. When Bagheera warns the wolves about their future, suggesting that the "madness" of overeating has damaged the wolves, he functions as the colonial voice disgusted with the urges of the mob. Again, we see how Kipling uses voice and position to highlight the "correct" use of masculine power: "Ye fought for freedom, and it is yours. Eat it, O Wolves" (95). With Shere Khan removed and Mowgli unwilling to take on pack leadership, the only social control left is to invoke the law. The logic of punitive conclusivity to curb excess is an essential part of Grahame's plotting as well as Potter's whole oeuvre. Grahame's unruly stoats and weasels, like the Wolf Pack, need leadership and Grahame, like Kipling, doesn't trust communalism. This same logic pervades Potter's stories where story after story uses this masculine idea of excess and development, punishment, reintegration with the system of order (matriarchal and female centered, in Potter's case). The sex of the author changed, but not the method of logic and reasoning to re-inscribe the social codes needed to keep order.

The power of social codes is impressive, particularly in *The Jungle Book*. Kipling shows that the Law of the Jungle is portable (like colonialism) when Mowgli revisits the village. He demonstrates the control of a colonial administrator: "Luckily, the Law of the Jungle had taught him to keep his temper, for in the Jungle life and food depend on keeping your temper ... only the knowledge that is was unsportsmanlike to kill little naked cubs kept him from picking them up and breaking them in two" (75). This curious mixture of English "sportsmanship" an food provision, as tied to the Law of the Jungle, create a Mowgli ready to serve in the outposts of empire. Kipling mixes his language of Englishness and primitivism in other places in the novel as well. We see an essential nod to his reading audience when Mowgli is taught by Father Wolf

> the meaning of things in the Jungle, till every rustle in the grass ... every note of the owls above his head ... and every splash of every little fish

jumping in a pool meant just as much to him as the work of his office means to a business man [15].

Father Wolf is hardly a businessman, but the English audience of the novel is being treated to a transposed logic where emerging boys become men through emulation of older male figures: in the jungle or in the city.

The noticeable absence of male figures as role models occurs in both Potter and Wilde's stories. Both writers set out male characters to experience the harshness of the world without the benefit of father figures knowledgeable in the "language" of masculinity and its connections to a larger, masculinized world of order. This absence reveals both writers' critique of masculinity as well as the vacuum, autobiographically, both writers experienced with their own father's inaccessibility. We can contrast this with Milne's world where older male mentor figures are nonexistent, but reveal a landscape more free of patriarchal influence to encourage play, satire, and experience: less of a critique of Victorian patriarchy, which we find in Potter and Wilde.

Kipling's use of language, as it is tied to law, reveals fundamental masculinized logic, which is more universal than mere English notions of maleness. In fact, the knowledge of languages would be of paramount importance for an English administrator in the colonies, and we could be witness to Kipling's subtle critique of colonial administration. Kipling's knowledge of Hindi and his experiences as a journalist gave him access and insight to colonial administration and the problems with administrators who had no knowledge of communities, language and history. It would be later that Kipling's views of colonial administration and the lapsidasical British public would spill over into poems like "The Islanders" and "Tommy." But in dying years of the nineteenth century, Kipling was still affected by his early colonial experiences and the "special calls [that] promise Masonic brotherhood with every species" (Nelson, "Sex and the Single Boy" 544). In the absence of a guiding religious philosophy, Kipling seems to have taken the masculinist schemes of brotherhood, hierarchy, and violence as venues towards an intersection of identity he found favorable. Language was a special vehicle towards reinforcing hierarchy and power, whatever tongue it may occur in. For example, Shere Khan is called "lungri"—the lame one—by his mother. And another female, Raksha, is the one to recall this for Mowgli. Tabaqui means "madness," and most importantly, disfigured and other characters, named in native tongue, become victims in the process by which masculine order is finally established. Language intersects with logic to produce the masculinized plotting and order Kipling so desires. For here, he can work out his views of how brotherhood should work: who can work together, who can be invited to participate, and who can be excluded.

In fact, Stephen Benson contends that the jungle is a "'central discursive space' where ... inscription and re-inscription takes place" (40). We see this in all of the pronouncements made (usually adults addressing Mowgli). The intersection of language, logic, and social codes reveal what Andrew Lycett claims as the social and legal structures Kipling always showed an interest in: "As a student of sociology he thought deeply about what holds a community together. In his research into the dynamics of society, he became convinced of the need for shared ideals and sense of power" (44). And despite the multicultural aspects of Kipling's work, this sense of power proceeds from an all-male lineage and is still unstable when we consider the perversions to law and English "sportsmanship." The logic Kipling builds for the expression of masculinities is aristocratic, centered on individuals and their motivations, and is inconsistent, not unlike what we find in Grahame's Riverbank where a development novel turns into a re-inscription of "shared ideals and sense of power."

Social codes and rules require inscription, and Potter, Grahame, and Kipling use punishment rendered on the body as their tools. Kipling is perhaps the most demonstrative, though Old Benjamin Bunny in Potter's work punishes both Benjamin and Peter with a whipping. Baloo's punishment is so severe that Bagheera labels the spanking as "bruises" (33). While Baloo is only reinforcing a code for survival, Laura Stevenson connects the punishment with Kipling's reputation as a writer:

> The beatings Mowgli undergoes in "Kaa's Hunting" are the recognizable product of the Kipling that C. S. Lewis called the "poet of work"— the writer who routinely presents the attainment of maturity from a disciplinary adult male point of view, likening it to breaking horses or reforming "raw cubs" [375].

To be broken means, in this case, to take an ungendered child and replace him with behaviors and reasoning that the group norms as "right," "productive," and truly "male." This is the same "breaking" of spirit that Potter employs in her tales: from Peter Rabbit to Jemima Puddle-duck to Mr. Jeremy Fisher.

Potter's re-inscriptions and "breaking" include, as in Kipling, psychological scarring. We have Peter Rabbit, in *The Tale of Benjamin Bunny*, illustrated with a red blanket, almost buried in a hole, clearly traumatized at the beginning of the story. Jemima Puddle-duck, at the end of her story, is described as a "bad sitter" and having "nerve" problems (172). Squirrel Nutkin loses his tail, a visual reminder to the other squirrels that being "excessively impertinent" and having "no respect" has physical costs. To describe Potter as a children's "writer of work" would be apt, not just because of these types of disciplinary scenes but also because her stories praise work and punish those who don't work. Her stories, much like Kipling's, continue to use a "central discursive space" where masculine codes of character building are repressive and retrogressive, inherited from an ethos of character building that includes punishment.

The more radical intersections of masculine logic and social codes occur in Oscar Wilde's stories. Tales like "The Happy Prince," "The Selfish Giant," "The Nightingale and the Rose," and "The Birthday of the Infanta" reveal Victorian codes of masculinity as targets for social critique. Whether to propose a masculinity that is supportive of spirituality over personal gain, romantic love over muscular manliness, the sacrificial main characters of many of Wilde's stories engage in resistance to social norms, which cost them their lives. Their stories aren't framed in control but in rebellion. Paradoxes arise from the critique of masculinity as normed in late Victorian England, and to be a "true" man in Wilde's stories means a character must sacrifice for beauty, for emotional effusion, for ideals centered on spiritual and romantic love rather than establish power centers, exert power for personal gain at the expense of others, or engage in solitary escape stories, which encourage misanthropy or social disengagement.

Victorian codes of masculinity and heteronormative schemes of manly logic are subverted through Wilde's creation of characters that either are ridiculous, created for specific satire, or characters that undergo a plainly visible transformation that doesn't include a "progress" to material success and the group's admiration, but undergoes a transformative experience where recognition of connections to groups, and success as measured by a character's sacrifice and devotion to others is a hallmark. For example, the Remarkable Rocket's egotism and ingrained sense of class are paraded in the story for comic effect and to demonstrate the essential lack of connection to groups for this character. In "The Devoted Friend," Water-Rat

Three • Reputation, Hierarchy, Masculine Logic, Law and Codes

represents a bachelor who is suspicious of married life. While seemingly a refutation of heteronormative unions, this character's hubris and egotism demonstrate that the sacrifice Hans made in the story isn't something the water rat is capable of. Wilde clearly proposes that devotion is no devotion, which is self-centered, but rather a masculine performance of sacrifice. In many ways, what Wilde demonstrates is that masculine logic should find Christ as a representative of what manliness should look like. That Wilde devotes so many tales for children with a sacrificial male (female character when we consider the nightingale) as the protagonist is remarkable. Ridiculing manliness, even such manliness that may represent Wilde himself (Water-Rat), becomes a rescripting of masculine logic where Darwinian individualism, class hubris, and the belief in English exceptionalism are questioned.

We see no such sacrifices in Grahame's novel. The class system is firmly in place, and the values of Darwinian consolidation of power are essentialized in the novel. While the Edwardian countryside has a legal system, evident in the trial of Toad with a severe sentence and a prison subplot, the logic of masculinity or manliness is more evident in the retaking of Toad Hall. Because the lower class stoats and weasels—seemingly an all-male grouping—ascend class and mock Toad and his pretensions, they must be "taken in hand." Though Toad escapes jail, he is never sent back in the novel. And the stoats and weasels are not only defeated but live in awe of the Riverbank Four? The "law" in Grahame's novel depends on which lens you employ. If Grahame wants us to identify with Toad and his plight (which he certainly wanted his son to identify with), then the rules and logic are more centered on the results: as long as class position and privilege remain in tact, transformations may do what they will.

Grahame's use of logic and law does allow for disruptions in heteronormative masculine performances though. The partnership of Mole and Rat are positioned with the inclusion of Pan in the novel. In this countryside setting, a Greek logic to nature worship with allusions to aesthetic masculinity are demonstrated. When we position Mole and Rat's companionship next to Otter's lost child, who is constantly adventuring, we may see that Grahame's representation of masculinity isn't entirely heteronormative. The multiplicity of masculinities is evident by the married Otter, old bachelor Badger, bon vivant Toad, and companions Mole and Rat. The Arcadian setting is more than a deeply sentimentalized and mysterious ode to nature; the setting allows for laws and logic that resist late Victorian patriarchy and demonstrate changing attitudes towards what being male could be.

Arcadian settings would seem to be the type of setting most suited to an absence of law and Milne's *Winnie the Pooh* is no exception. The fluidity of rules and logic may be nonsensical, but like all well-constructed nonsense, it's forms reveal central themes Milne found in boyishness: play, adventure, discovery, and companionship. We may even trace the rebellion of the toys in Milne's forest to heteronormative logic to Wilde's works directly. In "The Selfish Giant," the main character has a sign in his front yard declaring "Trespassers Will Be Prosecuted," revealing Wilde's sly rebellion to both capitalist land ownership and a mockery of both adult authority and Victorian codes of punishment. In Milne's story, law and land ownership give way to Milne's gentle critique of childhood innocence and purity in a more modernist fashion:

> Next to his [Piglet's] house was a piece of broken board which had: "TRESPASSERS W" on it. When Christopher Robin asked the Piglet what it meant, he said it was his grandfather's name, and had been in his family for a long time. Christopher Robin said you *couldn't* [Milne's italics] be called Trespassers W, and Piglet said yes, you could, because his grandfather was, and it was short for Trespassers Will, which was short for Trespassers William [34].

Milne's play with circular logic and run-on sentences mimic the thoughts of a child, especially when they are lying. But the logic Piglet improvises with the old family home as well as his grandfather's name, and mocks the "family home" and the adoption of civilized responses that can prove false so much of the time.

Milne's codes and logic of masculinity include satire and nonsense and logic centered around play, whether that play be linguistic or in terms of rationality. This play is subversive to previous notions of masculinity (adventure story, school-boy hero, moral/bildungsroman plot) and, again, reveals a shaky hierarchy among language users and actors in *Winnie the Pooh*. Linguistically, Milne mocks the polite, adult conversational routines. For example, the literalist Eeyore responds to Pooh's question concerning how he is doing, "Not very how ... I don't seem to have felt at all how for a long time" (45). Subversively, Milne destabilizes order in both plotting and in his use of language, giving masculinity a representation that more closely approaches a critique of society rather than a support for the prevailing social codes. When the group readies for the "Expotition to the North Pole," Piglet philosophizes "blowing happily at a dandelion, and wondering whether it would be this year, next year, sometime or never" (114). While we may read this scene as nonsensical, it is important to consider another frame: Piglet's "being" masculine is different from the adventuring plot, which dominates this chapter of the novel, espousing a masculinity not tied to the adventure story tradition or necessitating action.

This is how Milne's novel espouses a different logic to the masculinity being represented. Another example of a disruption in a heteronormative masculine logic would be Milne's use of egotism. When Pooh longs for honey and asks Christopher Robin for a balloon, Christopher Robin responds, "But you don't get honey with balloons!" (12). "You" refers to society or civilized norms expressed in rationality and common sense, considered masculine in John Stephens' schemata discussed in the introduction to this book. Pooh's response effectively subverts the norm: "*I* [Milne's italics] do" (12). Pooh's response is a counterpoint to accepted logic and demonstrates an egotism that marks him as a liminal character, certainly outside the "you" collective pronoun Christopher Robin employs. Milne has famously claimed childhood had an egotism that was "ruthless" (*Autobiography*, 238), and Milne makes use of this egotism in his satire of both childhood and group ethos in Pooh's egotism. While the satirical spirit of Edwardian writers like Evelyn Waugh and E. M. Forster are more evidenced in characters like Eeyore, Pooh's egotism critiques accepted codes of rationality in conversation and revives the use of nonsense as an antidote to adult notions of accepted behavior.

This isn't to say that traditional ways of the performing male aren't evident. The independent, active, strong, analytical performances of Pooh are, again, consistent with the schemata John Stephens proposes in "Gender, Genre and Children's Literature" (18–19). The egotism of Pooh never ascends to synthesizing information and reflecting on relationships that abound in the novel. Milne recreates, in some measure, the same system of manliness that rewarded Toad for his egotism and bachelorhood, with many of the same characteristics and performances of masculinity: boasts, songs, and independent actions away from the group. The privileged bachelor logic that is expressed by Toad, critiqued by Badger in Grahame's *The Wind in the Willows* and underlies the punishment and critique of Jeremy

Fisher in Potter's *The Tale of Mr. Jeremy Fisher* is reissued in the masculinized plotting in Milne's tale, particularly as it is expressed in speech acts.

Another aspect of traditional masculinity is the logic of competition scripted into the stories. While competition is evident in human behavior on many levels, its use as an organizing device for privilege and ordering is a representation of masculinity we see in late Victorian and early twentieth-century British literature. Competition is satirized by Wilde in "The Remarkable Rocket," exposing the ridiculousness of male vanity. Wilde does this in "The Selfish Giant" and "The Star-Child" as well. The title characters in all three stories perform in flat, folktale-like ways that enable Wilde to parody both adults and manliness. But a more serious investment in competition as a form of masculine logic is evident in Kipling's *The Jungle Book*. Here, competition drives Mowgli's battle for control of the Wolf Pack. And, as mentioned previously, breaking rules, violence and rise in hierarchy attends the competition between Mowgli and Shere Khan. Strangely, the result of Mowgli's competition with Shere Khan is that he becomes disillusioned with the Wolf Pack and democracy, refusing leadership of the group, and strides into exile and independence by the end of the story. The state of independence achieved at the end of the novel makes competition seem damaging to a character's quest for identity. Competition is also evident in Potter's stories, but the competition that attends such tales as *The Tale of Samuel Whiskers*, *The Fierce Bad Bunny*, or *The Tale of Timmy Tiptoes*, for example, involve more prey-predator plots, not as intricately investigative of psychological motivations as of that seen in Kipling. Of course, anxiety over masculine and national identity marked Kipling's life as well as his fiction, while Potter's tales are not apology tales for Edwardian masculinity, but a critique not often that subtle.

We see competition in Grahame and Milne as well, but both aren't as framed with violence as Potter and Kipling. Toad's competitiveness with Badger is a frequent refrain in Grahame's novel, Pooh refuses to collaborate on a gift for Eeyore, and Piglet rushes to give Eeyore his gift "before Pooh did: for he thought he would like to be the first one to give a present, just as if he had thought of it without being told by anybody" (83). Male characters in Grahame and Milne's novel frequently analyze situations, but don't often synthesize information. In this vein, their egotism and competition conforms to expectations of gender in their readership, and also demonstrate the differing zeitgeists of their respective ages. Gone may be the violent adventures of the high seas, the English boy abroad, and more nuanced depictions of masculinity may be evident in the texts, but competition and individualistic plotting demonstrate a logic to gender that still relies on masculine privilege.

Heteronormativity in Milne's Hundred Acre Forest mirrors two aspects of Grahame's depictions of established male relations as well, i.e., the noticeable absence or minimalization of women and the resistance to male hierarchy. The code of masculinity that is enforced in both tales also reveals that females are to be taunted and taken advantage of, as in the bargewoman and the theft of Roo from Kanga. And the protagonists, younger male characters, are active and supersede their pretentious and outdated older male characters (Badger, Owl, Rabbit). Both characterizations demonstrate a heteronormativity as expressed in Edwardian tales.

Heteronormativity, like gender, is a fluid term and demonstrates what one may age may define as normal. But even in this slippery categorization, only one particular author's mind and philosophy can remotely be examined. Heteronormativity as a term or process of logic in espousing, inscribing, and contesting manliness can reveal what laws, social codes; what logic, how language is used; and what perversions to logic and law abound. Kipling's Law of the Jungle, initially stated, inscribed, and witnessed in the early chapters sought to provide a framework for social harmony in the jungle life. But with all of the disruptions (Shere Khan, Mowgli's divided mind, Kipling's prejudiced English imagination), the law doesn't hold and becomes a system to be used by one to further one's own goals. The power of social codes is made more dire in Kipling because of the violence and death evident in the text, but social codes and logic as tied to masculine representations linger in Wilde, Grahame, and Milne's work as well.

The Christ figure so prevalent in Wilde's work becomes a message as to the logic a male character should employ in dealing with love, social injustices, and transformation. The "discursive space" of the body is the same canvas for both Kipling and Wilde, but Wilde's subversion of accepted materialistic, individualistic, and class-biased notions of masculinity is evident. The satirical and humorous characterizations of those male characters invested in their own egotism is contrasted with self-sacrificing characters in Wilde's stories. No such sacrifice is evident in Grahame's stories. And despite his softened characterizations of Edwardian bachelors, a firm power structure is in place, and is eventually restored by the end of the novel.

In addition to Wilde's subversive scripting of an alternative logic to manliness, we may read Milne's verbal play as revealing a rejection of Victorian moralities. Milne's characters mock civilized, adult conversation with their nonsensical speech, the companionship plotting of Pooh and Piglet (resembling the companionship plotting of Mole and Rat), and the use of egotism to challenge expectations of the public; these are all evident in *Winnie the Pooh*.

Finally, Potter's critique of masculine logic and law is ubiquitous. While she writes books where opposite-sex couples, sometimes with children, are seen as the epitome of what a child/listener could hope for, she also doesn't make the frame heteronormative entirely. The females are as active as the males, frequently are as violent, and though assuming domestic duties considered feminine in the early twentieth century, Potter's establishment of a domestic logic that takes precedent over privileged boyhood logic reflects changing notions of gender in the age.

Conclusion

> Men have come to see power as a capacity to impose control on others and on our own unruly emotions. It means controlling material resources around us— Michael Kaufman, "Men, Feminism, and Men's Contradictory Experiences of Power."

In the stories I've examined, reputation and hierarchy are inextricable and continue to sort or categorize. Reputations for higher-level characters include privileges of leadership, killing, economic security, and respect. Kipling's jungle uses reputation and hierarchy to sort out a Darwinian struggle for both survival and the raising of a boy into a man. The methods of hierarchizing include speeches, modeling, violence, and punishment. In many ways, Potter doesn't differ from Kipling in this use of sorting or categorizing characters. She uses violence, punishment, and gender-bending characters to sort out new hierarchies, usually situating a mother or leading female character at the top of the order. In many of the tales Potter wrote, she undoes traditional reputations or masculine representation of men as businessmen and providers. But both writers, Kipling and Potter, seem inextricably bound by their desire to maintain order where the sacrifice of others is necessary.

Wilde's use of hierarchy positions characters who must sacrifice themselves, to become leading men. And included in his Christ-like characters is a female character, the Nightingale. That Wilde was writing such androgynous manliness into his characters at the same time Henty and Stevenson were publishing tales where masculinity would be more muscular and less Christian is a poignant illustration of Wilde's critique of Victorian ideals of masculinity. In his more humorous stories, Wilde mocks hierarchy and reputation, viciously so in "The Remarkable Rocket." Framed next to the satire of the rocket's aristocratic beginnings and pretensions is a female duck character, reminiscent of the "New Woman" character demonstrating that reputation and hierarchy (Remarkable Rocket) are preposterous markers of identity next to social connections and activity (Duck).

While academics would be loath to use such a word, love becomes part of the formula in the logic of masculinity. Wilde has several stories where romantic love, brotherly love, and spiritual love dominate the frame of the story. Love becomes the reputed raison d'etre, proposing an alternative code to masculinity and identity, which rewards accumulation and power strategizing. Adventuring takes a backseat to helping out the outcasts in "The Happy Prince"; love initiates the sacrifice, causing the death of the Nightingale in "The Rose and the Nightingale"; and the return of the resurrected Christ figure in "The Selfish Giant" transforms the masculinity of the Giant as he dies.

In terms of law, logic, and rules, all the authors examined maintain strict codes of conduct that are consistently undone. Employing "inscriptions" on the body (Foucault, Butler), Kipling and Potter create powerful social codes, which serve as antidotes to freedom and democracy (Kipling) and as antidotes to unlicensed masculine privilege (Potter). Both writers inscribe powerfully through violence, threats, and death. Stephen Benson described Kipling's jungle as a "discursive space" where the intersection of language, logic, and social codes create a virtual space for becoming a man. Potter's countryside could easily be seen in the same light: her Edwardian countryside is daubed in beautiful watercolors but full of "natural" inscriptions for the unregulated character. While Kipling works with order and brotherhood, Potter imbues her landscapes with order that has to be reestablished, often dealing in the punishment system thought to be "natural" for boys.

Wilde's stories provide an interesting way to look at Grahame and Milne's use of hierarchy and reputation. Grahame's squirearchy does effectively close the opened loop begun by Mole's "escape" from spring cleaning, but reputations prove to be unstable, even Badger's. Traditionally seen by critics as a patriarchal character, Badger, as described by Grahame, has more of a reputation for such, and less violence is actually attributed to his character. The need for control, to curb and contain reputations, is evident in *The Wind in the Willows* (much like we see in Kipling's work). With Toad and Mowgli, subversive masculinity is too much and must be either removed (monkeys) or "taken in hand" (Toad).

Milne's novel certainly has subversive expressions of masculinity, but they are framed in the sentimental, Arcadian forest with an all-male cast (with the exception of Kanga). The absence of laws in Milne provide a challenge to masculinity based on common sense, rationality, and reserved emotions. Through nonsense, word play, and egotism, Milne challenges pervading notions of what it meant to be manly and effectively satirizes adult codes of conversation and manners. While Pooh resembles Toad in his unchallenged bachelor privilege, both Grahame and Milne owe much to Wilde in how their boy characters begin to see companionship and collaboration as expressions and representations of manhood and identity.

Four

Collaboration, Compromise, Group Performances

Collaborations (and compromises and group performances) seem appropriate not only as a lens into viewing masculinity as it grapples with identity, but in terms of the various ways masculinity defines itself against prevailing norms, particularly the changing landscape of domesticity. Characters in this study display anxiety over identity and how to work in groups. These groupings can be represented in scenes of collaboration and compromise. Whether an animal character is hunting, providing for his/her family, or engaged in adventure together, masculine performances in group or partner settings provide a different vision of how traditional, subversive, and inconsistent masculinity is represented by the authors in this study.

This chapter will reveal that hunting, whether in earnest (*The Jungle Book*) or in play (*Winnie the Pooh*), allows for an author to promote visions of masculinity that can be conflicting as well as consistent. Endemic to children's literature is the scripting of characters in search of an audience, even if the audience is only one other character. This type of characterization is a collaboration where what it means to be a man changes as the character must engage in performance that differs from isolated adventure or play.[1] But both hunting and the need for an audience reveal a different sense of collaboration and reveal different performances of masculinity.

In terms of hunting, "the hunt" can act as a central metaphor for masculinity. With hunting scenes and overall structure devoted to hunting, an author like Kipling can link survival to codes of masculinity (as he did in *Stalky and Co.* as well). Hunting, in Potter, Kipling, and Milne situates characters in schemes where they must collaborate, compromise, and reconfigure hierarchies. Hunting can be collaborative and allegorical, can suppress decadence and behaviors considered suspect. But if we trace hunting from Kipling through Potter to Milne, we can see how masculinity changes. Critique of violence and overly masculinist performances of hunting result in humorous and subversive accounts of manliness.

As characters seek to understand themselves (an object lesson in much of children's literature) through their interactions with other characters, they also reveal a need for audience. For Wilde, Grahame and Milne, their familiarization with the theater (writing and acting) results in characterizations of males who provide "spectacle" and "camp" sensibilities. While most of the performativity of this variation of masculinity is humorous, the masculine need for audience also makes hierarchy and hegemony cohere (Mowgli as audience for Kaa's slaughter of the monkeys), reorganizes the regulation of masculine desire into a Christian framework of selflessness (Wilde), and provides a critique of aristocratic, privileged masculinity (Toad and Remarkable Rocket). A more nuanced examination of the masculine need for audience can be found in Potter's stories. Here, punishment follows the overly spectacular and attention-seeking characters (Squirrel Nutkin). The audience that females can provide for masculine performance is poorly formed or partial in Kipling and Grahame, whose females live through reputation (and are not allowed to act: Raksha in *The Jungle Book*) or perform as helpers, dupes, or caricatured "others" (*The Wind in the Willows*).

We also witness, in these stories, where collaborative masculinity reveals problematic aspects on identity formation. Beatrix Potter punishes "buddy" plots and uses violence to regulate unchecked masculine desire. In Grahame's work, the temptation of other males (Sea Rat) to upset both balance and a self-regulated life figures prominently in the re-inscription of Rat's identity but also illustrates Mole's collaboration towards the same-sex union that he and Rat enjoy. The critique of group mentalities is evident in Milne, though suppressed by his humorous characterization (in Rabbit's plan to steal Roo and the leadership of Rabbit and Christopher Robin in the "Expotition" chapter). And certainly both Kipling and Grahame had no trust for mob rule or group mentalities as witnessed in their critiques of the wolves (Kipling) and stoats and weasels (Grahame).

We do witness traditional unions (male/female) in Kipling's *The Jungle Book* (seemingly the exception rather than the rule), in Grahame's *The Wind in the Willows* (Otter and Mrs. Otter), and in Potter's tales, most notably *The Roly-Poly Pudding* and *The Tale of Two Bad Mice*. In these representations of masculinity there is still wide variance. Kipling's Raksha

Four • Collaboration, Compromise, Group Performances

is a critique of the New Woman and a rejection of masculine identity, as influenced by softening "feminization" at home. Father Wolf, like Otter, is a vigorous model of fatherhood, teaching masculinity in the natural world, but also insufficient to the Spartan training Mowgli needs to survive as a colonial administrator. And Potter's depictions of heteronormative couplings remakes the balance of power between husband and wife, recalling the moral centeredness of women in these unions, while also investing these unions with tolerance for subversive aspects of performativity (anger, violence, play) from female characters. Potter distrusts decadent masculinity in much the same way Kipling does, but her intertwining of play with coupling is unique among these authors: exhibited and acted out in the real time of the stories and not just a legend (Raksha, *The Jungle Book*).

The most transgressive unions would be the same-sex unions witnessed in Wilde, Grahame and Milne. Capitalistic and accumulative masculinity is re-scripted in favor of sacrificial and transformative characterizations in Wilde's tales. In fact, leading Victorian critics like Herbert Sussman, Eli Adams and John Tosh have all recognized and discussed the "brotherhood" motif in Victorian literature and society. In these "brotherhoods," the "homosocial continuum" proposed by Sedgwick can be historically located from the Knights of the Round Table to the Pre-Raphaelite Brotherhood. The historical inheritance of the Pre-Raphaelite brotherhood includes not only aesthetic tenets but ideas surrounding modes of production; it is a critique of capitalism in its productive heart. We may also see this masculinity as a forerunner to the socialist masculinity that critics like Karen Hunt see as problematic and transgressive to society's norms ("'Strong Minds, Great Hearts, True Faith and Ready Hands'? Exploring Socialist Masculinities before the First World War"). But this extended notion of "brotherly masculinity" still minimizes the feminine.

While Grahame scripts the same transformative plotting for Mole and Rat (in both individualistic and homosocial development) in his novel, the avoidance of feminine influence and the illustration of the resistance to marriage is more visible in Grahame and Milne's work than we see in Wilde's work. Same-sex unions have to be carefully written, as both Grahame and Milne illustrate; using animals and toys to stand in for boys/males is but one way. Framing same-sex unions next to bonding scenes/plots and outrageous humor is another way to "manage" the homosocial and homoerotic depictions that Grahame and Milne use.

Finally, collaborative masculinity includes the ways that groups function to perpetuate hierarchy and keep social and political control. In both Kipling and Grahame, we witness group censure as a liberating agent to permit violence against "othered" groups. Even characters within the hegemonic group must be "taken in hand" sometimes, like Toad and Tigger. What emerges when groups attempt to impose order and halt individualistic development of male characters is how hypocritical, paradoxical, and ironic these attempts are. The logic of "loose common" language as natural and to be employed to halt Rat's poetic and aesthetic sentiments can be paired next to the highly organized and class-mannered attempt to rein in Toad after his motoring accident. The "Law of the Jungle" is hardly noble in the killing of the monkeys or the revenge killing by Mowgli of Shere Khan. What we find is that group norming needs an "other," and most often this "other" includes elements the British public would consider feminizing influences: play, emotional effusion, non-utilitarian expressions and behavior, and most damning, a disregard or challenge for/to hierarchy.

Hunting for Nobility and Nonsensical Critiques

Kipling scripts hunting as epic, glorious, and a collaborative activity in *The Jungle Book*. Hunting begins the novel with the "Night Song in the Jungle," a song which celebrates "the hour of pride and power,/ Talon and tush and claw./ Oh, hear the call!— Good hunting all/ That keep the Jungle Law" (3). While the law is invoked a number of times in the novel, particularly as it relates to hunting, group hunting is only as glorious as suffering is individual. The same song warns that "the bullock can toss you, or the heavy-browned Sambhur can gore" (3). The threat of death makes hunting a sport for real men, a sport which must be played fairly while retaining the wounding, scaring, and death that sanctions maleness in Kipling's universe. This epic quality of hunting requires group involvement to make it heteronormative (as opposed to the monkey's effeminacy), revealing what the often rebellious and individualistic Kipling found more appropriate for a child audience.

And, of course, in Kipling's conception of collaboration, males swirl and congregate around other males in patriarchal dissemination of power and reciprocity. John Kucich recalls Noel Annan's take on Kipling as "the

Four • Collaboration, Compromise, Group Performances

sole analogue in England to those continental sociologists—Durkheim, Weber, and Pareto—who revolutionized the study of society at the beginning of the century" (Annan qtd. in Kucich, 323–324). Annan claimed Kipling saw group relations superseding class, race, and national interests. This sociological interest of Kipling's is easily reflected in Mowgli's early life in the Wolf Pack where he is absorbed into a group of animals that hunts together (much like Kipling was absorbed into the life of colonial India). While there is hierarchy with Akela as the leader of the pack, the wolves hunt together, both males and females, in Kipling's jungle. In the "Hunting Song of the Seeonee Pack," Baloo sings about he duties of a scout, then sings about the duty of one wolf reporting to another, and finally he sings about the hunt together. In some ways Kipling reflects a dominant ideology of his age. During this period in British publishing history,

> Juvenile literature ... revered athletics and significantly rated rowing, cricket and football as more "manly" sports than ... boxing and shooting.... Above all, team sports were identified as the most important experience of character building as a process, comprising an ethos of loyalty, team spirit, patriotism, pluck and manliness [Springhall, 66].

This ennobling of the group hunting dynamic is Kipling's paean to masculinity in congress or united in brotherhood for a common, noble cause. We may reason that this is what unites Bagheera and Baloo in the story, two seemingly very different male characters: bachelor teacher and former enslaved, feared black panther. The team approach that these characters take includes Mowgli's education and mentorship.

The collaboration between Baloo and Bagheera is also centered on continuing patriarchy. In many ways, it is to the detriment of the jungle as a whole. Bagheera acknowledges Mowgli's power, particularly through his stare, and his eventual ascendancy, but with Baloo's instruction (and we reason that Baloo's reputation as a teacher means that this cycle of male training has been continuous for some time), the two of them have united in continuing patriarchy. Baloo and Bagheera are, even from the beginning of the novel, fighting the decadent and suspect masculinity of Shere Khan and his "lameness" (in both physical attributes and his failure to adhere to the hegemonic good of the whole). The collaboration of Baloo and Bagheera pits two seemingly different males together, united in one goal: to protect Mowgli, teach him the ways of the jungle, and ensure his ascendancy.

Masculinity in Children's Animal Stories, 1888–1928

We are actually only shown two hunting scenes in the novel, both involving unusual collaborations. By unusual, I mean these collaborations don't coalesce well with the firm "Law of the Jungle" and training that Kipling has imposed on Mowgli, but also, paradoxically, demonstrate that the central tenets of communication and hierarchal leadership are a matter of life and death. When Kaa joins to hunt down Mowgli and help Baloo and Bagheera rescue him from the monkeys, all three characters join in the battle. But it is the communicative skills of Baloo and Bagheera that both secure Kaa's participation (embellishing and lying about names and insults from the monkeys) and the communicative skills of Mowgli (using the "Master Word" to communicate his abduction to Baloo and Bagheera to Chil the Kite). The threat of death lingers in the slaughter of the monkeys, so that even Bagheera and Baloo are both companions to Kaa in the hunt and possibly food to him had Mowgli's "humanness" not saved them from the hypnotic spell of Kaa.

In the other hunting scene, the strategized killing of Shere Khan, Mowgli assembles some faithful wolves and uses the herd of cows and buffaloes to hunt Shere Khan. He ambushes the overfed tiger in a ravine, using the wolves like dogs to run the herd into a stampede death for the tiger. This hunting is a revenge hunt (no one feeds or is described as feeding from this hunt) and, again, the communicative skills of Mowgli are what set up the strategy where Grey Brother and Akela run the herd into the waiting tiger. The epic quality of Kipling's song is translated into two visible hunting/death scenes where nobility is more grounded and more centered on brotherhood than individuality. But the hunting scenes pair together males as hunters, well-versed in what is required to pull off the hunt. Kipling makes full use of both of these scenes with post-fight scenes where Mowgli thanks Kaa, Baloo and Bagheera with his promises of future hunts and leaves his village, for the last time, on the individualist path of the warrior he has molded himself into, despite these visible collaborative hunt/fight scenes.

We could easily contrast the heroism attached to Kipling's version of the hunt with Milne's version in *Winnie the Pooh*. When Pooh attempts to steal honey from the bees, he tries the deception or camouflage of appearing as a cloud. Even when Christopher Robin questions him, his stock response is "you can never tell with bees" (14). Pooh's ignorance, while humorous, recalls the ignorance of patriarchs and paternalists who would

Four • Collaboration, Compromise, Group Performances

rather not be questioned and when questioned, can't produce an answer. The failure, in this hunting scene, is how Pooh hunts and may be drawn by Milne to show that "naturalness" in the depiction of a male hunting is problematic and, ultimately, false.

As a collaborative representation, Pooh and Piglet's hunting of the Woozle produces a clear picture of satire as it concerns hunting and male collaboration in the hunting performance. Milne applies a heavy, faux verbal lacquer with his word choice as the two proceed on their misadventure: "tracking," "watching," "sudden," and "puzzled" (38). Milne's word choice mocks both hunting and the traditional "boys in the woods" plot of literary works like *Bevis, The Wind in the Willows, The Jungle Book*, and contradicts the popular fervor of the overly masculinist schemes of Lord Baden-Powell's Boy Scouts, as if mastery of the outdoors were overrated and unjustifiably elevated by adults when children, represented by Pooh and Piglet, will more often than not mis-perform as hunters (and both survive and actually bond in the process).

Clearly Milne won't provide a model for hunting, even from Christopher Robin (who has no trouble with expeditions and parties). In many ways, mentorship is challenged as a collaboration worth undertaking in Milne's world (Rabbit, Owl) for the more boyish characters, Pooh and Piglet. Both Pooh and Piglet misperform hunting, but clearly don't have a mentor and even benefit from the absence of a mentor as they more firmly establish their own relationship and collaboration, their own identities away from the models of pedantic blowhard (Owl) or know-it-all, organizer/planner (Rabbit).

As mentioned earlier, this could certainly be linked to violence, but Milne's casting of authority as problematic and not necessary for collaborations reflects his own experiences with authority, war, and violence. His service at the Battle of the Somme (1916), poem "OBE," play *A Boy Comes Home*, and *Peace with Honour* (1934) all deal with the atrocities of war, the questioning of nationalism and group mentalities (as would his poem "The Norman Church" (1952)). Collaborations between males, whether it was in profiting from the war or using the Old Testament to revisit an Evangelical tradition of judgmental religion, were problematic for Milne. He clearly was not investing his novel with the machismo and hegemonic male grouping that repeated violence as an act towards establishing gender identity. Jeffrey Richards has classified the Victorian male as "*puer aeternus* [Richards's italics], the boy who never grew up. It was not just the all-male society in which he functioned, it was also his preferred activities (hunting, empire-building, exploring, warring)" (106). Milne softens the aggression of the previous century's depiction of masculine aggression while continuing the exploring aspects of collaboration. And Milne's experience demonstrates the "boy who did grow up" and brought his experience to bear in his authorship of male collaborations.

In many ways, through fantastical settings and the use of localized adventure schemes, the team/athletic literature that dominated boys' magazines and public schools from the late nineteenth century into the Edwardian Era is evident as an influence and a point of departure for the hunting scenes of *The Jungle Book* or the recapturing of Toad Hall in *The Wind in the Willows*. But there are other philosophies afloat in Kipling and Grahame's work. As James Managan's study of the zeal for athleticism and boys' development literature in "Play Up and Play the Game: Victorian and Edwardian Public School Vocabularies of Motive" reveals, nationalism became linked with "the schools' secular trinity [of] imperialism, militarism and athleticism" (324). In the use of hunting, late Victorian attitudes of manliness are reflected in Kipling's hunt scenes, while modernism rejection of imperialism, militarism and athleticism are rejected in Pooh and Piglet's mock heroic hunt scenes in Milne's 1926 novel. But both writers project both fantasies of what being male means and what anxieties attended one's development as a male.

An Audience Required

In grouping, males look to other males as both audience members and fellow participants in initiatory experiences. When Mowgli is rescued from the Monkeys, Bagheera and Baloo have to fight to get him back, and they make sure they make public their scars: "he [Mowgli] has cost us heavily ... in good hunting, in wounds, in hair..." (66). Kipling seeks to remind us of what teams demand, in terms of commitment, and what happens to other team members (Bagheera, Baloo) when individuals don't follow their commitment (Mowgli). Masculinity, as represented in these group scenes of *The Jungle Book*, demonstrates that stoicism is only as good as the audience. In the poem before the "Tyger! Tyger!" chapter, the narrator invokes the audience necessary for Kipling's warrior society: "Brother, it [blood, power] ebbs from my flank and side./ Where is the haste that ye hurry by?/ Brother, I go to my lair—to die!" (70). Bodily harm and epic masculinity are intertwined in Kipling's conception of masculinity. The "sharing" of stories, scars, and battle demonstrates that despite the "solitude" of the hero in the adventure story tradition, manliness is built from the sharing of masculine codes, not from initiation experiences kept in isolated and solitary memory. For Mowgli, despite the epic trimmings Kipling provides for his picture of the feral child, is sheltered in most of the novel by Baloo and Bagheera, and once properly exposed to how to be masculine performs his masculine act of revenge in concert with and for the wolves.

For Kipling, establishing manliness includes the use of audience: to be a male means bodily sacrifice and harm; this sacrifice requires a group, either as witnesses or as eventual storytellers, and this sacrifice needs to be retold so that the establishment of masculinity is more complete. We can see this in Kaa's dance in *The Jungle Book*. Kaa's hypnotic dance is certainly based on the tradition of snake charming and hypnotism Kipling encountered from his time in India. In this scene of the book, literally, performance is the most deadly weapon a male has at his disposal. Dance as a weapon is a rarity in a children's story by a British writer, but Kipling blends allusive connections of dance as seduction and weapon (Salome) with his project in heteronormativity. And this is what Laura Stevenson and Andrew Lycett, to name a few critics, see as part of Kipling's narrative strategy and artistic temperament: the use of contrasts and dichotomous pairings. As Lycett contends, we can witness these perspectives: "one that married rationality and fantasy, western and oriental philosophy and the male and female sides of his personality" (*New Statesman*, 44). Kaa's uninscribed body is freed in gender blurring performance dancing a slaughter and punishment for the "undesireables" (monkeys), for Bagheera and Baloo who become suspect in the hierarchal order due to their vulnerability, and for Mowgli who is continuing his apprenticeship in how to be a male.

In many ways, the sharing of epic masculinity and the need for an audience is visible in Wilde's work as well. Though, we might reason, his depictions of this aspect of masculinity problematize both masculinity and the need for an audience. In "The Star-Child," Wilde's protagonist leads the children, like a Pied Piper character, into acts that are cruel and vindictive, thus calling into question masculinity that relies on both heteronormative consolidation of power and the performance necessitating an audience. The same could be said of "The Fisherman and His Soul." In this story, the Soul goes on these separate adventures, away from the Fisherman who has chosen a heteronormative marriage/pairing with a mermaid. It is the extensive cataloguing and exoticizing of the Soul's adventures, *as he recalls them to the Fisherman,* that illustrates, boasts and, more importantly, invites the audience to recognize how masculine these adventures make the Soul (which could all be the Fisherman's if he would renounce his love). Both of these characters' obvious needs for audience also allow Wilde to re-organize regulation of masculine desire into his larger Christian morality of these stories.

As a critique of aristocratic masculinity, two of the most conceited characters in this study make audience almost a pre-requisite in their search for identity: Toad and the Remarkable Rocket. Toad's performances — in song, speeches, actions, retelling of his actions — demonstrate not only an affinity for showing off, but a necessity towards establishing his hegemonic masculinity. Toad's need for audience validates his masculinity (and social position) while also calling attention to its liminality. We could classify Toad's performances as camp as Sedgwich sees it : "A gayer and more spacious angle of view" (*Epistemology of the Closet,* 156). But with this camp, we contend with the child reader/listener and the time of publication where "camp recognition" and "spaces and practices of cultural productions" (Sedgwick, *Epistemology of the Closet,* 156) intersect. In this way, both camp and the antithesis of the Edwardian gentleman, as Grahame constructs him, combine. In this way, we may read the troubling masculinity of Toad linked to his failure to perform, without an audience, the duties of his class and position. Not only do other characters know this about Toad (Badger, Mole, Rat, the stoats and weasels), they mimic him, deride him, and seek (I argue, ultimately, unsuccessfully) to contain his camp run afoul. But Toad's need for audience is a critique on the part of Grahame that is reflected in early children's fiction, most notably Wilde's "The Remarkable Rocket."

Wilde's Remarkable Rocket could easily pass for the literary model for Grahame's Toad. The Remarkable Rocket is such a comical figure that even Wilde's descriptions minimally amount to "supercilious" several times in the story; the real characterization takes place in his dialogue. Much like Toad, their speeches are egotistical in nature, centered on their accomplishments and what others may or may not have said about them. In a different vein, the Remarkable Rocket's speeches are directed less at a need for immediate audience in the story, i.e., another character, and more at the social sensibilities of the reading audience, most pointedly, the adult reader. The Remarkable Rocket critiques everyone in his witty, anti-masculinist manner from "I often have long conversations all by myself, and I am so clever that sometimes I don't understand a single word of what I am saying" to "I have no sympathy myself with industry of any kind, least of all with such industries as you seem to recommend.... I have always been of the opinion that hard work is simply the refuge of people who have nothing whatever to do" (359). I quote both of these to show that the literary model of masculinity Wilde represents contradicts the utilitarianism of Mill and Bentham, as well as the bourgeois sentiments of the reading public, thus establishing a mirror for a masculinity Wilde finds humorous and reprehensible.

Much of Milne's work demonstrates that masculinity needs an audience. Pooh frequently bursts out into song, writes poems and odes, and looks to implant himself in the lives of others as the days unfold in the forest. Eeyore's speech in the "We Say Goodbye" chapter demonstrates that even the reluctant cynic, Eeyore, wishes to be included in the group, for recognition, and to compete with Pooh for attention. Milne's career as a dramatist certainly may have influenced his writing of Pooh's character, but the idea of audience for masculinity is evident in Grahame's Rat (poet, songwriter) and in Baloo (teacher and songwriter). Rat, in *The Wind in the Willows,* is even ostracized to some degree because of his artistic temperament, but he isn't actually punished. And Baloo, like Pooh, is known for his songs and his performances (as a teacher), even respected. Pooh also demonstrates, in the mode of Toad, that having oneself for an audience is enough. While Pooh's declarations aren't as vindictive or posited against an other, as Toad's are, they both establish their identity in performance for themselves, revealing a self-collaboration in the establishment of Edwardian and Georgian maleness that seems inherited from Wilde, passed down to Grahame, and reconfigured in Milne.[2]

But one key element missing in Grahame's tale is the collaboration with females. Wilde's Star-Child is tempered by a fairy-tale mother disguised as a beggar woman who helps him transform. In Milne's novel,

Masculinity in Children's Animal Stories, 1888–1928

Roo is constantly interacting with Kanga who provides guidance as a mother. Roo certainly needs an audience for his playfulness (seen several times in the novel, most notably in the "Expotition" chapter), but his audience for the majority of the novel's length is his mother. When the feminine influence is exerted, we see Portly off on an almost deadly adventure, Toad nearly imprisoned for life, and Mowgli left to desolation and self-created crisis. The escape from domesticity and its influence as an audience seems to be a central theme in both Grahame and Kipling's works.

Where we witness a critique of masculinity that requires the collaboration with an audience is in Potter's work. We see this most evidently in her story, *The Tale of Squirrel Nutkin*. Nutkin consistently dances, sings, and taunts the owl, Mr. Brown. But he performs his carnivalesque flaunting in front of all the other squirrels "bobb[ing] up and down like a little red *cherry* [Potter's italics]" (25) and "danc[ing] up and down like a *sunbeam* [Potter's italics]" (33). Potter finds the impertinence of youthful masculinity too much and codifies performative masculinity with intense physical inscription as Nutkin's tail is taken by Mr. Brown. The story works, thus, doubly: revealing the necessity some boys/males feel in establishing an audience for their rebellion and active posturing as well as revealing a societal mechanism to curb such rebellion, i.e., an audience to scare into accepting the code.

As with much of Potter's work, subtlety or indirect attention is affirmed. Moppet and Mittens are renowned in the village as rat catchers (with a smaller illustration than the key scenes of *The Tale of Samuel Whiskers*). Contrast this with Benjamin Bunny and Peter Rabbit's audience of each other in pursuing their masculinist adventure scheme and you can see how using audience is affirmed in Potter's work. Much like Potter's life, drawing attention to oneself or needing audience to understand, develop or, even, test one's gender construction is problematic and is rarely sanctioned.[3]

Audience, as it is used by these various authors, demonstrates that the growing cult of fame and its connections to monetary compensation had taken hold, particularly for writers like Wilde and Kipling. But as writers like Grahame and Milne craft masculinity, audience serves as both a reinforcement of masculine privilege (to be seen and heard is gloriously masculine) and a critique of masculinity that overly relies on audience as a consolidation of self-image (the Remarkable Rocket, Toad, Benjamin

Bunny, Squirrel Nutkin). Whether overly audience-oriented behaviors are punished (as they are in Kipling's novel — Tabaqui and monkeys and in Potter's stories) or whether they are elevated as essential to masculinity (as they are in Wilde, Grahame and Milne's novels), the need for audience to exert privilege and hegemonic power is still evident, from Wilde to Milne.

The Boys Are Back in Town: Problematic Male Collaborations

One of Beatrix Potter's primary critiques of masculinity is a critique of males together in unlicensed play or exploration. More than willing to use violent inscription, when we pair together males in her stories, we see a distinct trend. Peter Rabbit/Benjamin Bunny, Timmy Tiptoes/Chippy Hackee, Ginger/Pickles: all of these male/male companionships, friends, relations, business partnerships produce near-death scenarios, violent punishments, and social isolation. In Potter's configuration, two males together usually means trouble, as they have no "checking" influence (female characters or home) and their pursuit of boyish behavior has to be curbed and punished. Collaborations between males, in Potter's work, is a merging of destructive psyches, which threaten the stability of the countryside. Consider, for example, how Ginger and Pickles end up hunting for food and positioned as a gameskeeper after their failed venture as businessmen (another collaborative venture males fail at together), and, as the narrator says, "In fact some people wish they [Ginger and Pickles] had gone further [away from the village]" (218). Because males in companionship challenge the authority of the domestic center and reinforce patriarchal ideas of freedom and privilege, Potter isolates them from the community and scripts near-death experiences for them (Chippy, Peter, Benjamin Bunny, Jeremy Fisher). When a character resists or rejects the ill-advised mentorship and collaboration with another male, they are rewarded like Timmy Tiptoes who returns home to raise his family and avoids the calamities that befall Chippy Hackee. In effect, females (and other forces of nature) regulate male desires in Potter's work.

In a similar vein, Grahame critiques ill-advised collaborations, particularly when we reconsider Rat and the Sea Rat. The influence of the Sea Rat almost results in Rat leaving his home and taking to the seas for adventure. This is quite similar to Mole's solo venture into the Wild Woods. What Grahame reveals is that there are influences on his characters and they can target an aspect of masculinity that can be quite troubling: the idea of living out one's life in adventure. Mole needs Rat to check him, and Rat needs Mole to check him: this is an essential part of their collaboration. In this manner, the feminine influence, oddly enough prevalent in Toad's adventures, is nullified as Toad merely takes advantage and aid from his interactions with females. And Mole serves as a "checking" influence on Rat and his ill-advised regression into exotic adventure story characterization. It may be a domestic force that connects Mole and Rat in their collaboration, but it is an all-male domestic collaboration centered on a sentimental and romantic-inspired living arrangement between the two.

Milne's characterization of boys in the forest would seemingly speak to a utopia of all-male collaborations. Except that Milne, ever the eye for satire, critiques aspects of masculinity from many different vantage points. When Pooh and Piglet follow Rabbit's lead to steal Roo from Kanga, Piglet reaps the punishment of disrupting a mother/son relationship. Because Pooh and Piglet don't question Rabbit, effectively, the humorous misadventure ensues. In many ways, we witness the critique mentioned earlier in this study where patriarchy and hierarchy are not only unstable but are ineffectual and dangerous as an influence.

The danger in this episode of Milne's novel is the transmission of xenophobia to Pooh and Piglet, as well as the directorial/authoritarian influence that Rabbit exerts. Milne uses nonsense and comedic actions to further the critique of Rabbit's masculinity, as well as to call into question the ineffectual collaboration of Piglet and Pooh in responding to Rabbit's directives. If we reason that from the initial all-male collaboration of Piglet/Pooh/Rabbit (which ends in disaster, certainly for Piglet), to the end of the story (where Pooh learns how to jump and practices with Kanga once a week, Rabbit takes care of Roo, and Piglet spends time with Christopher Robin), we see how Milne seeks to rework collaborative masculinity into a direction that is more collaborative (including Kanga and Roo) and less xenophobic and isolationist. It is as if Milne saw the problematic nature of an isolated community and added characters (Kanga, Roo, Tigger) that challenged a sentimental, isolationist reading of his novel.[4]

Four • Collaboration, Compromise, Group Performances

Kanga, the only "adult" character in the forest, must contend with this collaborative masculinity gone astray. And while Peter Rabbit gets bed and chamomile tea in Potter's story, Kanga physically punishes Piglet, though in jest. Much like Potter, physical punishment attends ill-conceived masculinity. Even with this humorous ending, Milne constructs a story where collaborative, all-male "adventure" that is threatening to another character, in this case a female mother, must be thwarted. In this episode, Milne is more consistent with the critique presented by Potter. Perhaps Carol Stanger is right in seeing Milne's work as a place where a feminist reading is appropriate.[5]

We certainly witness a critique of patriarchy and adult authority in the "Expotition to the North Pole." Christopher Robin pulls Rabbit aside, away from the group, and admits he doesn't know what the North Pole is. While Rabbit doesn't either, both characters demonstrate a feigned authority through silence. They collaborate to hide their ineptitude (very different from the flagrant displays of innocence and naiveté from Pooh, Piglet, and Eeyore). This regressive representation of masculinity reminds the reader of another episode in British history where major involvements of groups of Britons, led by adult males, went unquestioned: World War One. I bring up the first war because the experiences figure so directly, in many ways, in Milne's handling of man/boy interactions in the text. As Christopher Robin is developing his sense of identity and masculinity, he is both caretaker of his toys and leader (expedition, celebration party at the end of the novel). To witness this carefully crafted critique, on Milne's part, is to witness a mirror Milne holds up to the British public: the failure to question adult authority and the disastrous consequences of blind patriarchy.[6]

Even Kipling is critical of collaborative masculinity, certainly in its blind adherence to futile leadership and its flirtation with unsanctioned hegemony. Fluidity in the way groups are establish and motivated in the novel (Wolves, attraction to Shere Khan and denunciation of Akela) reveal a masculinity that has elements of fluidity but retains, even in its critique of collaboration, its interest in perpetuating patriarchy. In many ways, like patriarchy, the character's name may change, but the organization of power remains the same. In the beginning of the story, Akela is presented as the head of the Wolf Pack. There is a power struggle where the other wolves protest and look to replace him with either Mowgli or Shere Khan.[7] Both of these characters would not be the lead hunter in the wolves' communal hunting practice, and thus, really don't emerge as clear leaders when paired with the needs of the group.

But the fluidity within the group, as regards to leadership, does give us an indication of one aspect of Kipling's ideas of masculinity: a suspicion of mobs, a suspicion of inherited royalty, and a belief in leadership by natural ability and talents. As Richard Kerridge has asserted in "Nature in the English Novel," Kipling offered "a myth of a renewed, primal aristocracy, drawing its energy and legitimacy from nature's hierarchies rather than from exhausted feudalism that had lorded over them in Britain" (153). There is no primogeniture, no ancestral home in this story. The Darwinian jungle, as a setting, attempts to strip some of the class, race, and nationalistic sentiment away from the creation of individuality. Kipling reveals the fluidity of leadership in this jungle, according to abilities. Mowgli ultimately establishes his claim to leadership with the skin of Shere Khan, collected only after the group hunt he has overseen.[8]

In fact, the leadership of the group is up for grabs between Mowgli and Shere Khan. Mowgli and Shere Khan could be doubles where the wolves need neither, but only to recognize the power of their collective masculinity to hunt and feed the pack when led by "nature" and not by degenerate masculine characters. Mowgli resembles Shere Khan, both by an exceptional birth story and as an outsider to the Wolf Pack. Both of these characters organize wolves outside the dominant social structure (the Wolf Pack) to further their own causes.

And this may be Kipling's ultimate critique: groups are too vulnerable to ineffectual leadership. A feral boy minimally invokes the use of friendship and collaboration to achieve the death of Shere Khan, and really never congeals with either his Wolf Family or the Wolf Pack. In fact, both Mowgli and Shere Khan share this aspect of personality: they can only work with a group as it furthers their aims, as neither is truly interested in the communal power structure of the wolves. We may consider this part of Kipling's Imperialist stance: the native Wolf Pack can't govern themselves. They are vulnerable to both demagogues (Mowgli) and dictators (Shere Khan). While Kipling creates an ideal society in its hunting and communication dimensions, the intrusion of power and chaos (masculine forces as represented by Shere Khan and the monkeys) reveal the underlying need for hierarchy, even if it is a new, skills-based hierarchy. This may account for both the ending of the novel and the shifting bases of power.

As John Kucich observed: "Readers have long recognized that Kipling held figures at the top of the political, military, or administrative hierarchies in contempt, but that he had a special regard for the middle-level professional" (48). I would suggest that as Kipling withholds his critique of individual masculinity or makes it manifest, that poorly administered social groups push masculinity to individual excess. In this excess, we witness all the fears and desires of colonialist ambition and the violence and isolation such an "ungovernable" situation demands.

Critiques of males in collaboration afford these authors an opportunity to license behaviors they found acceptable (witnessed in the next section of this chapter). More importantly, they allowed these authors to punish and curb behaviors they found dangerous to the child. Whether the influence of chaos is at stake (the easily led Wolf Pack) or the blind following of patriarchy (Rabbit and Christopher Robin), collaboration must be sanctioned by the adult authors who read parental, nationalistic, and patriarchal disapproval into their texts.

Marriage, Same-Sex Unions: Boys Who Like Girls Who Like Boys Who Like Boys

Re-envisioned unions of males pervades the texts in these studies. In each of these authors' works, heteronormativity is neither "hetero" nor "normative" in regard to the different unions. While masculine privilege extends through homosocial and homoerotic bondings (Wilde, Grahame, and Milne), the picture of domesticity and male and female authors' reactions to domesticity reflect a changing culture. As John Tosh has asserted,

> Middle-class domesticity in Victorian England could hardly be described as an unqualified endorsement of patriarchal privelege.... The prestige of motherhood was greatly increased; housewifery was redefined as the art (or even the science) of household management; and the local standing of the family became more than ever dependent on the social skills of the wife [145].

Off-screen and minimalized opposite sex couples demonstrate one aspect of the resistance to the changing laws and burgeoning suffragette movement. But the characterizations of unions also includes homosocial and homoerotic couplings where male companionship demonstrates both fluidity in these couplings, in terms of power, and in terms of dynamic characterization: "maleness" is, again, unstable, even in the Christian symbolism and capitalist critique inherent in Wilde's male-male couples. We also witness, through Potter's writings, a re-envisioning of power relations in couples that include masculine participation, tolerance, and even encouragement of the domestic center as a place to perform masculinity: a masculinity more attuned to provision and more equal collaboration.

One of the heteronormative unions in this study is the union of Raksha and Father Wolf in *The Jungle Book*. But it is a union with a decidedly blurred gender past and with a subtle critique of the feminization of literature and of the changing roles of females in Britain. Raksha, the mother/female wolf, has a reputation as an excellent hunter (in her bachelorette years). Her hunting prowess was so revered, Father Wolf had to "win" her in marriage. Critics like Claudia Nelson still recognize the patriarchy inherent in the beginning of the novel ("Sex and the Single Boy: Ideals of Manliness and Sexuality in Victorian Literature for Boys.") And we can certainly read the "temporal and contingent" gender forces at work, which retire Raksha, the hunter, and produce Raksha, the mother. But Laura Stevenson in "Mowgli and His Stories: Versions of the Pastoral" posits that the story changes from a more mid–Victorian setting and characterization to a story that demonstrates the influence of the Colonial mission and a critique of overly "feminized" literary depictions of male and female characters in late nineteenth-century novels. In the first draft, Stevenson reveals, "Father Wolf complains about hunting alone, and Mother Wolf says the children are too little to leave — an obvious glance at Victorian domesticity" (365). After Kipling abandoned this conventional marriage dialogue and characterization, his subsequent draft "demonstrates the way resonance [artistic] can create a story independent of authorial control" (Stevenson 366). Raksha is characterized in epic masculine terms for her hunting prowess; Kipling contains her patriarchal and separate sphere containment as a mother, but also challenges the domestic, separate sphere role formation, at the very least, when we consider Raksha's past. We might consider this as a Victorian reading of Raksha, but would miss the Imperialist sentiments possibly at work. The new "Imperial" mother needs to be capable of violence because the empire requires violence, not Gilbert and Sullivan, "New Women," *Tom Brown's School Days*, and other concerns of the provincial minds in an island nation.

Four • Collaboration, Compromise, Group Performances

But, in this chapter, the importance of Raksha lies in her domestic coupling with Father Wolf and the past where they hunted together. Kipling provides at least one model for fatherhood that resembles a nuclear family and encourages a collaboration where fatherhood and provision are key elements of masculinity, as well as the initial influences Father Wolf has on Mowgli (his influence will give way to the more draconian and intense training and experiences Mowgli has with Baloo and Bagheera).

But Kipling isn't the only one to script collaboration in mating pairs of animals. Otter and Mrs. Otter have both a domestic union and a son, Portly, in Grahame's *The Wind in the Willows*. But Mrs. Otter is never seen (and heard only through indirect speech). It is almost as if marriage and heterosexual coupling is a myth in Grahame's novel. To say that the novel is tentative about heterosexual coupling is to put it mildly. The depictions of heterosexual coupling where mothers/women get to speak is limited to the collective "mother weasels" who bring their children to witness the struttings of the "Hegemonic Four" at the end of the novel, and more of a caricature than a characterization. Grahame's minimalization of marriage reflects both autobiographical issues with marriage and an era's questioning of heterosexual coupling, as both males and females begin to see marriage as problematic and unnecessary.

And nowhere is the questioning of marriage more evident than in Grahame's pairing of Mole and Rat in *The Wind in the Willows*. Judith Butler has argued that "there are structures of psychic homosexuality within heterosexual relations" (155) and Grahame's novel, at a minimum, illustrates this. But the use of animals in a pederastic fashion —(certainly from Wilde's influence), Rat as teacher to Mole — is a clever way to express admiration for same-sex coupling. The interesting intersection of rural sentimentality and "psychic homosexuality" becomes most explicit in the novel on the caravanning trip:

> The Mole reached out from under his blanket, felt for the Rat's paw in the darkness and gave it a squeeze. "I'll do whatever you like, Rat," he whispered. "Shall we run away tomorrow morning, quite early — very early — and go back to our dear old hole on the river?" [37].

Touching, companionship, support, escape: the assumption of both home and same-sex collaboration is established early on in the novel between Mole and Rat. The first person, "our," tells us that there has been a new establishment of identity for Mole, at least. But freedom is still at stake, as Anthea Trodd has commented on societal expectations: "pastoralism and male friendship offer images of a freer, nobler world outside the confines of bourgeois society and marriage" (58). This coupling of Mole and Rat reveals that collaborations can be a refuge, of sorts, from the adventure/domestic dilemma and from marriage, and demonstrate an avoidance of the "marriage plot" that dominates many Victorian and Edwardian novels.

We have already discussed the influence of Grahame on Milne's work and this is nowhere more evident than in the structure of his story where the Hundred Acre Wood is populated by all males (with the exception of Kanga). In Milne's world, male collaboration and male companionship are essential parts of his children's story. The consistent return to bonding and cooperative plots, even in stories where individual desires initiate subplots, are ubiquitous. From Pooh's visit to Rabbit's house to the great flood, the characters cooperate to make each other secure or further emotional/psychological needs of individual characters such as Piglet, Eeyore, or Pooh. For instance, in "*In Which* Piglet is Surrounded Entirely by Water," Piglet reveals both his insecurities as well as this central construction of Milne's masculine character:

> If only ... I [Piglet] had been in Pooh's house, or Christopher Robin's house, or Rabbit's house when it began to rain, then I should have had Company all this time, instead of being here all alone, with nothing to do except wonder when it will stop ... it wasn't much good having anything exciting like floods, if you couldn't share them with somebody [130–131].

While Piglet's confession reveals a masculinity that is more reminiscent of Wilde than Kipling, we see that the stoic, individualist masculinity of late Victorian Imperialism has been shed for a sentimental, homosocial version of masculinity where males may depend on one another for emotional and material support. As Carol Stanger has commented, "What strikes me most about the Pooh stories is that they are about building a community" (40). And this community is one where heteronormativity is a performance of normativity in homosocial guise, consistent in the all-male bachelor communities of Wilde and Grahame.

But the principal relationship in Milne's novel is the relationship between Pooh and Piglet. This relationship may rely on some form of mentorship on Pooh's part towards Piglet, and is clearly homosocial, but the pederastic angle, as with Mole and Rat, has been exorcised. Ann

Four • Collaboration, Compromise, Group Performances

Thwaite contends that Milne grew up in an environment that fostered companionship rather than competition: "Alan grew up to hate being in command as much as he hated to be commanded. He really only felt happy in relations between equals—in side-to-side relationships" (31). Except that like Christopher Robin and Pooh, Milne's relationship with Christopher Milne was hardly "side-to-side," and Piglet's relationship with Pooh with Pooh's primacy as the protagonist in so many of the episodes of the novel, make their relationship unequal. Foucault, Sedgwick and other theorists have posited that power is fluid and never static. Even current sociologists, such as Deborah Kerfoot, see a fluidity in how males understand collaboration:

> Erotic love as sociability requires ... that each is "attuned" to, and in tune with, the embodied subjectivity of the other — always shifting and in motion — doubly reinforcing its link with the practical aspects of care and underscoring the effort that is required to engage in emotionally intimate encounters [246].

And this certainly accounts for one reading of the relationship between Pooh and Piglet as mutually reinforcing — Pooh needing Piglet as audience, companion, and housemate (as we see in *The House at Pooh Corner*) and Piglet needing Pooh for companionship and security. Santanu Das, in examining the gender behavior of World War One, concludes that "homoeroticism has to be understood within new conceptual parameters and a different economy of emotions" (55). The day-to-day body contact of soldiers, coupled with the body contact of wounding and death produced an "eroticism [that] should not be understood solely in contrast to heterosexuality, nor viewed through the lens of gender and sexuality. Such intimacy must also be understood to exist as a triumph over death" (Das, 55). In other words, Piglet and Pooh's relationship, in its collaborative sense, could easily mirror the reconfiguration of masculinity Milne may have endured as a returning soldier from World War One, and their relationship (as well as the sentimental and Arcadian setting and mood of the novel) may be best classified as a resistance to the morbid landscape of both war and unchecked masculine aggression that led to that war.

The struggle for equality in collaboration or relationships, though, isn't as evident as the give and take, alternating roles we see with Grahame's characterization of Mole and Rat. Milne, as a humorist, used the inequality for plotting purposes (Piglet's insecurities are supposed to be funny and incite some conflicts in many episodes). The humor in the relationship interactions between Piglet and Pooh effectively allow for intimacy without the stain of homosexuality: both because these are toy/animal characters and the humor is paired so closely with the seriousness of sentimentality. The ease of Pooh and Piglet's coupling removes both the avoidance of marriage and the feminine influence, as well as the anxiety of a patriarch like Badger. In Milne's novel, the collaborative face of masculinity is a virtue that supersedes all others, even with the problematic issues of xenophobia, sentimentality, and misogyny that this all-male "group" engenders.

To claim that Milne inherited the same-sex coupling theme from Grahame seems plausible enough. To posit that Grahame inherited the same from Wilde would seem problematic, but for the mention of intertextual allusions from Wilde on both Grahame and Milne.[9] We may read the collaboration and companionship of these principal couples as inherited from romantic literary biography: Coleridge and Wordsworth or Shelley and Byron — all with bachelor, absentee fatherhood, and gender-defying behaviors.

While many of Wilde's tales follow traditional folktale plotting where an individual character goes through an experience leading to a transformation, Wilde also wrote stories where collaborations illustrate more humanitarian representations of masculinity, within same-sex companionship. In "The Happy Prince," the Prince and swallow collaborate on good works in the city as the swallow resists his earlier desires for individualist discovery and pleasure through travel. With this story, pederasty, or a relationship between an older male and younger male, is evident. Naomi Wood sees this ideal as inherited from Wilde's education: "The all-male culture of Oxford University, its tutorial system, and its emphasis upon the transcendent value of the 'Greats,' particularly Plato, provided fertile breeding ground for a pederastic code that eventually informed an apt pupil in Oscar Wilde" (159). This notion of influence, as a mutually reinforcing expression, didn't affect just Wilde, it was part of the *esprit du temps*: Locke and Rousseau's work had influenced the "Wordsworthian Romantic tradition that privileged childhood over adulthood and innocence over experience" (Wood 159). Yet, the swallow needs to be taught about the humanitarian aspect of his masculinity that he only learns from the influence of the Happy Prince. And, the hierarchy of the Prince as a

Four • *Collaboration, Compromise, Group Performances*

gender-blurring patriarch is still retained; there is no group collaboration to decide on how to solve the societal ills of the city the statue saves.

Posited next to the Prince and the swallow is the community of town males in the story whose practicality and hegemony illuminate the sacrifice of the main characters. The anthropomorphosized statue and swallow not only recall the Christian myth of Jesus and his disciples, but also the tradition of pederasty as the "Swallow kisses the Prince before he dies ... a rare male-male kiss in children's literature" (Wood 165). The older, wiser statue has given the youthful swallow his wisdom and receives an erotic reward before his death. And we are introduced to the swallow first, so while there is a recognizable journey of a young male to adult male, this journey into identity and sexuality the swallow makes is from hetero interests (the first love interest is the feminine reed) to same-sex collaboration and eros.

The same-sex coupling of the Selfish Giant and the boy in "The Selfish Giant" illustrate many of the same principles found in "The Happy Prince": compassion, maleness as a performance of companionship, and the lessons one male passes on to another. In this case, the story actually has more of a pederastic notion that privileges the youthful boy. In this story, the Christ figure of the boy teaches the Selfish Giant compassion to compensate for his earlier life of selfishness. While the giant is rewarded with a kiss, he also opens his garden to all the children following this brief, erotic moment. The young boy (Christ) returns and rewards the Selfish Giant's selflessness with transcendence: an ultimate Romantic configuration of the innocence of children as instruction for the more experienced.

In both of these stories "The Happy Prince" and "The Selfish Giant," the Christian representations of the prince and giant are obvious, the kisses not of betrayal but of love, and the teaching aspect of collaborative masculinity scripts performances of maleness that aren't rooted in bourgeois Christianity or capitalism. In the unions, resistance isn't framed as a masculine response to intimacy—erotic or psychologically. Wilde risks, in terms of the middle-class audience, his creation of couples who engage in collaborative plots, which emphasize understanding over material gain, and connection versus competitive ambition, accumulation, or physical dominance. Jeffrey Richards, in examining "manly love," posits that "the love of women is sexual and therefore inferior; the love of a man is spiritual, transcendent and free from base desire" (93). These two unions sublimate the competitive and individualistic notions of masculinity for "higher" performative goals on Wilde's part.

In fact, by contrast, we can examine the individual tales where males exude a masculinity that is competitive, individualistic and without collaboration. In the "The Star-Child," "The Nightingale and the Rose," and "The Remarkable Rocket," individualist schemes dominate the stories. Wilde reveals a resistance from characters as they interact with differing communities (or as these communities interact with them). In these characters' resistances to the variety of communities and collaborations that present themselves, Wilde seems to position the child as both needing community and in danger of the isolation which produces spoiled children, i.e., the Star-Child, the Student, and the Remarkable Rocket. This solipsistic version of masculinity is critiqued through the wider angle of relationships in both collections by Wilde.

One example of a story where individualism is critiqued would be "The Star-Child." In the story, the title character has to undergo a painful transformation to becoming connected to family and shedding the violent cruelty of his earlier characterizations by reuniting with both the feminine forest, as healer and instructor, and his mother and father. Wilde goes so far as to label his developmental tale as a "fire of his testing" (314), which cost him his life. The Star-Child is doomed to isolation and early death because there is only passing collaboration in pursuit of his quest. The Student in the "The Nightingale and the Rose" literally abandons love and passion for his beloved for the solitary pursuit of a scholar; the collaborative product of the Nightingale and the red rose tree lies seemingly wasted. And the Remarkable Rocket's journey allows him several opportunities for compromise and collaboration but ego and vanity prevail; he, like Toad, really represents a monstrous and selfish performance of masculinity tied to class and class distinctions as well as illustrates a competitive ambition that comes at a price. Contrast the selfishness of central male characters in "The Remarkable Rocket" and "The Nightingale and the Rose" with "The Selfish Giant," and you can see how this last tale merges elements of both collaboration and selfishness that demonstrates the influence of folk and fairy tales on Wilde, the moral atmosphere in which his children's works were published, and his aesthetic and ethical concerns in the creation of fiction.

In many ways, Wilde's works for children challenge traditional sto-

Four • Collaboration, Compromise, Group Performances

rytelling structures where males pursue individual goals. In "The Selfish Giant," a bachelor giant does recognize his error and knocks down the wall after realizing that the return of spring, the children in his garden, and his thawed-out heart aren't merely coincidence. Paradoxically, the giant longs for the return of the child who kissed him and his longing is rewarded with death as the boy returns as a Christ figure ready to take the giant to heaven. In this manner, Wilde challenges the construction of masculinity that seeks material or psychological rewards for efforts and change. To reward a character with death is to challenge our notions of what reward and desire are. To reward a character with death, for a supposedly Christian reading public, is to remind them that masculinity's highest cultural figure is centered on sacrifice and abandoning of personal desires. This transgressive performance by the Selfish Giant is rooted in both Romantic notions of childhood innocence and a lightened pederasty. The child teaches the giant to step out of his solitude and break the hold winter has over his garden and the hold his capitalist land-owning jealousy has over the capacity for children and nature to renew him. In this way, and in many others, Wilde's use of collaboration may rely on common themes and displays of morality (selflessness, compromise, purity of spirit) we witness in writers like Kingsley, Sarah Trimmer, and Thomas Hughes, but his aesthetic and psychosexual interests in homoerotic and transformative experiences are evident in how his collaborations pair boys and men together. As much as we can consider these characterizations as evidence of slipping or loosening gendered depictions for males, the kiss framed next to the sacrifice of Christ-like figures is nothing new. Betrayal isn't at stake in either "The Happy Prince" or "The Selfish Giant"; in both stories, dedication is the representative quality of masculinity we are supposed to take away from the endings. What Wilde does, ultimately, in these collaborations is remind the Victorian reading public that one of the qualities of masculinity inherited from the tradition of chivalry, inherited from the lessons of the life of Jesus, is the notion of dedication to a fellow man is manly, and this dedication serves as an extension to a dedication to humanitarian causes, not always rooted in personal growth tales as connected to our expectations from fairy tales. Wilde also illustrates that pederasty could be, in the words of C. S. Lewis, "the only counterpoise to the social struggle; the one oasis ... in the burning desert of competitive ambition" (106).

But as far as traditional expectations of couples or unions, we would have to nominate Potter as the creator of heterosexual couplings most recognizable by the Victorian reading public. It would seem that Potter praises the heterosexual couples, in this study and males who act collaboratively in unions. In one example, *The Roly-Poly Pudding*, the rat couple argue over how to make a dish, then finally collaborate in getting the butter, rolling pin and dough. They roll Tom Kitten up, together, preparing the food in teamwork: a blurring of gender roles and an absence of separate sphere roles according to sex. In *The Tale of Two Bad Mice*, both Tom Thumb and Hunca Munca collaborate in their destructive impulses, ransacking the doll's house in the beginning of the story. Tom Thumb joins Hunca Munca in "deconstructing" the house — taking apart the feathered pillows, moving the bolster down the stairs of the dollhouse, even moving the bird cage together out of the house. The story was modeled after the situation Potter found herself in: Norman Warne, Potter's first fiancé, was unacceptable by her parents, and thus Victorian practicality and hegemonic masculine family control prohibited an outward engagement and romance. The collaboration between Warne, as builder of a dollhouse he photographed for Potter to create a story around, even mimics, to some degree, the collaboration of Tom Thumb and Hunca Munca. Thus, autobiographically at least, we see the collaborative nature of unions, shared power, and collective expressions of violence and anger permissible in Potter's depictions of unions. This, Potter depicts, as play and this "concept of play and playfulness in subject positions [can] overturn conventional relations grounded in hierarchy and inequality" (Kerfoot, 246). Not only are males expected to contribute to family economy, collaborate and take direction in projects, they are supposed to allow play, which includes anger and aggression from females, as well as regulate their own anger and aggression appropriately.

 If we consider masculinity as only existing in relationship to femininity (see Whitehead, Connell, Nodelman), we might envision the expressions of anger and violence in Raksha; various witches, infantas, and plants in Wilde's stories; Kanga in *Winnie the Pooh*; and the bargewoman in Grahame's novel as foils for the construction of masculinity in these stories. Collaboratively, none of these female characters is paired with a male character in production, creation, or expression of connection; rather, the female characters are castigated as "Others" to the dominate plotting of the stories and as forces, which interrupt or challenge patriarchy (even

Four • *Collaboration, Compromise, Group Performances*

Raksha, with all of her challenge to Shere Khan, has to be married and imprisoned in a cave of sucklings so dangerous to her reputation). Only in Potter's stories with couples do we see females capable of expressions of violence *both tolerated by males and supported by males.* In this way, Potter demonstrates one of my central theses to the book: authors use animals to depict representations of gender that would have been questioned had the characters been human children/people. That these characterizations are hidden in the beautiful watercolors of Potter's artistry doesn't negate the fact that their best-selling status and quintessential Englishness isn't a lasting portrait of a picture of masculinity removed from the urban centers of the early twentieth century.

Not all of the characterizations require violence in collaborative unions. *The Tale of Timmy Tiptoes* depicts the same home economics we see in *The Tale of Two Bad Mice* and *The Roly-Poly Pudding*—a couple working together to secure the family store or home. In this tale, Timmy and Goody collect nuts together, depicted against an illustration showing naked, presumably male squirrels collecting nuts individually, while the illustrations at the end of the story demonstrate that separate spheres re-emerge. Timmy and Goody start their family: Timmy checking the lock on the nut store, guardian of the home, and Goody pushing two baby squirrels in a swing with another coddled in the crook of her arm. All of these stories feature children of the respective couples, an essential feature of Potter's collaborative unions. And while each may have a certain bit of energy, danger, and violence, they return to the family and provision of the family as a central representation of masculinity as it is tied to female partnership.

Certainly we ascertain that Potter praises masculinity in terms of provision and partnership. One need only take a look at the illustrations of *Two Bad Mice* or *The Tale of Timmy Tiptoes* to see pictures that depict couples comfortable in their couplings. She, in effect, shows both the coupling she yearned for in her own life — a different configuration than the marriage she witnessed between her mother and father — and the coupling she found in her marriage to William Heelis when she was forty-seven. Potter's conception of marriage and domestic sexual politics may have been a reaction to the aesthetic bachelor or even the burgeoning socialist movement in England. She may have feared what Karen Hunt classifies as socialist masculinity:

Masculinity in Children's Animal Stories, 1888–1928

> What made a good socialist might not necessarily make a good marriage. And what was so important in a masculine man — that he presided over his home — had to be sacrificed if he was to organize collectively with other men to create a society in which true manhood could be expressed [208].

Thus, it isn't just Grahame and Kipling who demonstrate an anxiety over the changing domesticity of the late nineteenth and early twentieth century. Potter's essential conservatism can critique bachelorhood and economic, problematic marriage schemes while her subversive feminism can challenge separate spheres while reinvesting the home with maternal power.

But opposite-sex unions are critiqued (as well as ill-conceived female rebellion) in Potter's work as well. In *The Tale of Jemima Puddle-Duck*, Jemima's union with the urban and sophisticated fox is a tale where collaboration can be a dangerous venture. Through this collaboration, Potter reveals that "gentlemen" are both suspicious and deadly. Only the intervention of Kep, the collie dog, and two fox hounds interrupt the ill-conceived plans of Jemima. A quasi-sexual predator (fox) requires a union with a killing squad (dogs) to restore the order of the farm. It is interesting to pair together Potter's tales of male and female unions because of the warnings and prejudices that emerge. Potter's distrust of the urban, sophisticated gentleman "slumming" it in the countryside is evident in the falsities the fox provides: a place to sit on eggs, a place to raise a family. And with Jemima's shaky representation by the end of the story, masculinity is paradoxically represented as a temptation and a solution, as an escape for Jemima, and as a corrective force in restoring the balance Jemima lost in giving into the temptation of the first masculine force, the fox.

But it isn't only a distrust of urbanity as associated with male characters that is problematic for Potter. In *The Tale of Ginger and Pickles*, the daughter of Mr. John Dormouse learns that collaboration in family can mean collaboration with a patriarch who is ineffectual. In *The Tale of Mrs. Tittlemouse*, the "most terribly tidy particular" (226) heroine constantly repels invaders, but her most problematic invader is Mr. Jackson, the toad who lives next door. Their failure at collaboration demonstrates a recurring them in Potter's work and a recurring illustration of masculinity: some males are prime examples of hegemonic masculinity where females and their desires are relegated as a male pursues his own desires. Mr. Jackson eats her food, makes a mess, then proceeds to attempt to re-enter when she has a party. That Mrs. Tittlemouse makes him sit outside is her compromise and rejection of future collaborations with him. Mr. Jackson doesn't collaborate the way Potter depicts in the previous stories I've mentioned.

In *The Tale of Timmy Tiptoes*, Chippy Hackee, the chipmunk, nurses Timmy after his fall, but wants him to stay in the hole with the nuts they've stored, escaping their married partners. Chippy even decides to camp in the tree after the wind blows off the top, to avoid home. Potter's illustration shows this masculine resistance to home in the picture of Chippy's wife prodding him with a branch as Chippy stores nuts for his camping escape. In *The Tale of Timmy Tiptoes*, the failure of collaboration by Chippy is framed next to the individual nut hunting the squirrels do; Chippy, it would seem, could go back and do this individual masculinity any time. Because Potter's many stories present different visions of collaborations between males and females, she is the only author of the ones I've included in this study who doesn't strip characters of family and family associations to establish masculinity; she encourages family and heterosexual unions with family to rework hegemony and establish the domestic center as the seat of collaborative power, roles and responsibilities.

It is easy to see the collaborations of Grahame and Milne, as well as Mowgli's young boyhood as reinforcing "self-engendering male communit[ies], a barely concealed apprehension about bourgeois marriage sapping male energy and domesticity vitiating male creative potency" (Sussman, 5). By comparing these different pairings we see that Grahame risked more intimacy and seriousness to his couple than Milne who chained himself to the humor of a post-war, disillusioned Modernist, but reveals both writers' hesitancy with bourgeois marriage. Wullschlager has contended that this comedic style of Milne's reveals the influence of history:

> Ending with a teddy bear sticking a twig in the ground ["Expotition to the North Pole"] — this would have been inconceivable amid the Edwardian gravity of Barrie, with his boys shrieking "Rule Britannia" as the pirates drag out the gangplank, and it is a giveaway that Milne was writing in the disillusioned, post First World War years [190].

To praise Milne as a writer who celebrates "community, the spirit of cooperation and kindness" (Thwaite 303) seems a bit much. He may celebrate these virtues, particularly when positioned next to Kipling and Grahame, but Potter and Wilde celebrate these virtues as well, and Potter includes characterizations of heterosexual couples. Grahame plots insurrection in the countryside, a real fear for both Grahame and the Edwardian reading public, thus embellishing and consolidating collaboration or camaraderie as an expression of masculinity as a vehicle for social and political control (and not merely for the good of two characters, Mole and Rat). Kipling's collaborations are paired against a backdrop of survival where the lessons of Jungle Law and life save Mowgli from certain death; thus, collaborations are a means to an end. In Milne, the crises experienced by characters are localized, much like Potter's world, and, unlike Potter's world, imminent death seems countries and ages away.

Perhaps the most traditional representation of collaboration, as the reading public would seem to want it, were the representations of heterosexual unions we see in Potter's work. As mentioned earlier, Beatrix Potter has several couples who collaborate on food provision and child-rearing duties, but she also characterizes unions with couples who both hunt together and act violently together. In Potter's life, she had two heterosexual couplings, but neither produced children. But she retained control of both her financial enterprises and her artistic production, which is mirrored in her female protagonists of several works (Mrs. Tiggy-Winkle, Miss Moppet, Sally Henny-penny). More importantly, when Potter scripts couples, she scripts shared power, even females who initiate adventure schemes, thus providing, at a children's literature level, anthropomorphic tales that depict heterosexual unions that aren't so deeply submerged in patriarchy and the fear of feminine influence.

Group Norms as Censure

This final section examines how males critique other males through groups and group censure. In this analysis, individualism must be stripped, usually painfully, from a male character to reinforce the group dynamic: from the needs of the Imperialist mission to the dictates of inherited gentry masculinity. Group norming can curb the adventurist impulse in a male character while also reinforcing the hegemony males fight to preserve whether in the jungle or along the riverbank. Most importantly, we witness ironies, paradoxes, and inconsistencies when characters try to enforce these dictates (largely through speech) against actions of boy/male characters whose impulses often demonstrate both a resistance to authority and an instability in gender formation.

Four • Collaboration, Compromise, Group Performances

There is a communality in group censure, particularly among groups of males to maintain the status quo. In *The Jungle Book*, Mowgli is told, "The monkeys never fight unless they are a hundred to one, and few in the Jungle care for those odds" (55). It is ironic that masculinity is praised — Kaa's use of the hypnotic dance — in one group while belittled in another. "Good hunting" is fine, but "fighting," even in defense of oneself or group is bad, particularly from the monkeys. John Kucich has examined the use of bullies and bullying groups and the "overt sadomasochistic preoccupations: the bullyings, beatings, and cruelty that pervade [Kipling's] work" (34). Kipling carries over boarding school sadomasochism into the jungle, where the prefects (Bagheera, Baloo and Kaa) dispense with violence as it benefits society as a whole, or as they reason is best for the whole. Kucich claims that this is a reflection of class politics imported from Britain, while I maintain that class politics offered a refuge for the ever-émigré Kipling who used the vehicle of middle-class bullying and the needs of the many superseding the rights of the few as a way to power and identity — for the child Mowgli and the Englishman abroad, at home, and at odds with the world.

This group censure is in effect at the end of *The Wind in the Willows* as well. The group of four retake Toad Hall because the stoats and weasels, like the monkeys in Kipling's novel, challenge hegemonic codes of masculinity. In Grahame's case, because his setting is the English countryside with representations of various professions, family structures, and characters with noticeable contrast in speech and behavior, class differences are raised. The irony, of course, is that Toad's behavior is presented as overly narcissistic and driven by class privilege and this is precisely what the stoats and weasels mock in their dinner scene before the group kicks them out.

But paradox and irony attend much of Kipling's efforts at establishing masculinity in Mowgli, as well. While Kipling scripts the monkeys' communality as dangerous, the use of grouping in Mowgli's hunting of Shere Khan doesn't seem to present the same problems. Mowgli relies on the other wolves, cattle and topography (using the ravine as a trap) to lure Shere Khan into a death by stampede. This is the "team" Mowgli assembles — all-male — to fight the insurgency of Shere Khan who is lethargic due to eating and drinking, hardly a noble prey. And instead of defending themselves, like the monkeys, Mowgli assembles this group and succeeds as a man through deception, timing, and sacrificing the village cattle for the death of a rival for power.

In many instances, the group ethos disrupts the development of the individual and promotes repetition of the groups' stricture, forcing the character into compliance with group or team dynamics. One finds evidence of this in Baloo and Bagheera's repeated warnings about the monkeys and the in the reference to the Jungle Law as the way or path for the individual. In Kipling's work, this group ethos, Jungle Law, takes an individual and curbs the excesses of individuality and rebellious choice, yet, for all of that, it still produces characters like the renegade wolves, monkeys, and Tabaqui. Badger does the same in *The Wind in the Willows*, with the same sense of inconsistency when we remember Toad and Rat, who begrudgingly or with resistance are pulled into the group dynamic, particularly with the retaking of Toad Hall. Not that all of the group dynamic as it affects one's identity is negative: Mowgli is taken into a society with this group dynamic and is inculcated into the system, which will help him survive (with many inconsistencies and individual rebellions), and Rat and Mole are saved by Badger in the Wild Wood in much the same way that Toad gets to go home at the end of the novel — according to the unspoken masculine privilege inherent in the gentry of the countryside.

The group halts not only developments in the countryside, it halts individual bildungsromans in *The Wind in the Willows*. During the first half of the novel, Mole stands center stage. By the end of the novel, he reports his spying activities to the group (looking for approval) and has effectively joined the heterosexual norm when he concurs with Badger about reining in Toad from his impulsive automobile adventures: "*We'll* [Grahame's italics] teach him to be a sensible Toad!" (107). In many ways, after this point in the novel, Grahame seems to inscribe gentry masculinity into Mole, a departure from his initial liberation. It is as if Grahame demonstrates that what is best in the countryside (and gentry masculinity, by extension) isn't what is represented by individuality, unchecked, and the technological invasion of the car, but in the group norm, most beneficial when united in purpose.

And though we witness collaborations in Wilde's stories, those stories don't reach, conclusively, towards a renewal of privilege and hierarchy. We are always aware of limits in a character as they must compromise themselves in Grahame's novel though. They are aware of this too: "... Mole saw clearly that he was an animal of the tilled field and hedgerow, linked to the plowed furrow, the frequented pasture, the lane of evening lingerings, the cultivated garden plot" (83). While Mole refutes the epicness of Toad's thoughts and protestations, the compromise between adventure and domesticity is rooted in a re-embrace of the pastoral while a same-sex companionship continues to take pace. The privilege of being able to contemplate adventure vs. domestic life is one afforded to the male characters in Grahame's tales, even Wilde's tales, if we consider the swallow's initial plans in "The Happy Prince." How to curb such individuality becomes a matter of group censure in *The Wind in the Willows*; how one escapes this condition is evident in the swallow's dedication and adherence to Christian principles of service to others.

This same sense of curbing individuality is evident in the two scenes where Toad must be "taken in hand." The same cast of characters with the same interventionist scheming is repeated. But, as the novel progresses, we can see Toad's lack of development (a condemnation on some part by Grahame of gentry masculinity) and Mole's capitulation to group norms. When he spies on the stoats we witness, for the first time, Mole's newfound classicism: "How they do laugh! That's what annoys me most!" (223). Michael Mendelson sees Mole's change as a transformation calling Mole "a convert to common sense and practicality" (134). In so many ways, the transformation of the homosocial Mole is regressive as he aligns himself with values inherited by Badger, the patriarch, in defense of class: values that are problematic (at best). These are the same values Badger uses to curb Rat's position as an aesthete and ineffectual soldier. In fact, I would argue that in Mole's questioning of his place and identity, he is led into the world of prejudice and stereotyping much the same way that Mowgli is led to stereotyping, "common sense and practicality" through the admonitions about the monkeys from Baloo and Bagheera. From the adventure into the Wild Woods to the retaking of Toad Hall, Mole's growing identity comes with the baggage of class prejudice and ordering less consistent with self-actualization and more consistent with group norming, despite the often transgressive representations Grahame constructs with Mole and Rat's same-sex companionship.

Group norming seems to also require denunciation of an "other." Both Toad and the Wild Wooders are cast as undermining the social codes of the rural Edwardian countryside. The working-class stoats and weasels, as well as rabbits are marginalized, often brutalized in the novel. In one scene Otter boasts "if I had had the luck to meet any of 'Them' [rabbits]

I'd have learned them some more — or they would" (74). Anthea Trodd sees the ending of the novel as nothing less than a state of class suppression: "Grahame revealed even the rural working class, the stoats and weasels, to be potential insurrectionaries, and restored a countryside thoroughly cowed by the gentlemen" (42). Positioned as revolutionists, the stoats and weasels mock Toad with a mimicking of his speeches and toasts as they ransack his kitchen and dining room. And while Grahame may have seen the retaking of Toad Hall as necessary to restore the group norm, it is problematic when we consider that Grahame plots the carnivalesque scene of roasting Toad next to the retaking of the home. The "carnival" thus comes to an end, but not before Grahame's critique of Toad's identity as a "dandy" is ensured, making the revolution seem warranted, in some measure.

A more gentle, yet visible critique of class is evident in *Winnie the Pooh*, as well. Rabbit and his extended relations may help Pooh out of a hole and join on the "expotition" but they are a group of characters that are indirectly mentioned, though directly illustrated. And Eeyore, who could be said to represent cynicism and common sense masculinity, finds their participation problematic: "If, every time I want to sit down for a little rest, I have to brush away half a dozen of Rabbit's smaller friends-and-relations first ... it's [the expedition] simply a Confused Noise" (116). This "noise" is a representation of a group that is both outside and inside the forest, and is a class of "others" who aren't even valued that highly by Rabbit. Individualism is valued in Milne's classic, even friendship, but not the friends and relations a character brings into the picture. After all, in the concluding chapter the friends and relations attend but they "spread themselves about on the grass, and waited hopefully in case anybody spoke to them, or dropped anything, or asked them the time" (153). The almost invisible "othered" characters, like the wolves, the monkeys, the stoats and the weasels, aren't individualized and are subject to the machinations of the group mentality of Milne, Grahame and Kipling.

I have spoken at great length about the monkeys' condemnation by Kipling and how they are positioned as an other to the group code of heteronormative masculinity. In an odd way, when we position the monkeys' play and song next to their slaughter, Mowgli's feeling of exile from the Wolf Pack, and his subsequent revenge tale, Kipling's dichotomous mind is evident again: while the monkeys are cast as "others," what is so beneficial about the masculine identity that Mowgli inherits? Surrounded with

Four • *Collaboration, Compromise, Group Performances*

English melancholy and colonial isolation, Kipling, like Grahame, characterizes masculinity as a problematized venture, whether it is the abrupt "ending" of Grahame's novel or the desolate sadness of Mowgli's leaving the Wolf Pack.

And while Grahame's ending to the novel positions Rat as inheriting part of the "patriarchal dividend" (Connell), Rat shows that there is a cost to masculinity as rendered in the group dynamic. As Badger re-enters the novel, the restructuring of hierarchy follows. Badger's consistent questioning of Rat's comments, thoughts, and actions reveal a severe critique of both the aesthete and a re-inscription of hierarchy proceeding from Badger's exalted position. But Badger reflects a strain of popular opinion on masculinity as society preferred "energetic action rather than unhealthy reflection and in much of the writing on manliness there is a persistent strain on anti-intellectualism, a suspicion of fine discrimination or expressed emotion" (Allen, 200). Grahame certainly constructs Rat as self-reflexive and capable of expressing emotion (unlike Badger). But this "fine discrimination and expressed emotion" isn't without pain for Rat. When he constrains Toad after he has been fooled earlier, he reveals, yet again, a sensitivity that is transgressive to group norms: "'No, not one song,' replied Rat firmly though his heart bled as he noticed the trembling lip of the disappointed Toad.... 'Please don't think that saying all this doesn't hurt me more than it hurts you'" (248). These famous last words often said before corporal punishment show that the body isn't the only place where punitive aspects of group identity establishment are rendered. What Rat demonstrates is that group censure requires the punished and punisher to undergo trauma in the inscripting process, as evidenced in Baloo's reconsideration of his punishments of Mowgli, and Rat's painful constriction of Toad's individuality. Was Grahame reiterating, in some way, the process of becoming male that he underwent as a mid-century Victorian? Was this representation a subversive revelation that masculinity is inconsistent and an attempt at imposing order on the chaos of identity formation? Or does masculinity necessarily constrain youth, females, and "others" in hopes of maintaining order as in this novel when "the friends set themselves up as a tribunal to defend the norm in opposition to individual expression" (Mendelson, 134)?

While masculinized communities dominate the children's works of Kipling, Grahame and Milne, the collaboration between characters demonstrates that there is fluidity, painful inscription processes, and suppression of individualist plots in these works. Hunting and masculine collaboration are integral parts of Mowgli's training in the jungle, but the "unnaturalness" of masculinizing a character is also integral, not only in Kipling's work but in Grahame's as well. Mowgli, Toad, and Rat are all characters who must suffer in the regulation of their behaviors and personalities to benefit the "common good." In Kipling's ethos the ends may justify the means, as Kucich claims, "Kipling ... frequently suggested that the most profound knowledge of all is the knowledge of cruelty and suffering. Many of his characters are gripped by melancholic convictions about the inevitability of suffering, which is the principal yield of their hard-won knowledge" (52). The problem is that the "ends" are boys/males who must live with their experience and knowledge in a curbed and regulated masculinity that doesn't understand itself.

A major differentiation among representations of masculinity is the pursuit of "common good" in the homoerotic/homosocial couples in Wilde's "The Happy Prince" and "The Selfish Giant." In these two stories, Christ figures lure other male characters into transformations that challenge their individual adventure schemes (swallow) and capitalist separation from society (Selfish Giant). Both of these collaborations stand in marked contrast to the individualist schemes of Wilde's other solipsistic characters (the Remarkable Rocket, the student in "The Nightingale and the Rose," and the Star-Child). Wilde's critique of bourgeois Christianity and self-concerned Victorian masculinity centered around accumulation are challenged by these same-sex couplings.

While Grahame and Milne were certainly influenced by Wilde and his same-sex characterizations — a reflection of the "bachelor" culture that pervaded the changing face of masculinity — they return to group censures and regulated behaviors to keep (or try to keep) the societal norms in place. In Grahame's case, it is a riverbank without revolution but wide latitude for male characters in male congregations. In Milne's case, idealized masculine representations removed, like Grahame's setting from the intrusion of marriage plots and feminine influenced, dominate the episodes of *Winnie the Pooh*, even if we read the novel with a feminist lens.

And though we may read Potter's works with an eye towards a return to and confirmation of heterosexual marriage, she combines the feminist influence of the Edwardian Era with an inclusivity for masculine participation in these unions. Potter's Hunca Munca, Anna Maria, and Goody Tiptoes all participate in unions that have separate spheres and collaboration: a fluidity in sharing and provision unseen in Wilde, Grahame, and Milne. Though Potter's stories don't seek to further marriage plots, they do set out parameters and warnings for the female reader as to the dangers in ill-considered unions (Jemima Puddle-duck).

As males collaborate with each other, we can tease out aspects of hegemony, subordination, complicity, and marginalization. The social organization of predominantly male communities (The Jungle, The Riverbank, The Hundred Acre Wood) make the varying positions of hierarchy and the actions of males in collaboration highly visible and rendered not only against femininity, but against class and hierarchy. Denunciations of collaborations abound, certainly in children's works, where the individual in pursuit of understanding, knowledge, or experience must go beyond a group or another individual in search of a goal. In this study, Mowgli, Toad, Rat, Peter Rabbit, the Star-Child, and others learn that groups, teams, families are to be avoided or, more surreptitiously, used in the pursuit of individual desires. Certainly Rabbit tries to use the group to steal Roo, Mowgli uses the group to enact his revenge scheme, and Toad can't retake Toad Hall without a group squad of "gentry" to help him. Toad illustrates, on different occasions, his use of others in collaboration where individual gains outweigh true collaborations. Edwardian gentleman, like Toad in *The Wind in the Willows* and the fox in *The Tale of Jemima Puddle-Duck*, will engage in collaborations only if it furthers that character's individual desires (particularly the use of women with these two characters). Toad uses the Gaoler's daughter to escape jail (along with a helping of maternal comfort), steals clothes from the bargewoman, trades her horse for food and sustenance, and even attempts to re-steal the car that landed him in prison in the first place. And we can't forget how he dupes his own friends with his feigned sickness, pleas for forgiveness, and mock-humility. This is the character that Grahame tries to corral by the end of the novel, into a group order Toad doesn't respect. But, if there is one representation that these authors all portray, it is the problems with males collaborating with males. In play, they learn to imitate animal calls (Mowgli), picnic and recite poetry (Mole and Rat), play with children in the garden (Selfish Giant), go on mis-adventures in the forest (Pooh and Piglet), and lose their clothes in mock battles with their sisters (Tom Kitten). When paired together, they incite and push each other to near-death experiences (Benjamin Bunny and Tom Kitten), torture and chastise "other" characters and nature (Star-Child, Toad, Mowgli), seek to suppress transformations and performances deemed unmanly (Kipling and Grahame), and isolate themselves in Arcadias (Milne).

CONCLUSION

The Hidden, the Subversive, the Traditional

When we consider the use of anthropomorphism, we have to contend with a long history of myth, religion, and fables. Whether we contend with the Ashanti use of Anasasi, the spider-trickster figure or monkey from the sixteenth-century Chinese author Wu Ch'eng-en, folk stories, fables, ghost stories, fairy tales, and fantasy have all made use of animal characters to teach lessons, to instruct readers on the nature of goddesses and gods, and to reflect the concerns of a particular culture in a particular time period. In British children's literature, the influence of John Locke is most pervasively seen in his recommendation of Aesop's fables and their ability to both delight and teach morals without the superstition or fantasy of fairy tales.

While "reason" may have trumped fantasy in the works of John Newberry (*A Little Pretty Pocketbook*, 1744, and *The History of Little Goody Two-Shoes*, 1765), the late eighteenth century and the "instructional" mode of writers like Sarah Trimmer (*An Easy Introduction to the Knowledge of Nature, and Reading the Holy Scriptures, Adapted to the Capacities of Children*, 1770) and Anna Letitia Barbauld (*Lessons for Children*, 1778–1779) were co-opted into the fantastical settings and characters of William Roscoe (*The Butterfly's Ball and the Grasshopper's Feast*, 1807), Lewis Carroll (Alice in Wonderland, 1865), and Charles Kingsley (*The Water Babies, a Fairy Tale for a Land Baby*, 1863). Didacticism fell out of favor, whether it be from the influence of the Romantic Era writers or the Victorian fascination with childhood. Anthropomorphism became less a vehicle of overt instruction and more of a imaginative engagement with the world where critiques of society could be subversively embedded.

In terms of sexuality, studies in psychology and sexology became more ubiquitous, not just in England but in Europe as a whole. The nineteenth century saw the works of von Krafft-Ebing (*Psychopathia Sexualis*,

Conclusion

1886), Havelock Ellis (*Sexual Inversion*, 1897), and a host of others. As sexologists sought to classify or pathologize sexuality, other thinkers, such as Herbert Spencer, sought to use Darwin's work to link primitive human nature to sexual instinct, directly establishing a relationship between science and patriarchy; hierarchy had a new tool that can be adopted for legitimizing patriarchy, social policy, and control. As Joseph Bristow has asserted, "Since early sexology often leant heavily on medical science, it had a marked tendency to codify certain sexual behaviors as categories of disease" (6).

Taken with sexology, the "fitness" of male Britons became an obsession that sprouted from the mid–1880s' scandals (1884 Dublin Castle expose, 1889 Cleveland Street Scandal) through Wilde's 1895 trial, where sexuality comes "out of the closet," into the media and popular culture. The reading public ingested this cultural landscape and "generally harboured anxieties about poverty and crime, about public health and national and imperial fitness, about decadent artists, 'new woman' and homosexuals. This loose assemblage of beliefs can be marked out as 'degenerationism'" (Greenslade 2). It is this background of "unfitness" and anxiety over how males were not ready to imperially rule the colonies that enters into popular opinion, particularly with rebellions in India, Ireland, and South Africa.

The "degeneration" of males was a launching point for Baden-Powell's Scouting Movement, but even this movement can't be lumped in with the common myths of middle-class anxiety. Baden-Powell was no "jingoist and disliked aggressive displays of national prowess. He did not want European war and was sickened by the consequent slaughter" (Pryke, 318). But it is as if the debates and anxieties over masculinity dictated a course towards war. Anne Windholz summarizes the chronology of both philosophical masculinity and its intersections with political change:

> Young men who came of age in England at the end of the nineteenth century did so as the very nature of masculinity was being contested in social, economic and sexual arenas. The ideals of British masculinity with which many of these youths grew up, traceable to the "muscular Christianity" of Thomas Arnold and Charles Kingsley decades before, were tested and challenged, redefined or reinforced, against backdrops at least superficially disparate: against the cultural boundaries being extended in a continental bohemia by the Aesthetes and Decadents, and against the Imperial boundaries being defined and defended across the globe by the soldiers and

adventurers of Victoria's Empire.... While the Decadent movement challenged entrenched gender norms and sexual prejudices in the realm of high culture, the literature of empire more fully permeated fin-de-siècle popular culture, not least as an antidote to the degeneracy perceived as threatening British manhood and, by extension, nationhood. Imperial masculinity captured the imagination of the public and was promulgated in the rhetoric of politics, literature, and even science. British manhood would bring civilization to the hinterlands of the world; in turn, the hinterlands of the world would save British manhood from civilization [631].

To blame all anxiety over the roles of males on Imperialism is philosophically simple-minded: the Industrial Revolution, changes in technology, increasing world cultural awareness, the extensive work and agitation of women in pursuit of the vote and in terms of improving women's legal rights, and workers' strikes all had been hugely influential in defining "maleness," as did research in sociology, sexuality, and psychology; the study of economics and class; and developments and debates in theology. Even children's literature was influenced by and contributed to the renegotiation of what it means to be male. It is no wonder that natural and Edenic settings figure largely in the tales I've examined because these authors could use animals and act out the anxieties they read about daily, sometimes even experienced firsthand.

In terms of literary masculinity, Claudia Nelson has argued that feminization of mid-eighteenth century masculinity occurred in conversations on masturbation, marriage, and spirituality. She sees a change in nineteenth-century literary expressions of gender:

> No longer is sexuality generally judged as male/strong/regrettable against an asexuality that is female/weak/laudable; by the end of the century the usual pattern is natural/heterosexual/good versus unnatural/homosexual/despicable. With this shift in definitions, the sissy becomes suspect and "androgynous manliness" turns into an oxymoron [546].

We see androgynous heroes in *Tom Brown's School Days* or *The Water Babies*. We can see the imperial masculinity of Kipling or the providing Englishman of Potter as examples of Nelson's assertion. But as societal ideas of manliness changed — ideas of manliness were changing — paradoxes and ironies abound in the confusion of these changes as evidenced in the writings of Wilde, Grahame and Milne. These writers demonstrated visions of sexuality that may still have privileged the representation of male heroes, replete with misogyny and avoidance of females, but they argue with the discourse of earlier writers, especially in the adventure story tradition.

Even when the emergence and continuation of all-male brotherhoods is considered, anxiety over how to express oneself, as a male, combined with culture:

> To become a man, the male must move from the homosocial, diffusely homoerotic world of adolescence into the adult world of compulsory heterosexuality.... In literature, this problematic of bourgeoise masculinity is played out in the conflict between the masculine plot and the marriage plot, in the ambiguity in Marryat between a vigorous life at sea and a land-locked life in marriage ... and ... the tension in the closure of *In Memoriam*, between the vision of a male marriage in heaven and an epithalamium for a heterosexual marriage on earth [Sussman 143].

To say literary masculinity is complex is an understatement, but to say that it demonstrates a variety of anxieties over a variety of influences seems quite reasonable. For this reason, it will be quite beneficial to reunite the categories of the chapters into the authors whose representations of masculinity prove such a rich picture of the struggle for identity.

Wilde

Oscar Wilde's use of Hans Christian Andersen's "The Little Mermaid," "The Shadow," and " The Nightingale" (among others), demonstrates the lingering influence of both fairy tales and the romantic imagination. Wilde's vision can be dark and optimistic, sacred and profane, liberating and constrictive. And his construction of masculinity through the use of animals mirrors this vision.

In Wilde's works for children, we read elements of the adventure story tradition (violence, adventure), particularly in the exoticism of landscapes, which he uses in "The Fisherman and His Soul" and "The Star-Child." Wilde uses off-screen violence in "The Fisherman and His Soul" to mythologize masculinity as the Soul recounts his adventures, as well as aestheticizes violence in "The Star-Child." Violence sustains hierarchies in Wilde's stories, hierarchies he largely undoes by the end of the stories. In many instances, Wilde carries on the tradition of violence we read in the Grimm brothers and in Hans Christian Andersen's stories. While Wilde does gothocize stories with the use of violence and doubles, he also ends stories with morals that reject such violence.

Wilde uses the epic, myth-creating tradition of storytelling or narration of off-screen adventures to both build character and engage in the commercially successful plot developments we find in the adventure story tradition. However, unlike Kenneth Grahame and Beatrix Potter, Wilde doesn't script escape plots. And while this may highlight how Edwardian masculinity sought a general escape from femininity or the feminine influence, it also reveals nuances in Wilde's transcriptions of the fairy tale and folktale traditions; Wilde plots his masculine characters, like his life, as if they must embrace their destiny. Wilde also reworks the adventure story tradition with pathos and emotional vulnerability.

Perhaps the most unusual aspect to Wilde's characterization of masculinity is his merging of pagan and Christian motifs and symbols. We witness a beautiful and beneficial paganism in the dwarf character from "The Birthday of the Infanta." Wilde, as he does in most of his stories, characterizes or animates flowers, trees, and other nonhuman characters to occupy a world, with emotional and spiritual significance, with humans. The pagan descriptions of the krakens and undersea setting of "The Fisherman and His Soul" provide an example of Wilde's penchant for folkloric settings and characters. What the child reader may see is that masculinity can be tied to artistic production — in song or in description. A dilemma arises in Wilde's work between paganism and Christianity: the same dilemma faced in Ireland as hegemonic culture sought to erase the "primitive" culture and its rituals and displays. Wilde's father was an ardent folklorist and his mother a strong supporter of the "Irish cause," and this is reflected in his work.

While Wilde critiques the church in his works for children, he does not minimize the volatility of paganism. Even landscapes are anthropomorphosized as evil and vindictive, though still rooted in the fairy tale tradition as much as a critique of masculinity, which needs a corrective force for regulation.

Wilde's creation of an "aesthetic masculinity" is a model we see critiqued, curtailed, and resurrected in the other authors in this study. One of the dangers of this aesthetic masculinity is the element of pederasty we find in stories like "The Happy Prince" and "The Selfish Giant." This "aesthetic masculinity," as it is expressed in Wilde's characterizations is more modern and self-aware, more self-reflexive than writers like Kingsley and even Carroll created. We can contrast the flatness and contained nature of Alice with the self-reflexivity of the swallow and see how "modern" a writer Wilde really was.

If we consider aestheticism as an expression of political and artistic philosophy as inherited from the Enlightenment Era, then we can see how Wilde's critique of mid–Victorian, Evangelical masculinity both mirrors changes in theological England as well as read a Catholic sensibility to his work. Iconography, description, ritual and performance all find a place in his stories. In terms of the representation of masculinity, Wilde mocks priests, soldiery, town fathers, narcissistic masculinity, capitalism, knowledge and practicality as he posits "true" Christian morality next to bourgeois Christianity.

In this way, Wilde reorganizes masculine desire into a moral, Christian framework, as well as demonstrates that community and companionship are preferred over isolation. The sacrifice of characters such as the Happy Prince and the boy in "The Selfish Giant," recall the reputation of manliness more aligned with common good than individual gain. Clifton Snider has posited that Wilde combined Eros (feminine principle espoused by Jung to be the "principle of connection") with Logos (masculine "principle of knowledge"). In this way, he sees the Selfish Giant's garden as an image of Eros where children play and the Selfish Giant reconfigures his masculinity from his authoritarian, controlling self (Snider). Several of Wilde's stories demonstrate this cycle of transformation, reinvesting masculinity with Christian morals and frameworks.

Finally, there is a variety of representations of masculinity in Wilde's work where we witness instability. Individualism and exceptionalism are still evident though hierarchy is so often challenged. Patriarchy, masculine privilege, and authority, in general, are rich sources of satire on competitiveness and independence for Wilde. Though we may consider the tales framed in the aesthetic need for individuality, the need or desire that masculine characters have for an audience makes masculinity, even Wilde's, tied to reputation and performance: two very unstable qualities in Wilde's scripting of manliness in these stories.

Kipling

Kipling certainly had his ties to the adventure story tradition, but when we read *The Jungle Book*, adventure is sublimated in favor of training because that is what this novel is: a story of training and how to masculinize a character into the "order" of things (or the Law of the Jungle, if you will). Like Wilde, Kipling doesn't highlight an escape plot in the novel; characters must face their destinies and the costs associated with imperial masculinity or manliness in the frontiers of the British Empire, absorbing masculine culture of other societies but ultimately imposing class-conscious, race-conscious patriarchy.

Kipling appreciates rebellion in many of his literary works, from *Kim* to "The Man Who Would Be King." We see this in how Raksha keeps out the invading Shere Khan in the beginning of *The Jungle Book*. We can see the class rebellion by the monkeys as elements of the carnivalesque in the novel, but the use of violence to eliminate them demonstrates, ultimately, that Kipling sought to portray Imperial masculinity as the way of manliness for the Englishman abroad.

Kipling also uses violence as a corrective force, particularly on Mowgli, as he is trained. But he also uses violence to enforce group norms and to establish hierarchy. But Kipling's violence is conditional and unstable: as a tool for education it is questioned by Bagheera (concerned over the corporal punishment used by Baloo) just before the monkeys are slaughtered by Kaa in front of Mowgli.

Kipling's worldview is complex, more along the lines of Wilde's blurring pagan and Christian sensibilities. Kipling's lifelong interest in the Free Masons reveals an appreciation for multivalent brotherhood, realized in *The Jungle Book* through characters like Kaa, Baloo, Bagheera and Akela. Kipling can critique both aesthetic play and deviant masculinity through the brotherhood of these characters in their mission to masculinize Mowgli. Despite Kipling's respect for Islam and Hinduism, he is aware of his Victorian Christian audience and links spirituality to control and order in the novel.

Even when Kipling critiques Hinduism, as he does through the behaviors of the Wolf Pack and the descriptions and characterizations of the villagers, we can see that masculinity is more concerned with connections between other men than it is with women and "othered" characters. But we see how this aspect of masculinity is unstable. Fraternity doesn't hold in the story, and the imperial masculine character is always in dis-ease, flirting between embracing more simplistic, traditional notions of manliness seen in cultures that challenge decadent, urban masculinity of the late Victorian age.

Conclusion

Kipling, like Wilde, also uses elements of gothic doubling in Shere Khan and Mowgli—both characters are outsiders, both outcasts, both cruel, both without honor in their killings. Interestingly, both characters are characterized in body and body reactions. Shere Khan, or "lungri" (lame one), is characterized as deviant from birth, while Mowgli's body, and its power, is linked to his ability to stare, which both separates him from the other characters of the novel, as well as reminds us he has a soul. Bodies act as a source for reputation in the novel: Kaa, Bagheera, and Shere Khan all are rendered by Kipling as containing power through their bodies, capable of death for "lesser" characters. Ironically, Kipling scripts Baloo as a maternal character through a gender-blurring role as mother to wolf cubs, and Raksha as bodily violent and masculine in her threats to Shere Khan in the beginning of the story.

Like Wilde, Kipling composed through dialectics and oppositions. We see this in how he uses reputation in the novel as it is positioned next to masculinity. Mowgli is given a front row seat to problems with disruptive influences on the development of his masculinity and maintenance of group norms when Baloo, Bagheera, and Kaa first censor then exterminate the monkeys. The power of reputation to curb individual masculine desire is quite evident: Mowgli must fall in line, and he does. But, posited right next to this scene, is Baloo's rejection of jungle society and its consideration of his reputation should they catch him upset, crying and disrupted, at the departure of Mowgli.

Kipling obviously prefers hierarchy in *The Jungle Book*, even with the mini-rebellions that emerge. We see how the hierarchy works well, even positioning the Wolf Pack as dangerous in its "mob mentality" without a "natural" aristocrat like Akela. But even that mode of hierarchy is unstable by the book's end. Because males can transform, as in Mowgli's case, they are doomed to repeat the cycle of violence and battle over hierarchy, even if they are in positions of Imperial leadership.

Power is fluid and unstable in the novel; there is a law, but it only works for a few characters. As much as Kipling makes language and law centerpieces to his Jungle Law, characters are made masculine in how they inscribe and become inscribed by either violence or in social relations. In many ways, we could read Mowgli's development as Kipling's demonstration of how a child's need to be "broken" from individual growth to fit the needs of society.

The Hidden, the Subversive, the Traditional: ... from Wilde to Potter

One way a character becomes masculinized in the novel is in social relations, particularly, in hunting. Kipling depicts hunting as glorious, almost epic in scope, but we learn early on that in the Wolf Pack, it is a collaboration with different individuals fulfilling different needs. Even Baloo and Bagheera are collaborating in Mowgli's ascendancy, though we could reckon this development in terms of continuing patriarchy. And, like Wilde, masculinizing requires an audience, whether they must witness the gender-bending dance of Kaa or the delivering of Shere Khan's hide by Mowgli.

Potter

Even when we read Potter's first story, *The Tale of Peter Rabbit*, we can witness a critique of masculinity as it is tied to the adventure plot. The mythologized father is illustrated as dead and in a pie, a foreshadowing of what adventure plots have in store for males. Paired with the rambling of Lucie In *The Tale of Mrs. Tiggy-Winkle*, the adventure story or plot is critiqued by Potter when males enter into it.

In many ways, Potter, like Grahame, scripts masculinity as escaping domesticity. The escape of Peter Rabbit, Jemima Puddle-duck, particularly framed with leaving the domestic home, is punished by Potter. One aspect of escape as a performance of masculinity is the noticeable absence of fathers: Peter Rabbit and Tom Kitten both have to navigate their masculinity as it intersects with domesticity. Both attempt to escape with disastrous results and psychologically traumatic illustrations afterwards.

Potter may be the author who most uses violence in this study. Much of this sentiment had connections with her careful observations of the natural world where birth, violence and death dominate the life cycle of animals. Violence, as in Kipling's work, is used as a corrective force (Peter Rabbit, Benjamin Bunny, Squirrel Nutkin, Jemima Puddle-duck, Jeremy Fisher), but violence is also linked to the female's progression in the farmyard. Potter scripts violence as a tool for mothers and even has them perform in transgressive ways when we consider their reputations as killers (Moppet and Mittens) and their boasts (Tabitha Twitchit) of violence used.

Potter also uses violence to penalize male characters who are suspect,

Conclusion

demonstrating a common aversion to "city" masculinity and its links to aestheticism and decadence. Jeremy Fisher and the fox, in *The Tale of Jemima Puddle-Duck*, demonstrate a suspicious masculinity, whether it is dandified bachelorhood (Jeremy Fisher) or having a predatory and urban disposition (the fox).

Potter also employs characterizations of violence in a class-biased manner. The chipmunks, Chippy Hackee and his wife are characterized as violent next to Timmy and Goody Tiptoes, who avoid violence and act as middle-class, burgeoning parents next to the smaller, less "accepted," childless Hackee couple.

We also find trickster figures and rebellion in Potter's work. Squirrel Nutkin resists the patriarchy of Old Mr. Brown, the owl, seeking an audience with his songs and taunts of the old patriarch who receives sacrifices from the other squirrels for their nut gathering on his island. But the truly subversive (and productive) rebellion occurs in *The Tale of Two Bad Mice*, where the dollhouse becomes a stage for the collaborative union of Hunca Munca and Tom Thumb. In a dollhouse, they wreak havoc on the play food and beds, using what they can for their own family, reveling in anger and desire, collectively. This is one of the central lessons of masculinity in Potter's stories: individualist adventures are punished, while collaborations that reinforce home and family are rewarded.

Potter critiques males when they collaborate with each other, with no feminine part to their union: Ginger and Pickles, Peter and Benjamin. She also critiques males who fail to perform as providers: Benjamin in *The Tale of the Flopsy Bunnies* and the ill-equipped bachelor, Jeremy Fisher, who misperforms masculinity in his fishing episode.

Potter has no trouble criticizing hierarchy. In *The Tale of Ginger and Pickles*, both the principal characters, leaders in the community, lose their store due to bad business practices. But Potter also critiques the patriarch, Mr. John Dormouse who stays in bed while his wife and daughter sell faulty merchandise: "not the way to carry on a retail business" (Potter, 221).

This critique of hierarchy is linked to Potter's code of heterosexual behavior in the countryside settings of her stories. Provision and partnership with female agency assured, even in anger and play, is rewarded and supported by Potter's characterizations. Her vision of masculinity punishes and "breaks" characters (much like Kipling's), demonstrating that masculinity is a performance that needs constriction of individualist desires running wild.

Stylistically, Potter's prose is unembellished and uncrowded with overly ornate language. Humphrey Carpenter has asserted that Potter's "deliberately flat, unemotional narrative voice" (297) was a guiding influence on twentieth-century writers like Grahame Greene and Evelyn Waugh. And this works in how she, without pity or judgmental tone, characterizes masculine excess and the corrective violence she uses.

Grahame

In Grahame's novel, the influence of the adventure story is evident in both the Sea Rat's stories that seek to entice the Water-Rat to give up his life of rural ease. But the mythologizing of maleness as the characters retake Toad Hall is both critiqued (the chapter is entitled, "The Return of Ulysses") and supported (they are firmly in control of the countryside by novel's end). Grahame is a master of both criticizing and writing to the expectations of the middle-class reading audience, which may account for this ironic ending.

Like Potter, Grahame scripts escapist tendencies in his masculinization processes. Mole escapes domesticity, only to return to it. Rat seeks to escape his "narrow life," only to return to it. Toad seeks to escape his class and expectations of a rural gentleman, only to be put back in power by novel's end. But all three characters escape marriage and female influence on their curious domesticity. In Mole and Rat's case, their escape of domesticity is an embrace of same-sex companionship.

Violence and the threat of violence are seen in both Toad's speech and his actions. Violence is promised by Badger and Otter when they talk about the "othered" characters in the novel such as the rabbits or stoats or weasels. Most noticeably is the violence of the stoats and weasels in their taking of Toad Hall and the seemingly justified use of violence when the principal characters retake the home. While Grahame may have fictionalized his story, the assassination plot he foiled in 1903 at the Bank of England, seems to indicate that a distrust of socialism and working-class mobs lingered for him.

Influenced no doubt by Wilde and Kingsley, Grahame's inclusion of

Conclusion

Pan in the novel has prompted much speculation. But the lure of paganism, in terms of how a character becomes manly, is paradoxical: Rat is at once possessed and maddened. Mole and Rat both demonstrate, in bowed heads and hushed tones, their subservience and spiritual rapture, but it is a curious rapture. On one had, it demonstrates that hierarchy still dominates masculinity, spiritually speaking, as the male Pan is the dominant deity in the novel. But the pagan vision is fleeting, contained: Pan doesn't speak, the whole scene is captured in a song (created by nature, not Rat or Mole), and the characters forget the episode. While some critics see this as Grahame capitulating to a middle-class readership (Moore), I see this as a true rendering of art for art's sake, more liberating than the legacy of Christian sacrifice (seen in Wilde) and a revival of aestheticism that contrasts with the militaristic, adventurist characterizations of masculinity in Kipling and the utilitarian representations of masculinity in Potter.

But, as with much of Grahame's plotting (as in Wilde's work), paradoxes and contradictions abound. Toad claims to need a "salon" and has been seen as a stand-in for Wilde (Knoepflmacher, Gauger, Lerer). But Toad allows for Grahame to critique aestheticism, more directly, and dandyism — not the poetics of the writing style or philosophy but the overly enthusiastic embrace of the public dimensions of fame. Toad also allows Grahame to critique modernism and industrialization in the caravanning episode as well as when Toad takes to the automobile. Though, it must be remembered, that Grahame does conditionally embrace Toad's metafictionality and self-reflexivity when the narrator asks the readers about the value of good storytelling.

And while the novel is devoid of Christianity, the vision of aesthetic brotherhood abounds, particularly in the partnership of Mole and Rat as well as the spirituality that is centered on companionship and not adventure and solipsistic masculinity. While this brotherhood is transgressive, as it was in the Victorian Era, the "squierarchy" wasn't and reflects either Grahame's capitulation to the audience and publishing market or a belief in the collectivity of gentry masculinity. Either way, it is unstable because the reinstatement of Toad into his home is clumsy and hastened.

The code of gentry masculinity is also contained in the legal systems and codes, which convicts Toad, yet allows him to escape and continue in aristocratic privilege. While codes of heteronormativity were changing in the Edwardian Era (but not the behaviors as exhibited by the egotistical and competitive Toad), the challenge to marriage and heterosexual unions by Grahame continues the same-sex unions we witnessed in Wilde's stories.

Perhaps one of the greatest pressures in Grahame's novel on masculinity is group censure. The group halts the rebellion of both Toad and the stoats and weasels. But group censure, as a system of hierarchy and privilege witnessed in Badger, also halts Mole's development in the story and produces a compromise in his character mid-novel. Group norming, in Grahame's novel, needs an "other," whether it is the stoats and weasels (Peter Green identifies them as representatives of mob mentality) or the bargewoman, for the values and privilege of middle-class masculinity to be reinscribed. But this group censure is painful and problematic, even as transformation and punishment are painful in Wilde, Kipling, and Potter's works. This demonstrates that each of these writers seems aware of the psychological aspects of masculinizing a character. But for Grahame, as he plots an Arcadian fantasy, the direct relationship of punishment and corrective that exists in, say, a fairy tale, is made more visible as the characters express reservations in the course of their censure (Rat, Toad).

Milne

Milne's novel could be considered as continuing the adventure story tradition, but only in a localized manner and without the exoticism, nationalism, and heavily masculinized subplots of earlier writers. He does use the body for inscription for characters, particularly Piglet, whose insecurities and size, render him a target for sentimental concern. But the episodes of the novel, even the adventurist impulse-laden ones, end with returns to homes or friends.

Milne critiques heroic masculinity through the frequent misperformances of hunting and "expotitions," demonstrating that the collaboration is more important than individual gain or exploitation of others. In this vein, we may read Pooh's self-aggrandizement quite differently than a character like Toad's: less harmful and less exploitative. The lack of violence in the novel, as a whole, reflects both Milne's life experiences and a war-weary British public. In this manner, the adventure story, as it was modified by Richard Jeffries' 1882 novel *Bevis*, continues to be modified by Milne and subsequently by Mary Norton, Richard Adams, and others.

Conclusion

We can see the influence of theater and Milne's dramatic writing in his prose style of the novel. The self-reflexivity of characters like Pooh, Piglet, and Eeyore are in marked contrast to characterizations of Christopher Robin, arguably more adult. This is but one characteristic of literary modernist techniques in the text (avoidance of teleology, free indirect speech, irony, punning). And Milne seems to write in a tradition of nonsense inherited from Carroll and Lear, with innocence as a camouflage for secular humanism. While a character like Eeyore critiques the "song and dance" of Pooh, Milne's novel reveals a less burdened aestheticism than Grahame's, and a lack of religious and socio-political control systems.

Similar to the other authors mentioned, Milne does include the use of the body and reputation, though it might be overshadowed by the humor. Pooh and Roo's delight in jumping, Piglet's traumatic scrubbing and forced medicine demonstrate that the body can be a source of both pleasure and pain in the construction of masculinity. Pooh also demonstrates, like Toad, that fulfilling masculine desire is more bodily constructed in Milne, and that boyishness is often physical and individualistic.

Milne's novel is the work most absent of law or a regulatory system. This allows for the play and discovery themes to emerge in contradiction to the importance of hierarchy, rules, and control we witness in the other authors I've studied.[1] Milne critiques hierarchy and its falseness: in the xenophobia of the more adult Rabbit, in the blundering faux-intellectual Owl, and in the supposed authority of Christopher Robin. If there is a code or system at work in the novel, it would be egotism and individuality. In this logic system, lying, embellishment, hiding a lack of knowledge, and following individual instinct are offered instead of gentry masculinity, Jungle Law, rural domesticity, and aesthetic elitism. Egotism emerges as a counter to collectivizing forces and the hierarchy that attends such constrictive systems.

Consistently, Milne posits a masculine need for audience in establishing identity. Pooh's need for audience runs from songs/poems performed for himself to songs/poems intended for the group. Roo's need for audience includes not only his mother, but the other male characters when he "swims" in the "Expotition to the North Pole" episode. Even Eeyore reflects a need for attention, though he condemns it in others. In this way, Milne demonstrates a variety of motivations for attention, but that the masculine need for attention in proving maleness is still evident.

While not as psychologically scripted as the homosocial and homoerotic unions in Wilde and Grahame, Milne's collaboration of Pooh and Piglet is a continuation of the earlier authors pairings. Milne removes the stain of homosexuality through homosocial behavior, as well as sanitizes their union through humor. Milne's couple, the forest in general, avoids the "burdens" of marriage and feminine influence through characterizations and the sublimation of Kanga, the only female in the forest.

Finally, Milne does provide group censure in his novel. It occurs in the way characters treat the rabbit and his relations in two separate episodes of the novel: the "Expotition to the North Pole" chapter and the "We Say Good-bye" chapter. In this manner, we might see how Grahame's disdain for the stoats and weasels emerges in the lower class relations of Rabbit as they are critiqued and characterized. But Milne is also careful to have the group not censure individuals and their misperformances, as we witness Eeyore and his speech at the good-bye party where characters realize the present Christopher Robin intends to give is not for Eeyore.

In many ways, we can read Milne as a product of all of these writers. He contests Victorian values and traditional representations of manhood, inherits the landscapes of Potter and Grahame, rejects the violence of Kipling and Potter, and continues the tradition of bachelor and homosocial manhood seen in Wilde and Grahame. I have tried in this book to present many of the dilemmas and plots of these narratives presented for male (and female characters) as they struggle, play, and suffer in the course of their respective developments. Uniting all these stories is the development of their central characters — a major concern for most writers of children's literature. One aspect of that development is how to make a boy a man or how to perform, represent, and critique modes of societal expectations of masculinity. Despite nonhuman and quasi-human exteriors, British children seem to lurk underneath the skins of the characters in Wilde, Kipling, Potter, Grahame, and Milne's works. The pleasures they enjoy, the pain they suffer, the confusion they exhibit, and the wonder they revel in tell us about a multi-faceted masculinity and forces on masculinity in the late Victorian, Edwardian, and early Georgian Britain.

Chapter Notes

Preface

1. In the Victorian era, muscular Christianity continued the idea of a physical manliness combined with an Evangelical belief in carrying out Christianity: at home or in the empire. In many ways, Wilde's characters could be said to inherit this tradition, even in anthropomorphic guise.
2. See Ellman and Killeen for Wilde's early experiences with Irish paganism.

Chapter One

1. Grahame had only recently left the city to move to the country and was living in an ill-conceived marriage, which suggests there is autobiographical influence in these conflicts that Mole and Rat suffer (see Green).
2. The Fisherman dies at the end of *The Fisherman and His Soul*, reunited with his Soul, but broken hearted and suicidal. Rat's psychological malaise is only broken by Mole's care and Rat's reunion with his writing.
3. More on the masculine need for audience and its relationship with performativity is covered in Chapter Four: "Collaboration, Compromise, Group Performances."
4. These escapist fantasies are evident in Mole's and Rat's sections of the narrative as they escape home (Mole) and into fantastical life (Rat).
5. Certainly the absence of father figures dominates *The Wind in the Willows*, framed more acutely by the emergence of and eventual control of Badger as hierarchal head of the River Bank. But this analysis of Potter posits more specific "child" characters as being without fathers.
6. His cousin Benjamin has to learn twice about the dangers of the human world: as a father, Benjamin lets Flopsy's bunnies eat and sleep next to McGregor's garden. Not as a result of an escapist fantasy, but just being a bad parent. Males rarely come off that well in Potter's work, specifically when they act without a female.
7. In fact, we come upon Peter again in post-traumatic condition as the beginning of *The Tale of Benjamin Bunny*.
8. Toad can't wash his clothes, and rather than learn, he gives in to his boyish impulsivity and mocks the bargewoman, steals her horse, and continues his escape. Grahame might even be said to condemn Toad's behavior as Toad is made to apologize and make restitution to the bargewoman at the end of the novel.
9. While I can find no evidence that Milne modeled this episode after Potter's story, suspicion lingers about the association between invading honey eaters into domestic spaces maintained by fastidious owners.
10. I examine the monkey's "aestheticism" and this form of rebellion later in my work.
11. Perhaps this is where Kipling remembered he was writing for children.

12. The essentially conservative Potter may give the best examples of transgressive performances of the authors I examine. But often a female performs transgressively, then reverts under social pressure (or through violence enacted by a male) to more heteronormative postures of femininity. In *The Roly-Poly Pudding*, Moppet and Mittens begin in normed depiction watching muffins baking: "They patted it [the rising dough] with their soft little paws — 'Shall we make dear little muffins?'" (177). They foreshadow what may happen to Tom and paradoxically what their "soft little paws" will be used for at the end of the story.

13. Potter's violence is scary because of the implications it has with motherhood. Jemima is allowed to hatch her own eggs though problematically: "Jemima Puddle-duck said that it was because of her nerves, but she had always been a bad sitter" (172). The problem is that Jemima didn't have problems with eggs surviving before. Potter seems to have punished her gullibility with the fox and for her precocious, individualist performance in the story.

Chapter Two

1. Thwaite chronicles the relationship with Barrie that Milne cultivated, as well as several instances where his work is compared with Wilde's.

2. Greek mythology in the case of *The Fisherman and His Soul*.

3. Though misperformance of masculinity is visible in Peter and Benjamin's adventure and in Pickles and Ginger's business practices in *The Tale of Ginger and Pickles*.

4. See Gillin, Richard. "Romantic Echoes in the Willows." *Children's Literature* 16 (1988): 169–75.

5. Later in this book, I demonstrate how group/heteronormative censure proves most heavy on Rat's identity as an artist/aesthete.

6. I don't include *The Tailor of Gloucester* in this part of my analysis because that story celebrates the tailor and his beautiful clothes, not the same motivation and philosophy behind "aesthetic" dress.

7. Kingsley's fairy does go on to say, "Whatever their ancestors were, men they are" (198). While Kingsley (1885) incorporates Darwin into his novel, Kipling (1894) could be critiquing India as much as he is critiquing "effeminate Englishness" in the more Darwinian landscape of Kipling's jungle.

8. This is not to say that Potter wasn't concerned with language, but her aims were less expressive than moral and, in terms of asserting feminine power, transgressive.

Chapter Three

1. Though I would contend that Rat's knowledge of River Bank history is similar to Badger's in how it expresses a logic of colonialism and class, Rat's knowledge and appreciation of Pan, artistic effusion, and individualism serves as a foil to a united identity and power system for much of the novel.

Chapter Four

1. One notable exception seems to be Toad in *The Wind in the Willows* and Pooh in *Winnie the Pooh*. Both of these characters perform, theatrically or otherwise, for themselves as often as they do for others.

2. This could certainly be where Milne could be criticized: that his use of Pooh's performances don't risk as much, in terms of humor, as Wilde's and Grahame's character and type assassination do.

3. In *The Tale of Mrs. Tiggy-Winkle*, the title character serves as a model for Lucie in domestic economy (and as an unregulated female entrepreneur, without male interference). In this story, Lucie journeys into an understanding of a way to be female whereas journeys into becoming male are rarely rewarded in Potter's stories.

4. I am not saying that Milne was successful, but he does expand his plotting to include the aspect of children (Roo) and others (Tigger and Kanga) by their inclusion and involvement in the episodes of both novels.

5. Though Kanga is an adult and a mother, she not only participates in the humor, she dishes it out physically, verbally, and in the same nonsensical vein that permeates Milne's text. This is quite different from writers like Carroll, Burnett, and Nesbitt (to name few): Kanga fully participates in the humor, and with physicality.

6. Interestingly, Pooh finds the pole, but it is the collaboration with Kanga that makes the rescue possible in this chapter of the novel.

7. It may be remembered that Akela is challenged for leadership due to missing a kill. He was cheated by Shere Khan, so "naturally" (for the reader, not the wolves) Akela was still fit to lead.

8. See Chapter Two, Aesthetic Masculinity

Conclusion

1. Even Wilde's texts lead, often in a satirical and critical mode, towards what "society" expects.

Works Cited

Adams, James Eli. "'The Boundaries of Social Intercourse': Class in the Victorian Novel." *A Concise Companion to the Victorian Novel.* Ed. Francis O'Gorman. Oxford: Blackwell, 2005: 47–70.
———. *Dandies and Desert Saints: Styles of Victorian Masculinity.* Ithaca: Cornell University Press, 1995.
Allen, Warren. "Popular Manliness: Baden Powell, Scouting and the Development of Manly Character." *Manliness and Morality: Middle-Class Masculinity in Britain and America, 1800–1940.* Eds. J.A. Managan and James Walvin. Manchester: Manchester University Press, 1987. 199–219.
Altick, Richard D. *Victorian People and Ideas.* New York: Norton, 1973.
Bakhtin, Mikhail. *Rabelais and His World* [1941]. Trans. Hélène Iswolsky. Bloomington: Indiana University Press, 1993.
Bauer, Helen Pike. *Rudyard Kipling: A Study of the Short Fiction.* New York: Twayne, 1994.
Benson, Stephen. "Kipling's Singing Voice: Setting the Jungle Books." *Critical Survey* 13.3 (2001): 40–61.
Braudy, Leo. *From Chivalry to Terrorism: War and the Changing Nature of Masculinity.* New York: Knopf, 2003.
Bristow, Joseph. *Sexuality.* London: Routledge, 1997.
Butler, Judith. *Gender Trouble.* London: Routledge, 1990.
Carpenter, Humphrey. *Secret Gardens: A Study of the Gold Age of Children's Literature.* Boston: Houghton Mifflin, 1985.
Clark, Beverly Lyon, and Margaret R. Higonnet. *Girls, Boys, Books, Toys: Gender in Children's Literature and Culture.* Baltimore: Johns Hopkins University Press, 1999.
Connell, R.W. *Masculinities.* Berkeley: University of California Press, 2005.
Cosslett, Tess. "Child's Place in Nature: Talking Animals in Victorian Children's Fiction." *Nineteenth-Century Contexts* 23.4 (2001): 475–95.
Darcy, Jane. "The Representation of Nature in *The Wind in the Willows* and *The Secret Garden*." The Lion and the Unicorn 19 (1995): 211–222.
Das, Santanu. "'Kiss Me, Hardy'": Intimacy, Gender, and Gesture in World War I Trench Literature." *Modernism/Modernity* 9.1 (2002): 51–74.
Fox, Paul. "Other Maps Showing Through: The Liminal Identities of Neverland." *Children's Literature Association Quarterly* 32.1 (2007): 252–268.
Friedman, Ellen, and Jennifer Marshall. *Issues of Gender.* New York: Pearson, 2004.
Gauger, Annie. *The Annotated Wind in the Willows.* New York: Norton, 2009.
Gilead, Sarah. "The Undoing of Idyll in *The Wind in the Willows*." *Children's Literature* 16 (1988): 145–159.
Gillin, Richard. "Romantic Echoes in the Willows." *Children's Literature* 16 (1988): 169–175.

Works Cited

Grahame, Kenneth. *The Wind in the Willows*. New York: Tempo, 1966.
_____. *The Wind in the Willows: An Annotated Edition*. Ed. Seth Gauer. Cambridge: Harvard University Press, 2009.
Green, Peter. *Kenneth Grahame, 1859–1932: A Study of His Life, Work and Times*. London: John Murray, 1959.
Greenslade, William. *Degeneration, Culture and the Novel 1880–1940*. Cambridge: Cambridge University Press, 1994.
Grinstein, Alexander. *The Remarkable Beatrix Potter*. Madison, CT: International Universities Press, 1995.
Hinojosa, Ramon. "Doing Hegemony: Military, Men, and Constructing a Hegemonic Masculinity." *The Journal of Men's Studies* 18.2 (2010): 179–194.
Hollindale, Peter. "Aesop in the Shadows." *Signal: Approaches to Children's Books* (1999): 115–32.
Hunt, Karen. "'Strong Minds, Great Hearts, True Faith and Ready Hands?' Exploring Socialist Masculinities before the First World War." *Labour History Review* 69.2 (August 2004): 201–217.
Hunt, Peter. "Dialogue and Dialectic: Language and Class in the *Wind in the Willows*." *Children's Literature* 16 (1998): 159–169.
_____, ed. *Understanding Children's Literature*. London: Routledge, 2005.
Kapler-Luce, Rebecca. "The Seeing Eye of Beatrix Potter." *Children's Literature in Education* 25.3 (1994): 139–146.
Kent, Susan Kingsley. *Gender and Power in Britain, 1640–1990*. London: Routledge, 1999.
Kidd, Kenneth. "Ways of Being Male: Representing Masculinities in Children's Literature (review)." *Lion & the Unicorn* 27.3 (2003) 433–437.
Killeen, Jarlath. *The Fairy Tales of Oscar Wilde*. Hampshire, England: Ashgate, 2007.
Kerridge, Richard. "Nature in the English Novel." *Literature of Nature: An International Sourcebook*. London: Routledge, 1998.
Kipling, Rudyard. *The Jungle Book*. London: Puffin, 1994.
_____. *Something of Myself*. Cambridge: Cambridge University Press, 1990.
Kaufman, Michael. "Men, Feminism, and Men's Contradictory Experiences of Power." Joseph Kuypers, Ed. *Men and Power*. Halifax: Fernwood, 1999.
Knoepflmacher, U. C. "Oscar Wilde at Toad Hall: Kenneth Grahame's Drainings and Draggings. *The Lion and the Unicorn* 34.1 (2010): 1–16.
Kucich, John. "Sadomasochism and the Magical Group: Kipling's Middle-Class Imperialism." *Victorian Studies* 46.1 (2003): 33–68.
Kutzer, M. Daphne. "A Wilderness Inside: Domestic Space in the Work of Beatrix Potter." *The Lion and the Unicorn* 21.2 (1997) 204–214.
Kuznets, Lois R. "Kenneth Grahame and Father Nature, or Whither Blows *The Wind in the Willows*." *Children's Literature* 16 (1998): 175–185.
_____, ed. *Kenneth Grahame*. Boston: G. K. Hall, 1987.
Landow, George. "Aesthetes and Decadents of the 1890s — Points of Departure." *The Victorian Web*. 17 Sept. 2002. Web. 11 May 2011.
Lane, Margaret. *The Tale of Beatrix Potter*. Middlesex: Penguin, 1986.
Lear, Linda. *Beatrix Potter: A Life in Nature*. New York: St. Martin's, 2007.
Lerer, Seth, ed. *The Wind in the Willows: An Annotated Edition*. Cambridge: Harvard University Press, 2009.
Lewis, C. S. *Surprised by Joy: The Shape of My Early Life*. New York: Harcourt, 1955.
Linder, Leslie. *A History of the Writings of Beatrix Potter*. London: Frederick Warne, 1971.

Works Cited

Lois, Margot. "Gods and Mysteries: The Revival of Paganism and the Remaking of Mythography through the Nineteenth Century." *Victorian Studies* 47.3 (2005) 329–361.
Lorber, Judith. *Paradoxes of Gender*. New Haven: Yale University Press, 1994.
Lycett, Andrew. "Just Not So." New Statesman, 128: 4452 (1999): 43–44.
———. *Rudyard Kipling*. London: Weidenfeld and Nicolson, 1999.
MacCormack, Carol, and Marilyn Strathern, eds. *Nature, Culture, and Gender*. Cambridge: Cambridge University Press, 1980.
MacDonald, Ruth K. *Beatrix Potter*. Boston: Twayne, 1986.
Mackey, Margaret, ed. *Beatrix Potter's Peter Rabbit: A Children's Classic at 100*. Lanham, Maryland: Scarecrow, 2002.
———. *The Case of Peter Rabbit: Changing Conditions of Literature for Children*. New York: Garland, 1998.
Mangan, J. A. "Play Up and Play the Game: Victorian and Edwardian Public School Vocabularies of Motive." *British Journal of Educational Studies* 23.3 (1975): 324–335.
McBratney, John. "Imperial Subjects, Imperial Space in Kipling's *Jungle Book*." *Victorian Studies* 35.3 (1992): 277–294.
Mendelson, Michael. "The Wind in the Willows and the Plotting of Contrast." *Children's Literature* 16 (1988): 127–145.
Milne, A. A. *Autobiography*. New York: Dutton, 1939.
———. *Toad of Toad Hall: A Play from Kenneth Grahame's Book*. New York: Scribner's, 1957.
———. *Winnie the Pooh*. New York: Puffin, 1992.
Nelson, Claudia. "The Beast Within: 'Winnie-the-Pooh: Reassessed.'" *Children's Literature in Education* 21.1 (1990): 17–22.
———. "Sex and the Single Boy: Ideals of Manliness and Sexuality in Victorian Literature for Boys." *Victorian Studies* 32.4 (1989): 525–551.
Nikolajeva, Maria. *The Rhetoric of Character in Children's Literature*. Lanham, Maryland: Scarecrow, 2002.
Nodelman, Perry. "Making Boys Appear." *Ways of Being Male: Representing Masculinities in Children's Literature and Film*. Ed. John Stephens. New York and London: Routledge (2002): 1–14.
Nyman, Jopi. "Re-Reading Rudyard Kipling's 'English' Heroism: Narrating Nation in *The Jungle Book*." *Orbis litterarum* 56 (2001): 205–220.
Parsons, Linda. "'Otherways' into the Garden: Re-Visioning the Feminine in *The Secret Garden*." *Children's Literature in Education* 33.4 (2002): 247–268.
Pater, Walter. *The Renaissance: Studies in Art and Poetry*. Oxford: Oxford University Press, 1998.
Philip, Neil. "The Wind in the Willows: The Vitality of a Classic." *Children and Their Books: A Celebration of the Work of Iona and Peter Opie*. Eds. Gillian Avery and Julia Briggs. New York: Oxford University Press, 1989.
Potter, Beatrix. *The Complete Tales of Beatrix Potter*. London: Frederick Warne, 1989.
Pryke, Sam. "The Popularity of Nationalism in the Early British Boy Scout Movement." *Social History* 23:3 (1998): 309–325.
Richards, Jeffrey. "'Passing the love of women': Manly Love and Victorian Society." In *Manliness and Morality: Middle-Class Masculinity in Britain and America, 1800–1940*. Ed. J. A. Mangan and James Walvin. Manchester: Manchester University Press, 1987: 92–122.

Works Cited

Robertson, Judith P., Tony Campbell, Eugenia Gritziotis. "The Psychological Uses of Ruthlessness in a Children's Fantasy Tale: Beatrix Potter and *The Tale of Peter Rabbit.*" *Changing English: Studies in Reading and Culture* 7.2 (2000): 177–189.

Roper, Michael. "Between Manliness and Masculinity: The '"War Generation"' and the Psychology of Fear in Britain, 1914–1950." *Journal of British Studies* 44.2 (2005) 343–362.

Scott, Carole. "Between Me and the World: Clothes as Mediator between Self and Society in the Work of Beatrix Potter." *The Lion and the Unicorn* 16 (1992): 192–198.

Sedgwick, Eve Kosofsky. *Between Men: English Literature and Male Homosocial Desire.* New York: Columbia University Press, 1985.

———. *Epistemology of the Closet.* Berkeley: University of California Press, 1990.

Snider, Clifton. (2009, August 3). "On the Loom of Sorrow: Eros and Logos in Oscar Wilde's Fairy Tales." Retrieved from http://www.csulb.edu/~csnider/wilde.fairy.tales.html.

Springhall, John. "Building Character in the British Boy." *Manliness and Morality: Middle-Class Masculinity in Britain and America, 1800–1940.* Eds. J. A. Mangan and James Walvin. Manchester: Manchester University Press 1987: 52–74.

Stanger, Carol A. "Winnie the Pooh Through a Feminist Lens." *The Lion and the Unicorn* 2.2 (1987): 34–50.

Steig, Michael. "At the Back of *The Wind in the Willows*: An Experiment in Biographical and Autobiographical Interpretation." *Victorian Studies* 24.3 (1981): 303–324.

Stephens, John. "Gender, Genre and Children's Literature." *Signal* 79 (1996): 17–30.

Stevenson, Laura C. "Mowgli and His Stories: Versions of Pastoral." *Sewanee Review* 109.3 (2001): 358–379.

Sussman, Herbert. *Victorian Masculinities: Manhood and Masculine Poetics in Early Victorian Literature and Art.* Cambridge: Cambridge University Press, 1995.

Tosh, John. *A Man's Place: Masculinity and the Middle Class Home in Victorian England.* New Haven: Yale University Press, 1999.

Trodd, Anthea. *Introduction to Edwardian Literature.* Calgary: Calgary University Press, 1991.

Wallace, Doris B. "Secret Gardens and Other Symbols of Gender in Literature." *Metaphor & Symbol* 3.1 (1988): 135–146.

Warren, Allen. "Popular Manliness: Baden-Powell, Scouting and the Development of Manly Character." *Manliness and Morality: Middle-Class Masculinity in Britain and America, 1800–1940.* Ed. J. A. Mangan and James Walvin. Manchester: Manchester University Press, 1987: 199–219.

Whitehead, Stephen M. *Men and Masculinities.* Oxford: Blackwell, 2002.

Whitlark, James. "Scriptural Paradoxes for Imperial Children." *Children's Literature Association Quarterly* 24.1 (1999): 24–33.

Williams, Raymond. *The Country and the City.* New York: Oxford University Press, 1973.

Windholz, Anne M. "An Emigrant and a Gentleman: Imperial Masculinity, British Magazines, and the Colony That Got Away." *Victorian Studies* 42.4 (1999/2000): 631–658).

Wood, Naomi. "Creating the Sensual Child: Paterian Aesthetics, Pederasty, and Oscar Wilde's Fairy Tales." *Marvels & Tales: Journal of Fairy-Tale Studies* 16:2 (2002): 156–170.

Zipes, Jack. *Fairy Tales and the Art of Subversion.* New York: Routledge, 1991.

Index

adventure story 7, 8, 16, 17, 23, 26, 28, 29–35, 38, 42, 49, 56, 93, 105, 111, 118, 119, 133, 138, 166–168, 171, 173, 175
Aesthetic Movement 66, 71, 75, 76, 81, 84
aestheticism v, 4, 12, 15, 18, 25, 50, 51, 58–63, 65, 67–69, 71–83, 85, 87, 89, 98, 108, 168, 172, 174, 176, 179
Arcadia 10, 17, 27, 28, 33, 61, 68, 76, 77, 81, 88, 117, 118, 124, 145, 162, 175

bachelorhood 5, 17, 36, 119, 152, 172
Baden-Powell, Robert S.S. 8, 12, 13, 49, 131, 164
"The Birthday of the Infanta" 62, 63, 69, 95, 99, 105, 108, 116, 167
blurring 63, 67, 101, 112, 133, 147, 150, 169, 170

Carroll, Lewis 163, 168, 176
Catholicism v, 59, 61, 62, 64, 69, 70, 84, 88, 168
Christianity v, 7, 12, 15, 18, 20, 58–67, 69, 71, 73, 75, 77, 79, 81–85, 87–89, 103, 123, 126, 134, 142, 147, 149, 157, 160, 164, 166–169, 174, 179
collaboration v, 12, 17, 19, 20, 62, 74, 124–133, 135–137, 159–162, 171, 172, 175, 177, 179, 181
collaborative masculinity 126, 128, 138, 139, 147
compromise v, 17, 19, 20, 28, 125, 127, 129, 131, 133, 135, 137, 139, 141, 143, 145, 147–149, 151–153, 155–157, 159, 161, 175

Darwin, Charles 7, 18, 43, 49, 54, 58, 76, 95, 101, 117, 122, 140, 164, 180
Darwinism *see* Darwin, Charles
"The Decay of Lying" 76, 81
degeneration 7, 8, 11, 13, 164
"The Devoted Friend" 74, 116
domesticity 17, 24, 27, 28–30, 35, 36–44, 49, 52, 54, 55, 79, 92, 94, 96, 100, 102, 107, 122, 125, 136–138, 141–144, 151–153, 157, 171, 173, 176, 179, 181
doubling 26, 27, 28, 170

escape 9, 10, 17, 20, 23–25, 27–31, 33, 35–43, 45–47, 49–55, 57, 78, 90–92, 95, 103, 104, 107, 111, 116, 117, 124, 136, 143, 152, 153, 157, 161, 167, 169, 171, 173, 174, 179

femininity 35, 40, 96, 122, 127, 136, 138, 146–148, 154, 160, 167, 168, 172, 177
"The Fisherman and His Soul" 25, 27, 30, 41, 50, 63, 64, 71, 87, 93, 105, 134, 166, 167, 179, 180
Free Mason 60, 84–86, 88, 106, 114, 169

gothic 25, 27, 51, 69, 70, 76, 170
Grahame, Kenneth 1, 3, 4, 9, 10, 12, 13, 15–17, 19, 20, 24–26, 28–34, 36, 37, 39–42, 45, 46, 50, 51, 56–63, 66–68, 70–79, 81, 83, 85, 88–92, 94, 95, 98, 99, 103, 104, 106, 108, 110–113, 115, 117, 119–121, 124, 126, 127, 128, 132, 134–136, 138, 141, 143–146, 150, 152, 153, 155–162, 165, 167, 171, 173–177, 179, 181; *The Wind in the Willows* 4, 12, 14, 15, 16, 18, 20, 27, 29, 36, 37, 39, 45, 46, 50, 56, 59, 60, 62, 66, 70, 72, 73, 76, 79–81, 83, 93, 99, 103, 119, 124, 126, 131, 132, 135, 143, 155, 156, 157, 161, 179, 180

"The Happy Prince" 4, 30, 41, 59, 65, 74, 92, 93, 105, 108, 116, 123, 146, 147, 149, 157, 160, 167, 168
hegemonic masculinity 3, 4, 24, 55, 90–92, 98, 104, 128, 129, 131, 134, 137, 143, 150, 152, 155, 167
heteronormative 6, 16, 20, 26, 27, 37, 42, 43, 45, 47, 48, 49, 57, 66, 72, 75, 79, 94, 96, 99, 100, 101, 105, 116–119, 122, 127, 128, 134, 142, 158, 180

Index

heterosexuality 20, 29, 30, 56, 143, 145, 150, 153, 154, 156, 160, 165, 166, 172, 175
hierarchy 11, 17, 19, 20, 24, 35, 43, 44, 48, 51, 52, 53, 57, 67, 72, 86, 87, 90–93, 95–99, 101, 103–111, 113–115, 117–124, 126, 128, 129, 138, 140, 146, 150, 156, 159, 161, 168, 169, 170, 172, 174–176
Hinduism 18, 85, 87, 169
homoerotic 4, 20, 127, 141, 145, 149, 160, 166, 177
hunting 43, 45, 48, 51, 52, 53, 60, 86, 96, 97, 101, 106, 112, 115, 125, 126, 128–132, 137, 140, 142, 153, 155,

Islam 18, 85, 169

The Jungle Book 4, 8, 14, 15, 18, 20, 31, 43, 48, 53, 60, 79, 84, 86, 87, 95, 97, 100, 112, 113, 120, 125–128, 131, 132, 133, 142, 155, 168–170

Kingsley, Charles 16, 58, 85, 88, 149, 163, 164, 173, 180; *The Water Babies* 85, 163, 165
Kipling, Rudyard 1, 3, 4, 8, 9, 12, 14–20, 24, 25, 31, 34, 37, 41, 43–54, 56–63, 70–72, 75, 79, 80, 84–92, 95–102, 104–106, 109, 110–116, 120–130, 132, 133, 136, 137, 139, 140–144, 152, 156, 158, 160, 162, 165, 168–172, 174, 175, 177, 180; *The Jungle Book* 4, 8, 14, 15, 18, 20, 31, 43, 48, 53, 60, 79, 84, 86, 87, 95, 97, 100, 112, 113, 120, 125–128, 131, 132, 133, 142, 155, 168–170

marriage 4, 5, 9, 10, 16, 20, 37, 45, 48, 55, 69, 127, 134, 141–144, 146, 151–153, 160, 161, 165, 166, 173, 175, 177, 179
Masonic Order *see* Free Mason
Masonry *see* Free Mason
Milne, A.A 1, 3, 4, 9–13, 16–20, 25, 32–35, 41, 43, 49, 56, 57, 59, 61, 62, 70, 71, 74, 80, 82, 83, 88, 90, 91, 104, 105, 108–111, 114, 118–122, 124–127, 130–132, 135–139, 141, 144–146, 153, 154, 158–162, 165, 175–177, 179–181; *Winnie the Pooh* 4, 11, 16, 18, 21, 33–35, 39, 49, 59, 61, 80–83, 105, 110, 118, 122, 125, 130, 150, 158, 160, 180
muscular Christianity 12, 15, 20, 58–60, 66, 82, 85, 88, 164, 179

nature 5, 6, 13, 18, 38, 44, 52, 62, 65–70, 72, 73, 75–77, 85, 90, 98, 112, 117, 118, 137, 140, 149, 162, 163, 174
"The Nightingale and the Rose" 93, 102, 116, 148, 160
nonsense 33, 61, 80, 82, 88, 118, 119, 124, 138, 176

paganism 18, 44, 59–70, 85, 88, 99, 167, 169
Pan 63, 66–68, 70, 76, 107, 117, 174, 180
Pater, Walter 12, 14, 27, 71, 72
patriarchy 13, 15, 32, 91, 114, 118, 129, 138, 139, 141, 142, 150, 154, 164, 168, 169, 171, 172
pederasty 14, 74, 75, 146, 147, 149, 167
performative 4, 5, 83, 136
"The Picture of Dorian Gray" 3, 14, 26
Potter, Beatrix 1, 3, 4, 9, 10, 12, 14, 15, 17–20, 24, 25, 29, 37–48, 50–57, 59–63, 66, 70–72, 75, 78–80, 83, 85, 88–90, 91, 92, 94, 99, 100, 101, 104, 106–108, 110, 111, 113–116, 120, 122, 123, 125–127, 136, 137, 139, 142, 150–154, 160, 161, 163, 165, 167, 171–175, 177, 179–181; *The Story of a Fierce Bad Rabbit* (1906) 53; *The Tailor of Gloucester* (1903) 180; *The Tale of Benjamin Bunny* (1904) 38, 39, 53, 94, 107, 116, 179; *The Tale of Ginger and Pickles* (1909) 107, 152, 172, 180; *The Tale of Jemima Puddle-Duck* (1908) 37, 55, 78, 152, 161, 172; *The Tale of Mr. Jeremy Fisher* (1906) 78; *The Tale of Mrs. Tittlemouse* (1910) 42, 152; *The Tale of Peter Rabbit* (1902) 29, 37–40, 94, 107, 171; *The Tale of Samuel Whiskers or, The Roly-Poly Pudding* (1908) 37, 53, 126, 150, 151, 180; *The Tale of Squirrel Nutkin* (1903) 44, 53, 136; *The Tale of the Flopsy Bunnies* (1909) 37, 66, 100, 172; *The Tale of Timmy Tiptoes* (1911) 55, 100, 120, 151, 153; *The Tale of Tom Kitten* (1907) 37, 40, 53; *The Tale of Two Bad Mice* (1904) 45, 47, 100, 107, 126, 150, 151, 172
Pre-Raphaelite 71, 76, 127

rebellion 17–20, 25, 38, 39, 42–49, 54–57, 59, 92, 101, 116, 118, 136, 152, 156, 169, 170, 172
"The Remarkable Rocket" 71, 99, 102, 116, 120, 123, 134, 148

Index

reputation 9, 17, 19, 43, 54, 90–105, 108, 122–124, 126, 129, 142, 168, 170, 171, 175, 176, 179
reversal 33, 42, 44, 51
Ruskin, John 12, 14, 27, 71, 72

"The Selfish Giant" 61, 64, 65, 93, 116, 118, 120, 123, 147, 148, 149, 160, 167, 168
socialism 18, 20, 46, 65, 73, 173
spirituality 18, 58–63, 65–68, 82, 84, 85, 87–89, 116, 165, 169, 174
"The Star-Child" 41, 49, 50, 51, 69, 71, 105, 108, 133, 148, 166
The Story of a Fierce Bad Rabbit (1906) 53

The Tailor of Gloucester (1903) 180
The Tale of Benjamin Bunny (1904) 38, 39, 53, 94, 107, 116, 179
The Tale of Ginger and Pickles (1909) 107, 152, 172, 180
The Tale of Jemima Puddle-Duck (1908) 37, 55, 78, 152, 161, 172
The Tale of Mr. Jeremy Fisher (1906) 78
The Tale of Mrs. Tittlemouse (1910) 42, 152
The Tale of Peter Rabbit (1902) 29, 37–40, 94, 107, 171
The Tale of Samuel Whiskers or, The Roly-Poly Pudding (1908) 37, 53, 126, 150, 151, 180
The Tale of Squirrel Nutkin (1903) 44, 53, 136
The Tale of the Flopsy Bunnies (1909) 37, 66, 100, 172
The Tale of Timmy Tiptoes (1911) 55, 100, 120, 151, 153
The Tale of Tom Kitten (1907) 37, 40, 53
The Tale of Two Bad Mice (1904) 45, 47, 100, 107, 126, 150, 151, 172

unitarianism 18, 39, 61, 85, 88, 108
utilitarianism 13, 18, 39, 59, 63, 72, 79, 85, 89, 135, 174

violence 4, 17, 25, 33, 39, 44, 49–57, 61, 62, 70, 81, 92, 93, 95, 97, 105, 106, 114, 120–128, 131, 141, 142, 150, 151, 155, 166, 167, 169–174, 177, 180

The Water Babies 85, 163, 165
Wilde, Oscar 1, 3, 4, 7–9, 11–14, 16, 18, 19, 24–27, 29–34, 41, 49–51, 56–59, 61–77, 79, 81, 83–85, 87–94, 99, 101, 105, 108, 110, 111, 114, 116–118, 120–124, 126, 127, 133–137, 141–144, 146–150, 153, 156, 157, 160, 161, 163–171, 173–175, 177, 179, 180, 181; "The Birthday of the Infanta" 62, 63, 69, 95, 99, 105, 108, 116, 167; "The Decay of Lying" 76, 81; "The Devoted Friend" 74, 116; "The Fisherman and His Soul" 25, 27, 30, 41, 50, 63, 64, 71, 87, 93, 105, 134, 166, 167, 179, 180; "The Happy Prince" 4, 30, 41, 59, 65, 74, 92, 93, 105, 108, 116, 123, 146, 147, 149, 157, 160, 167, 168; "The Nightingale and the Rose" 93, 102, 116, 148, 160; "The Picture of Dorian Gray" 3, 14, 26; "The Remarkable Rocket" 71, 99, 102, 116, 120, 123, 134, 148; "The Selfish Giant" 61, 64, 65, 93, 116, 118, 120, 123, 147, 148, 149, 160, 167, 168; "The Star-Child" 41, 49, 50, 51, 69, 71, 105, 108, 133, 148, 166
The Wind in the Willows 4, 12, 14, 15, 16, 18, 20, 27, 29, 36, 37, 39, 45, 46, 50, 56, 59, 60, 62, 66, 70, 72, 73, 76, 79–81, 83, 93, 99, 103, 119, 124, 126, 131, 132, 135, 143, 155, 156, 157, 161, 179, 180
Winnie the Pooh 4, 11, 16, 18, 21, 33–35, 39, 49, 59, 61, 80–83, 105, 110, 118, 122, 125, 130, 150, 158, 160, 180

www.ingramcontent.com/pod-product-compliance
Lightning Source LLC
Chambersburg PA
CBHW032102300426
44116CB00007B/861